WRONGFUL DEATH

A MEDICAL TRAGEDY

WRONGFUL DEATH

A

MEDICAL TRAGEDY

SANDRA M. GILBERT

W. W. NORTON & COMPANY

NEW YORK/LONDON

Copyright © 1995 by Sandra Gilbert
All rights reserved
Printed in the United States of America
First Edition

The text of this book is composed in Photina
with the display set in Fenice
Composition and manufacturing by The Haddon Craftsmen, Inc.
Book design by JAM Design

Library of Congress Cataloging-in-Publication Data

Gilbert, Sandra M.
Wrongful death : a medical tragedy / by Sandra Gilbert.
p.   cm.
1. Medical personnel—Malpractice. 2. Gilbert, Elliot L.
I. Title.
RA1056.5.G54 1995
346.7303′23—dc20
[347.306323]   94-26732
ISBN 0-393-03721-5

W. W. Norton & Company, Inc., 500 Fifth Avenue, New York, N.Y. 10110
W. W. Norton & Company Ltd., 10 Coptic Street, London WC1A 1PU
1 2 3 4 5 6 7 8 9 0

In memory of Elliot Lewis Gilbert
1930–1991
and with love and gratitude
for Dick and Leah Asofsky
and Bob Griffin

In a wrongful death action, grief or sorrow of the heirs is not a proper element of damage.

—Canavin v. Pacific Southwest Airlines,
1983, 148 Cal. App. 3d 512, 196 Cal. Rptr. 82

One of the limits of detection most often explored [is] the difficulty of converting knowledge into proper action. . . .

A work of detective fiction is after all constructed to lead up to the revealing of some previously hidden truth. Since anything that follows this revelation tends to be an anticlimax, the actual business of converting that truth into action—into, say, the capture and punishment of the criminal and the 'healing' of society—is often left as a kind of afterthought for the last few paragraphs of the story. . . .

[But] there's no necessary connection between the ability to discover knowledge and the ability to apply it.

—ELLIOT L. GILBERT,
A Guide: The World of Mystery Fiction

"None of the doctors told me," said Camelia's mother, Andrea Plaza. "I asked them what really happened to my baby. . . . I asked them crying and I asked them OK and I asked them mad. And they didn't tell me."

—SAM STANTON,
" 'What Really Happened to My Baby?' "
Sacramento Bee (November 7, 1993)

CONTENTS

PREFACE

Two days after my husband died, my friend and former colleague Toni Morrison—a storyteller I respect more than any other—called me from New Jersey to express her sympathy.

I was in shock, almost inarticulate, but I murmured gratitude as she spoke her condolences.

Then, just as we were about to hang up, "Now I want you to do all the mourning things, Sandra," she suddenly added, with tender authority.

"Mourning things?" I stammered.

"Well, I know you'll do all the right things, the public things," she explained, "but I want you to do the *real* mourning things."

"What are those, Toni?" I asked, bewildered.

"He'll tell you," she said quietly.

And she was right. He did. In whatever strange way the dead communicate with the living—through our deep knowledge of them, through our intuitions and memories of their needs, their passions, their desires—my husband spoke to me and told me to write this book.

The real mourning thing.

And because I know there are many other survivors of what is legally called "wrongful death," death that appears quite clearly to result from medical mistakes or negligence, I hope I have done this "mourning thing" for them, too.

As the wide-ranging and passionate debate surrounding the Clinton health care proposals has made plain, our country is in the midst of a virtually unprecedented health care crisis. So far, discussions of this problem have focused on the key issue of insurance coverage, of *access* to medical attention. And of course, like most other Americans, I believe this is a crucial matter. (Two of my children, through no fault of their own, have medical histories that mean we are afflicted with constant and absurdly unjustified worries about health insurance.)

Yet as the story I tell here will show, there is another aspect of our national health care crisis, one a number of researchers have discussed extensively in specialized books and professional journals but which has so far escaped widespread media attention: the problem of medical negligence, or what is usually called "malpractice."

I have sought in this book to dramatize this relatively unpublicized aspect of our health care crisis not through an accumulation of statistics and "case histories" but by recounting the wrenching experiences my children and I underwent as we struggled to understand what killed my basically healthy, sixty-year-old husband on February 11, 1991. And to emphasize the brutal reality of this medical tragedy, I have told my story as fully and frankly as I can, withholding no facts except the amount of the relatively small sum my children and I received as compensation for our loss, a sum that the terms of a legal settlement forbid me to name.

As we painfully learned, in an increasingly depersonalized and bureaucratized medical system, too many doctors are indifferent or careless, maybe smug, maybe overworked, maybe just forgetful of the famous admonition to *at least do no harm*. Responsibility in the often miraculous but always highly technologized realm of modern medicine is so dispersed, so fragmented, that finally it accrues to no one.

The services of the hospital in which my husband spent twenty-four fatal hours and of the code team that strove for fifty-five minutes to resuscitate him when he was dying cost our insurance company $102,113.07, almost as much (according to one expert) as a heart transplant then cost. Yet most members of all the teams who cared for him (including the surgery team and the recovery-room team) remain to this day nameless and faceless to me and my children. (Nor are these medical "teamsters" known to the insurance company itself, which has in any case no right to seek reimbursement from the hospital, even if there has been demonstrable negligence.)

Yet when I was growing up physicians still made what were quaintly known as "house calls," a practice symbolizing an "I/Thou" relationship between doctor and patient. Of course, there never was a golden age of medicine, certainly not when I was a child and people still died (even, indeed, in hospitals) of pneumonia, tuberculosis, rheumatic fever, and other illnesses that have largely been conquered in recent years. Now, though—with, or perhaps because of, all his or her new skills— the doctor is an institution, sometimes a corporation, sometimes a "team," and the patient often no more than a stripped body on an examining table or gurney.

Perhaps it's easier for a "team" confronting a depersonalized body to be indifferent or careless than it would be for a single responsible soul facing another known, and trusting, soul. Equally to the point, perhaps it's easier for a "team" to forget about, or to repress, the desperate needs of a mortally ill patient's family. To forget, indeed, those fundamental obligations implied by the ancient warning to *do no harm*—obligations that clearly include the *moral* obligations summarized in the phrase "medical ethics."

To be sure, the patient's needs must always come first; every physician's primary responsibility is obviously not just to seek to heal but also to avoid medical disaster in the course of treatment. But neglect of the problems of relatives, in particular the pain of those who have survived an unexpected medical calamity, is at the very least venial. For me and my children, certainly, the utter mystery that surrounded my husband's death intensified grief. And it seems likely to me now that the dispersal of responsibility among a number of different "teams" made it especially hard for us to find out what had happened.

Where *all* are accountable, it turns out, *none* is accountable. In a way, indeed, this paradox of nonaccountability is a central issue at the heart of the story I have narrated in these pages. And another of my key themes is the deep shock—the numb bewilderment, the ache of loss exacerbated by confusion, even astonishment—with which I and my children, and indeed many of our friends, responded to the mystery that confronted us.

As a participant in the tale of medical tragedy that I am telling here, I was in many ways a kind of zombie when I began this book. Stunned by what professionals call "unanticipated grief," unable to grasp what had happened to my husband and *why* it had happened, I was also unable to understand what had happened to me and the kids. Nor, as I see when I look back now on the events of 1991, was I able in any but the most rudimentary fashion to comprehend and control what was *happening* to us.

In the beginning, then, writing down some of the details of my loss forced me to define the trauma, if not to master it. At the same time, more than most memoirists, I was and am profoundly indebted to many people whose goodness not only fostered my writing but helped me live through the story itself. If, at various points, my struggle to survive grief and surmount confusion appears to have been eased, that is because there were those who conspired, often without my knowledge, not just to comfort me—to feed me, nurture me, stay with me through many dark weeks and months—but also, so far as was possible, to simplify the complications of what began to seem like an unusually bizarre bereavement.

14

To be more specific, as I grappled with the outline of this story—the "adverse event" that killed my husband, the process of discovery that gave us some inkling of what happened, and the claim we finally felt we had to assert against his doctors—I was supported, consoled, and advised by an astonishing array of colleagues, friends, and relatives. Among associates in the English Department at the University of California, Davis, who helped me cope with personal and professional problems posed by my husband's death, I want especially to thank Peter Dale, Michael Hoffman, Michael Kramer, David Van Leer, Joyce Wade, Jean Walraven, and Alan Williamson, as well as numerous other faculty members, students, and staffers in both the department and the U. C. Davis Humanities Institute. Among the many friends who (as I often put it to myself) "saved" me in the months following this terrible crisis, I must offer particular gratitude to Gina Campbell, Moneera Doss, Dorothy Gilbert, and Elizabeth Parr—and gratitude, too, to Richard Adams, Jonas and Milly Barish, Wendy and Larry Barker, Joan and Shelley Baumrind, Elyse Blankley, Chana and Ariel Bloch, Zelda Boyd and Dick Frieden, Duncan Campbell, Gianna Celli, Julie Cummings, Luise David, Joanne Feit Diehl, Sid Gershgoren, Todd Gitlin, Husain and Diana Hadawi, Shirley Kaufman, Susan Kolodny, Don Lazere, Guille Libresco, Jo and Larry Lipking, Erle Loran and Ruth Schorer, Diana O Hehir, Ruth Rosen, Peter Dale Scott, Ellen Stekert, Garrett Stewart, Ruth Stone, Phyllis Stowell, Effie Westervelt, Joe Westlund, and Florence and Alex Zwerdling.

For research assistance, and/or for advice with problems ranging from computer glitches and journalistic practices to legal issues and the economics of medical malpractice, I thank Rebecca Asofsky, John Beckman, John Currie, Karen Gale, Lenny Gubar, Lisa Harper, Paula Harrington, Deirdre Loughman, Christer Mossberg, Bob Pollak, Howell Raines, Kate Remen, Jeanne Scholz, Renee Schwartz, Christopher Sindt,

Jeanette Treiber, Kent Van den Berg, and Dan Wenger. For providing safe and pleasant spaces in which this book could evolve, I am grateful to the Bellagio Study Center of the Rockefeller Foundation, the corporation of Yaddo, and the MacDowell Colony. For handling our family's case with tact, expertise, and *élan*, I thank my attorney Dan Kelly, along with his associates Wes Sokolosky and John Link. And for both supporting and critiquing my manuscript with warmth, dedication, and incisiveness, I thank my agent, Ellen Levine, and my editor, Jill Bialosky.

I must, though, offer special gratitude to the friends who scrupulously read or reread and discussed my drafts of this book—Ben Bagdikian and Marlene Griffith, Carolyn Heilbrun, Toni Morrison, and Jerry Richard—as well as to the members of my literal and figurative family, who read, commented, and persistently strengthened me: my courageous mother, Angela Mortola; my remarkable children, Roger, Kathy, and Susanna Gilbert; my longtime comrade and collaborator, Susan Gubar, *sine qua non;* my wise and loving companion, David Gale; and (always insouciantly providing a reason to live) my grandson, Justin Valentine Gilbert.

Finally, my deepest debts are reflected by my dedications: to Dick and Leah Asofsky, who analyzed and energized, sustained and inspired me when I was most bewildered; to Bob Griffin, who cooked and comforted, counseled, consoled, and indefatigably "Yaddoed" when (I'm sure) I was most bewilder*ing;* and to my late husband, Elliot L. Gilbert, who taught me how to write and told me, as Toni promised he would, to do—and how to do—what has been, for me, the *real* mourning thing.

PART ONE

ADVERSE
EVENT

*We defined injuries due to medical manage-
ment . . . as adverse events. . . . We defined an
injury caused by the failure to meet standards
reasonably expected of the average physician,
other provider, or institution as a 'negligent
adverse event.'*

—HOWARD H. HIATT, M.D. et al., "Special
Report: A Study of Medical Injury and
Medical Malpractice," *New England Journal
of Medicine,* August 17, 1989

1

*Mr. Quayle, an earnest look on his face, began to fidget. "I, I
can't tell you exactly what we do on that pain and suffering
in the—" the Vice President said, his voice trailing off as he
looked offstage toward Kevin E. Moley, the deputy secretary
of the Department of Health and Human Services, who has
been coaching him. "Kevin, what do we do on the pain and
suffering on our malpractice proposal?"*

—*New York Times*, Wednesday, October 7, 1992

SUNDAY, FEBRUARY 10, 1991, 7 P.M.

First thing tomorrow morning my husband, Elliot, is scheduled
for major surgery at the medical center associated with the University of California, Davis, where he and I both teach. Our two
daughters, Susanna, twenty-six, and Kathy, twenty-eight, and
Kathy's roommate, Liz, are watching TV with us in his comfortable hospital room. Our thirty-year-old son, Roger, who lives on
the East Coast, can't be here right now, but we just had a pleasant phone conversation with him.

It's twilight in Sacramento, California, blue and windy but not
cold, when Dr. Jack Reitan, the chief of anesthesiology, comes by
in a sweater and blue jeans to chat and check Elliot's throat and
lungs. Last week, when Elliot's routine operation for prostate
cancer was originally scheduled, the procedure had been halted

by a technical problem about "intubation"—introducing a respiratory tube for anesthesia—and tonight Dr. Reitan wants to reassure my husband that he and his associates are prepared for any difficulty.

Since Dr. Reitan and Elliot are colleagues, both professors on the same campus (my husband is the chair of the English department), the two men enter into a particularly amiable discussion. Dr. Reitan confesses that he was once a graduate student in literature. My husband asks him about the state of medicine. Reitan explains that malpractice suits have recently become serious problems for physicians, noting that "we all have to practice defensive medicine nowadays."

My husband, a robust, gray-bearded man of sixty, laughs and agrees. He has been on at least one university committee dealing with this sort of issue. He is looking especially handsome, or so it seems to me, in the blue and silver striped terry-cloth robe that I bought him for Christmas, in anticipation of this hospital stay.

Perched on the windowsill next to his bed are two stuffed toys that my daughters and I brought him for good luck: a newly purchased Raggedy Andy, one of his childhood heroes, and Orlando Furrioso, a hairy orangutan that he gave me last Christmas.

———

MONDAY, FEBRUARY 11, 1991, 8:15 P.M.

A little more than twenty-four hours later, my husband is dead in the recovery room, after what my daughters and I had been told was successful surgery.

We don't know this, at least not right away. The surgeon, Dr. Ralph W. deVere White, has spoken to us several times during the day, always assuring us that everything is all right and urging us to leave the hospital, where we've been waiting since Elliot was taken to the OR—the operating room—at six in the morning. Telling us to go out for lunch, for a nap, for dinner, while the recovery-room nurses are "waiting for a bed in the Intensive Care Unit."

In fact, it isn't until nine P.M., February 11, that the elevator doors in the hospital lobby slide open and Dr. deVere White, the surgeon, strides grimly out in a dark gray suit, flanked by his white-coated resident and a harried-looking, unfamiliar woman carrying stacks of papers.

My daughters and I have come back from the meal we were told to go out for only to discover that "the doctor is coming down to see you," so I am standing at a long counter near the elevator, biting my nails, when the door gapes wide and the three emerge.

The surgeon, an Irishman, becomes oddly hearty.

"We've had a problem, luv, a *big* problem," he begins briskly, as he steers me out of the lobby and down a hospital hall I didn't know existed.

I manage to say "What—what—?"

"Dad's had a heart attack," he replies, shaking his head with what seems to be strange ruefulness.

"But what, but what are you—?" I begin.

In the background, from the pastel depths of the empty late-night hospital lobby, I hear the screams of my daughters, who are talking separately to the white-coated resident.

The harried-looking woman and the Irish surgeon are struggling to open the door of a secret room that turns out to be hidden in the hallway just off the lobby.

I begin to cross myself compulsively. "Are you trying to tell me, Doctor," I whisper, "that my husband is *dead?*"

In the lobby, one of my daughters has flung her shoulder bag across the floor. Keys clash on the ceramic tiles. Her wallet flies open. IDs and credit cards spring out. She and her sister and her sister's roommate are screaming and screaming.

I am still crossing myself as the doctor and the harried-looking woman and I finally enter the secret chamber, a small reception area with straight chairs ranged stiffly along the walls. As the unfamiliar woman comes toward me to take my hand, I see that she is wearing a badge which says "Carolyn, Office of Decedent Services," and she is carrying a large folder labeled "Bereavement Packet."

My daughters and their friend are brought down the hall by Dr. Poonamallee, the resident, who hovers beside them in an uneasy silence. Looking around the room, I notice that there are no tables or magazines in here at all, not one of the *Times*, *Newsweeks*, or *Sunsets* that we associate with "waiting rooms." This is the room, I realize, where you don't wait any more. This is the room where they tell people that people are unexpectedly dead.

And this is the room where you may begin to understand what "medical malpractice"—or call it "negligence" if you like—might really mean.

Although we don't yet suspect it, we are going to learn within the next month that my husband didn't die from a "heart attack." On the contrary, he evidently died as a result of medical neglect; indeed, he may have died because someone in the recovery room failed to get the results of a simple blood test. Failed, in other words, to notice that amidst the efficient bustle of a modern recovery room, in a major American medical center—indeed, a teaching hospital—while my daughters and I were dutifully picking at the restaurant dinner the doctor had told us we should go out and eat, my husband was in truly mortal danger.

Had something gone wrong in the surgery? If so, why hadn't we been told? How could the doctor have repeatedly urged us to leave the hospital when my husband wasn't (to say the least) doing well? And why had he told us that Elliot had a heart attack when, as he must have understood, we'd soon find out he hadn't?

Most horrifyingly, why and how had a supposedly sophisticated team of nurses, residents, surgeons and anesthesiologists let things get to such a pass that when at 7:20 P.M. they finally invoked "the code" (to bring a rescue team for an emergency), it was too late to resuscitate someone who had twenty-four hours earlier been vigorously healthy?

These are questions that will haunt us for years to come. What Dr. Reitan had so jovially called "defensive medicine" has turned into *offensive* medicine. And it has changed my life, along with the lives of my children, forever.

———

Every year, it is conservatively estimated, more than one out of one hundred Americans admitted to a hospital will suffer from the calamitous effects of medical malpractice—negligence, incompetence, carelessness, indifference—leading to what researchers in the field call "adverse events" or, more specifically (referring to difficulties caused by medical mismanagement), "negligent adverse events." Some will die: one of the most important current surveys suggests that *one in every 388 hospitalizations* issues in death resulting from an adverse event caused by medical negligence. Others will be temporarily incapacitated; still others permanently injured or even seriously disabled. Yet according to a recent study, "Less than two percent of people who are harmed by incompetent medical care file malpractice suits, suggesting that the legal system rarely holds bad doctors accountable for their mistakes."

These figures imply, further, that many, perhaps most, victims of "adverse events" don't even know they're victims, suggesting that in the face of legal inaction, the medical profession itself feels relatively free to overlook even death-dealing (or at least egregiously life-threatening) errors committed by its members. Nor do any significant laws require that physicians inform patients and their families about the true nature of so-called "negligent adverse events."

Thus, as Harvard researchers argued not long ago in the *New England Journal of Medicine*, "the civil-justice system only infrequently compensates injured patients and rarely identifies and holds health-care practitioners accountable for substandard medical care," while both the law and the medical system in effect conspire to perpetuate this situation. Yet, as one commentator observes in a useful, recent collection entitled *Medical Accidents*, "it is the question of accountability which has proved to be [of most importance] to victims. Accountability from the victim's point of view means simply that something is done to ensure that those responsible . . . are required to give an account of themselves, that an explanation is given to the victim or family, and that steps are taken to try to avoid a similar accident happening again."

Nevertheless, as Dr. Reitan and my husband agreed on that windy night of February 10, the malpractice "crisis" is big news—though mostly, I must now add, for the wrong reasons. It is this "crisis," we are told, that has forced doctors all over the country not only to practice what Reitan called "defensive medicine" but also to pay escalating insurance premiums which in turn (or so the story goes) drive up patients' medical bills. Just a few years ago, in fact, President George Bush and Vice President Dan Quayle jumped on the "crisis" bandwagon to propose an elaborate new set of federal controls that would help keep health care costs down by severely limiting compensatory payments to patients and families who have been the victims of medical malpractice. More recently, although the Clinton health care proposal commendably avoids ceilings on compensation, the administration's plan calls for attempts at alternative dispute resolution in the hope, evidently, of keeping such payments down.

In fact, as we were to learn, compensatory limits have already been established in the state of California for survivors of someone who has died what is known as a "wrongful death." Here, despite popular belief to the contrary, relatives cannot sue even the most negligent of hospitals for punitive damages, cannot seek awards for the often quite considerable pain and suffering inflicted on dying victims of medical carelessness, and cannot ask to be compensated for their own pain and suffering.

Of course, the California law is perfectly reasonable in implying that no financial compensation can provide emotional consolation to those who have been traumatized by an unexpected and unnecessary death. Yet as the authors of the Harvard study remark in the *New England Journal of Medicine,* society requires "credible systems and procedures . . . to guarantee professional accountability to patients." How, my children and I began to wonder as we were forced to confront the enormity of the "mistake" that had killed my husband, can a seemingly indifferent medical institution be held responsible for its errors if there is neither a law (with "teeth") that requires disclosure of negligent adverse events nor a financial punishment commensurate with the crime of what we understatedly define as "negligence"?

That, despite the outcry over escalating malpractice claims and the concomitant need to practice "defensive medicine," there is for the most part neither an effective disclosure requirement nor a meaningful financial punishment may be indicated by a recent report: far from being in the red, "California's four doctor-owned medical malpractice insurance carriers" have been earning good profits. "With cash reserves and earnings up and damage awards capped," noted one observer not long ago, "each carrier paid a dividend in 1990: the Doctors' Company, $25 million; Norcal, $24.6 million; Medical Insurance Exchange of California, $16 million; Southern California Physicians Insurance Exchange, $15.2 million for a total of $80 million."

Until the spring of 1991, I, like many other citizens, had usu-

ally read newspaper accounts of malpractice suits and settle-
ments with bemused ambivalence. Yes, I'd regretfully agree, you
certainly couldn't trust some doctors. But no, I'd think, many of
these people who sue are probably just greedy, or they're the
victims of cold-blooded, ambulance-chasing lawyers who are
themselves even greedier. With most Americans, I shared the
belief that, as the editor of the *Harvard Medical School Health
Letter* put it in a rueful summary of public opinion, "malpractice
suits are a vulgar effort to capitalize on misfortune." And anyway, *caveat emptor.* If you choose your physician and your hospital wisely, if you're an "intelligent consumer" of medical care,
you're bound to be okay.

Now I feel differently. Now I know that most victims of medical negligence and other forms of malpractice don't even realize
that they *are* victims. And the majority of those who do probably
aren't "greedy" plaintiffs. They're angry, vulnerable, thirsty for
justice, desperately wishing that someone really *had* practiced
"defensive medicine."

For what is "defensive medicine" anyway, and why should
the need for it be so irritating to doctors? Surely it's just *good*
medicine.

2

"We're not God," says Robert Derlet, director of the emergency department at the U. C. Davis Medical Center in Sacramento. "We can't take care of everybody."

—*Newsweek*, October 14, 1991

MONDAY, AUGUST 21, 1990, 10 A.M.

Good medicine is what we thought we were getting when we walked into the office of Ralph W. deVere White in the long, low professional building that sits across a crowded parking lot from the recently renovated glass and concrete six-story hospital that is the centerpiece of the University of California, Davis, Medical Center in Sacramento. As always in California's Central Valley in summer, it was searingly hot outside, nearly a hundred degrees, so that rescue helicopters, which regularly land on the hospital roof with emergency cases from all over the northeastern part of the state, seemed to glow and shimmer in the haze, the roar of their blades almost a palpable weight in the already heavy air.

The associate dean of the medical school met us cordially just outside the door to the building. Tall and freckled, with white-blond hair, he shook hands with my husband, whom he already knew from their joint service on several university committees, and welcomed me back to the U. C. Davis faculty. After four years in the English department at Princeton, I'd returned permanently to my old post at Davis because I so much disliked being in a commuting marriage. Now, of course, I was especially relieved that I was here to be a help to my husband.

"DeVere White is waiting for you in his office," the dean said. "He already knows about your case."

My husband had been diagnosed with prostate cancer on July 30, less than a month earlier, and we were coming to see Dr. deVere White, the chief of Urology at the U. C. Davis Medical Center, for a consultation.

Although it has received relatively little publicity compared to, say, AIDS and breast cancer, prostate cancer is both a widespread and a puzzling disease. It strikes one out of eleven men (making it analogous to breast cancer, which strikes one out of nine women) and kills some 38,000 Americans a year. Worse, where oncologists dealing with breast cancer have developed fairly clear-cut treatment "protocols," physicians haven't been able to agree on any preferred approach to prostate cancer. Depending on the stage and grade of the disease, some advocate radical surgery; some, various forms of radiation; some, so-called hormone blockers; others, a combination of two or three of these; still others, chillingly, what is known as orchiectomy (surgical removal of the testicles—in other words, castration). And what makes one's choice of treatment particularly daunting is the fact that to date no chemotherapy has been shown to be effective in the battle against this cancer.

By the time we made our first appointment with Dr. deVere White we knew all this. Dr. Humphreys, Elliot's regular urologist in Berkeley, had filled us in on a great deal. But as alert consumers of medical care, we'd also been determined to review and research all Elliot's options ourselves. We called an old friend, a pathologist at the National Institutes of Health (NIH) in Washington, and asked his advice about doctors and treatments. After conferring with an associate at the National Cancer Institute, he came up with a few names in northern California and a general outline of current thinking about this illness. At the same time, through other friends, we were assimilated into an informal prostate cancer network, local survivors of the disease who were glad to talk in person or on the phone about the choices they'd made.

Then, like the good academic researchers we were, we did an on-line computer search of the medical literature ourselves, using resources from the U. C. Davis Medical Center that were available to us on campus. Just a week before, Elliot had brought home a thick stack of books and articles. He was too anxious and distressed to read most of them, but though they often contradicted each other and were sometimes so technical as to be incomprehensible to me, I had ploughed through them all. In fact, right now, as we hurried toward deVere White's office, I was carrying a copy of an article that had seemed to me, even as a medical innocent, to hold out some hope of an effective and comparatively painless cure.

DeVere White was the third doctor we'd seen in three weeks, and in the next few days we were to meet with several more, in our determination to make the right decision about the management of my husband's case. Dr. Humphreys in Berkeley had recommended surgery and scheduled an operation for September, so Elliot was already donating blood in preparation for the procedure. But Humphreys had also warned about the special risks of prostate cancer surgery, not so much the usual dangers of clotting or the side effects of anesthesia that attend most major operations but two particular consequences of the operation that, not surprisingly, struck terror into my husband's heart: a three-to-five percent chance of incontinence, and an almost one hundred percent likelihood of impotence.

Faced with such risks, who wouldn't seek advice from expert

after expert? Perhaps, I speculated at the time, it was the specter of these potential assaults on crucial aspects of a man's sense of himself—his adulthood, his sexuality—that had so far kept prostate cancer a relatively unpublicized killer and an underfunded field of investigation. Maybe, I thought, no one, especially not middle-aged male journalists (who should be writing more about the disease) and legislators (who should be allocating more moneys for research) wanted to contemplate such deep-seated sources of masculine anxiety. It had, after all, taken women decades to come together as a community and confront the devastating impact not just on health and life but also on images of femininity that are associated with breast cancer. Now they had begun to do that. But men are notoriously reluctant, even recalcitrant, about what we feminists call "consciousness raising." And I knew that, besides the inevitable fear of cancer, it was the likelihood of impotence together with the threat of incontinence that haunted my husband as we went from doctor to doctor.

Elliot had no physical symptoms at all. His malignancy had been detected during a routine checkup, appeared still to be a treatable stage B or C tumor (cancers that reach stage D, the most severe of four stages, are not considered operable), and had not shown signs of metastasis. Yet after Dr. Humphreys recommended surgery, perhaps to be followed by radiation, we'd consulted with a physician at U. C. San Francisco who'd actually proposed that even at this comparatively early point orchiectomy might be the best and surest treatment. Plainly we needed a third opinion, and a colleague had referred us to the well-known chief of Urology at our own institution. Thoughtfully, he'd cleared the way for us by talking to the associate dean we'd met outside the professional building, who had in turn alerted deVere White that a fellow faculty member at U. C. Davis was coming to see him today about what had been tentatively diagnosed as a stage B or C prostate cancer.

MONDAY, AUGUST 21, 1990, 10:45 A.M.

Scorching as it is outside, it's cool and comfortable in the medical office building. Feeling self-consciously special, we've been ushered through the crowded waiting room into the usual small bare utilitarian examining room, where deVere White is to join us. I am sitting next to a table in the corner, clutching, as if for comfort, the Xeroxed article I've brought and a notebook in which I've been scribbling the opinions and suggestions of various doctors. Elliot is on the other side of the room, staring at, but not reading, a pamphlet about penile implants. Considering our usual mode of exuberant talkativeness—always interrupting each other to agree or disagree or make new points—we are both surprisingly silent.

DeVere White makes a dramatic entrance, bustling in with clipboard in hand and a nurse at his heels to whom he is noisily giving instructions. "Tell them oi'll be there at three. . . ."

A short, stocky balding man with a longish, very British-looking scallop of gray hair and a very Irish-looking turned-up nose, he dismisses the nurse with a wave of his hand, seats himself on a metal stool, scoots it toward Elliot, and looks directly into my husband's eyes. "Ye're Professor Gilbert? I'm Ralph deVere White. Now, d'ye want the prostate cancer talk or d'ye want to ask me questions?"

My husband sits a bit straighter and permits himself a small smile. I can see that he has already begun to be won over by a practitioner who has what is perhaps the liveliest and most charming bedside manner I've ever encountered.

Elliot says that yes, we do have a lot of questions but first we'd like to hear "the prostate cancer talk," since deVere White has offered to deliver it.

Scooting his stool even closer to my husband, the Irishman launches into an animated lecture on prostate cancer: its nature, its consequences, its statistics, its management, and the prognosis for sufferers in various age-groups. Like the other physicians we've spoken to, he concedes that there is little general agreement on the efficacy of surgery versus radiation, although it is clear that (also like the other doctors we've met) as a surgeon himself he advocates the operation known as a radical prostatectomy.

Because prostate cancer is as a rule relatively slow to grow and metastasize, he explains, men over seventy-five should usually elect radiation, which does not cure the malignancy but in effect "holds" it at a harmless stage for eight to ten years. Statistically, he notes, these older men are as likely to die *with* as *from* the disease.

But about someone in my husband's age-group—Elliot is fifty-nine, three months from his sixtieth birthday—he becomes surprisingly vehement. "Ye're a young man. Ye should have twenty or thirty years left," he says earnestly, insisting that in a case like this only radical surgery, followed if necessary by radiation, can effect the complete cure that would make possible those extra decades of life. "A young man like yerself," he reiterates, this time with a heartening grin, *"deserves* a cure."

Youth is relative. My energetic, passionate, sometimes irascible husband certainly doesn't think he's *old*—a fifty-nine-year-old man is hardly old in our society—but he looks younger, less harried, as he smiles back at the doctor.

The conversation moves to other matters, to *the* other matters that are worrying Elliot. Incontinence. Impotence.

A very minor chance of incontinence, deVere White remarks, at Elliot's age and with his sort of tumor, especially if the surgery is skillfully done. Really, despite scary statistics sometimes promulgated, only one percent of men like Elliot suffer from this problem. Of course, he adds wryly, "If it's *you*, it's one hundred percent *you*."

I think, well, not that reassuring, but honest, anyway.

And impotence? Although this has long been almost an invariable side effect of prostate cancer surgery, because in order to excise the malignant gland the doctor has to sever the nerve that controls a man's erections, we have heard from the prostate cancer network about a new "nerve-sparing" surgical procedure that leaves the crucial nerve intact, thereby preserving potency.

DeVere White shakes his head vigorously. "No, no, no." The nerve-sparing procedure isn't radical enough, he declares. It doesn't let the surgeon take "wide margins"—in other words, it means that in order to circumvent the nerve he might have to leave some deadly cancer cells in the body.

Elliot grimaces. I stare at the ceiling. This doesn't seem to me to be a situation where a wife can comfort her husband in front of a stranger.

Of course deVere White senses the tension. "Now what're ye worryin' about?" he demands, turning his back to me and fixing his eyes even more intently on my husband. He lowers his voice a little. "Y'know," he confides, "even with the nerve-sparing ye'll be a stuffer instead of a poker. But in any case, after a radical, I can give ye the best erection of yer life." He gestures toward the penile implant pamphlet Elliot is holding. "There's the implant, there's the injection."

We've heard about both: the implant, which permanently hardens a man's penis, and the injection, somewhat sardonically praised by several members of the Network, which artificially induces a two-hour erection.

"My wife has a question about an article she's been reading." Elliot obviously wants to change the subject.

"Yes," I say, handing deVere White my Xerox. "I wonder about *this*."

It is an article about the benefits of a three-month course of preoperative combination hormone therapy for sufferers from early stage (A to C) prostate cancer. According to the authors, clinical trials have shown that such a course of treatment shrinks both the tumor and the prostate, making radical prostatectomy significantly easier and less complicated. After this therapy, they assert, the time in surgery is some two hours shorter and the surgery itself far less complex and bloody than it would otherwise be. In every case, they observe, they've had excellent results, including higher rates of cure.

"Ah." DeVere White closes his eyes theatrically and intones the name of the principal author. "Monette, Monette, Monette, they're doin' interesting work." He opens his eyes and shrugs. "Well, ye could try that if ye want to," he says somewhat surprisingly.

"But would you advise it?" my husband wants to know.

"If ye like, if ye like," deVere White reiterates. "It can't hurt and it might help."

Both Elliot and I are a little taken aback by the idea that we should make an unassisted decision in this matter, but then, as we were to reflect later, Elliot is after all not deVere White's patient, he is Dr. Humphreys's case and deVere White is only a consultant. At least at this point.

The conversation strays to other subjects. DeVere White mentions that he himself is from a literary family, so he feels a kind of bond with us. His father is a well-known novelist and travel writer in Ireland and England. His stepmother is an even more well-known feminist biographer. I am unaccountably pleased. I've always admired her work and had met her on the East Coast less than a year ago.

Elliot asks who the most highly regarded surgeons in the field are. Our eyes meet as we suddenly realize that this is probably a tactless question, since deVere White himself may well be one of them.

But the doctor is insouciant about the query, as if he doesn't consider it a blunder. "Cut*terrs*, now," he begins, rolling the "r"s in his Irish brogue. "Good *cutterrs*—" and reels off a short list of specialists around the country.

Cutters. I dutifully take down the names in my notebook, then, feeling queasy, begin to doodle on the margins of the page.

"And you?" Elliot wonders, recovering from his embarrassment. "Would you be willing to do the surgery?"

Although Dr. Humphreys is already scheduled to perform the operation, Elliot has clearly begun to think that deVere White might be a more polished practitioner.

"Well, it's up to you, up to you," deVere White replies. "Of course, I do it all the time."

We rise to go, shaking hands all around. I tuck my notebook and the article into my briefcase.

Dr. deVere White makes us promise to keep in touch, let him know what we decide to do. "Safe home," he says, an Irishism I find far more endearing than "Take care" or "Have a nice day," its American equivalents. "Safe home." Get home in safety, journey without risk.

At the door, Elliot turns and says again, with just a hint of anxiety, "So you'd do the surgery? I could move it up here from Berkeley?"

DeVere White smiles and holds up his hands. They are clean, pink, strong-looking hands with blunt, well-manicured fingers. Surgeon's hands, I tell myself.

"I'm not sayin' these golden hands will save ye," he answers, smiling. "I'm not sayin' these golden hands will save ye. . . ."

But he is.

3

In both sudden death and anticipated death, there is pain. However, while the grief is not greater in sudden death, the capacity to cope is diminished. Grievers are shocked and stunned by the sudden loss of their loved one. . . . If you are such a griever, you probably are suffering extreme feelings of bewilderment, anxiety, self-reproach, and depression, and you may be unable to continue normal life.

—THERESE RANDO, *How to Go On Living When Someone You Love Dies*

MONDAY, FEBRUARY 11, 1991, 9:45 P.M.

We are standing beside my husband's body, in a small private room on the surgery floor, down the hall from the recovery room proper. I am still crossing myself compulsively, and out of some archaic, nearly forgotten impulse from my Catholic childhood, whispering fragments of the Our Father and the Hail Mary to myself.

Elliot has been carefully covered with white sheets and a white hospital blanket, as if some tender attendant feared he'd catch cold.

Cold. He is warm but getting colder. I kiss his mouth, his beard, his beautiful thick gray curls, which seem to have been combed by someone. The skin of his face is soft—have they also shaved his cheeks, above his beard?—but has the sort of fresh chill that it would have if he'd just come in from a long walk in the snow, at Lake Tahoe, say, this time of year.

He appears to have a small, secret smile on his lips.

Later, I will wonder if such a "smile" is only what he was referring to when he used to joke (mysteriously, I thought) about a "rictus of a grin." The rueful grimace of the dying one?

The clean white coverlet has been tucked around his neck, like a bib or a ruff.

My daughters and their friend are sobbing, gasping, even cursing next to me. We stand in a row on the side of the bed nearest the door, clinging to the iron bedrail that has been drawn up on both sides of his body. Are the nurses afraid he'll fall out of bed?

Dr. deVere White, his silent staring resident, and the woman from Decedent Affairs face us, on the other side of the bed. Behind them, through a large, uncurtained, icy-looking window, we can see the lights of the parking lot.

Just eight hours ago, deVere White had told us Elliot's surgery was successful, and we'd jubilantly activated a telephone tree for friends and relatives. You call one person who calls two others, each of whom calls others in turn. The word had gotten out. Tokens of love and friendship have already begun to arrive. Now my daughter Kathy is carrying a fancy potted plant that someone in the English department had sent to speed Elliot on his road to recovery, and my daughter Susanna is incongruously clutching the string of a shiny helium balloon that says "GET WELL SOON!"

"What happened? What *happened?*" Susanna demands. Her eyes are swollen, red, and drenched. The balloon bobs with every jerky distracted move she makes.

DeVere White shrugs his shoulders, hangs his head. "I don't know, luv," he says almost plaintively. "He was making good

water, the anastomosis was fine. But his pressure dropped. . . .
His heart . . ." He pauses a moment, then adds, "Nothin' like this
has ever happened to me."

In the midst of my Hail Marys and Our Fathers I stare at his
suit. Its dark gray cloth is expertly tailored. I've never seen him
in street clothes before. In the office he wears khakis and the
usual starched white coat. But I remember that Elliot had said
the doctor had visited him in the hospital ten days ago in his
"conference clothes."

DeVere White was running a urology meeting at Tahoe last
week. That's why we'd had to reschedule the surgery for today.
The surgery that was supposed to have happened on January
30.

"I don't know, luv," he reiterates. "His pressure just dropped,
his pressure dropped, and his heart—a heart attack. . . ." He
glances down at a gold watch, which seems to complement his
suit.

I don't think he's anxious to get out of here. I think he just
doesn't know where to turn his eyes. I keep on crossing myself.

"We must have done the wrong thing," I say in an urgent
undertone to deVere White. "He should have had radiation instead. He shouldn't have had surgery."

DeVere White shakes his head with surprising passion. "No,
no, it was the right decision. The right decision."

"Daddy, daddy, my daddy . . ." Kathy is breaking down, weeping uncontrollably. Her roommate, Liz, weeping herself, takes
the potted plant from her and puts it on a chair in the corner.

Susanna has moved to the other side of the bed, next to deVere
White. She is stroking her father's face and, through her tears,
peering intently at the pillow under his head. "There's blood
here, blood on the pillow," she says severely to the doctor.
"What's this blood?"

Again he shrugs helplessly. "They tried to get a pacemaker in.
The code team."

A nurse I hadn't noticed materializes out of the shadows in a corner of the room and places a towel over the blood on the pillow.

I begin talking to my husband. He looks so—so *close,* I'm sure he can hear me. "Baby, my baby, why did you do this stupid thing? What kind of stupid thing have you done, baby, sweetheart?" I say this over and over again, in a low rapid murmur, as if it were another prayer, like the Hail Mary. Evidently, with so many other survivors of a shock like this, I believe the whole business is *Elliot's* fault. "How could you do it, darling, baby?" I whisper, bending closer to him.

My daughters are keening again, but suddenly Susanna stops and glares reproachfully at deVere White. "He looks funny," she snaps. "Puffy, bloated."

Kathy and Liz agree. His face is puffy, they say.

I stop my frantic whispering for a minute and glance at deVere White. "Is his face swollen, Doctor?" I ask, as if I need someone else to tell me what my husband ought to look like.

DeVere White gestures quizzically. His elegant suit seems to comment that *he* doesn't know how Elliot should look, *he* doesn't know what "they" did, he wasn't there, he only knows what "they" told him—about the pressure, the good water, the heart attack, the pacemaker.

"Perhaps you . . . would you like a glass of water?" The woman from Decedent Services leans toward me nervously.

Poonamallee, the resident, still stands like a stone next to deVere White, gazing wide-eyed at us.

"I know, I know, for you this is unpleasant, awful," the doctor resumes clumsily, "but believe me for me it's *shattering.*"

Kathy has pulled herself together and is placing calls from a phone at a desk discreetly hidden behind a screen at one end of the room.

"Don't worry about the long-distance charges," says the woman from Decedent Services.

So far, Kathy has reached her brother, Roger, who, 3,000 miles from here, in Ithaca, New York, has started weeping and booking flights. Now she's trying to get in touch with Elliot's brother in Georgia, Susan Gubar—my best friend and frequent literary collaborator—in Indiana, and the English department administrative assistant down the road in Davis.

The "arrangements," I realize in the part of me that notices things, are being made. The "arrangements" one hears about have begun.

But most of me just keeps on murmuring to my husband, stroking him, murmuring to him.

Susanna, Liz, and the doctor are conferring quietly with the Decedent Services woman, but I can't listen to what they're saying. Only the resident seems as rooted to the floor as I am.

Now we're all moving toward the door, somehow they've pried me away from the bed, and out into a glaringly white corridor where a gray-haired, sallow woman lies half propped-up on a gurney with oxygen tubes in her nostrils and what seems to me to be a ghastly look of alarm in her eyes.

DeVere White has given me a paper cup half full of water, and I'm trying to swallow it as we all crowd into the elevator. He is asking me if I'm okay, do I feel okay, and the girls are telling him they're worried, urging him to check my pulse. I suppose I must be pale.

Now we're all standing in the parking lot. I'm lighting a cigarette and so is the Decedent Services woman, and then deVere White is clasping my wrist, taking my pulse. Kathy has gone to get the car. Does he think I'm dying too? Can he tell from my pulse?

Poonamallee isn't here, didn't get into the elevator with us. Is he still keeping his strange vigil at Elliot's bedside?

DeVere White has let go of me. I must be all right, I guess. He is telling us that a coroner's autopsy will be necessary, since

Elliot has only been in the hospital for twenty-four hours. That's the law in California, he explains. Any death within twenty-four hours of a hospitalization requires a coroner's autopsy.

I hardly understand what that might mean but I nod numbly. "Coroner's autopsy" sounds like something from Ellery Queen, and one-half of the writing team known as "Ellery Queen" was a good friend of my husband. Elliot occasionally wrote detective fiction and now and then taught courses in the subject. Perhaps such a procedure would be somehow appropriate.

Our battered Toyota pulls up, with Kathy looking puzzled and frowning in the driver's seat, as if she's surprised that such ordinary objects as cars and steering wheels are still left in the world.

Oddly, Susanna hands me the long string that holds the "GET WELL" balloon. I decide to let go of it. It rises eerily over the parking lot, and we all look up, following its wavering ascent, until it disappears.

"Go, Elliot, on your dark journey," I say to myself theatrically, meaninglessly. For of course there is no journey. Elliot is waiting just upstairs, waiting for me to come back tomorrow with another balloon.

Liz opens the door of the car. I am supposed to get in. But first I have to say goodnight politely.

I shake hands with the woman from Decedent Services, who finally pushes the folder labelled "Bereavement Packet" toward me. I give it to Susanna. Then inexplicably I step forward and embrace deVere White. We have, after all, been in this together for the last four months, I reason. I must produce a proper farewell. And it is comforting to hug him and be hugged by him. As if Elliot were giving me the hug he was supposed to give me tonight, after his triumphant departure from the recovery room.

Now I am sitting in the front seat of the car, next to Kathy, and the others are in the back with the "Bereavement Packet" and the potted plant. Though, as I notice for the first time, it's chilly and breezy out here, I roll down the window so I can light another cigarette without offending my family.

Dr. deVere White bends toward me, elbows on the door frame, and leans in. "I couldn't feel worse if it were me own father," he says. Then, as Kathy releases the clutch and steps on the gas, "Safe home," he adds.

4

In unanticipated grief, you are unable to grasp the full implications of the loss. Your adaptive capabilities are seriously assaulted . . . and the death may continue to seem inexplicable.

—RANDO, *How to Go On Living*

MONDAY, FEBRUARY 11, 1991, 11:45 P.M.

The four of us are sitting in the bright, freshly decorated kitchen of the Davis condo that Elliot and I bought last spring, when he decided that, as department chair, he'd need a "pad" nearby so he wouldn't have to commute every day from our house in Berkeley. A carefully symmetrical arrangement of copper pots and pans—Elliot believed deeply in symmetry—gleams on one wall, over the mail-order butcher-block cabinet he put together only last month.

To an outsider, our conversation might seem to be peculiarly animated, but we ourselves know that it is circular, repetitious, pointless. Over and over again, each of us murmurs the same refrain—"What happened? What could have happened?"—as if these words are a kind of talisman we're passing around the table from one person to another.

"What happened? What could have happened?"

"Daddy didn't have a bad heart. He never had a heart problem."

"Anyway, don't they check someone's heart before surgery? They do all these tests, don't they?"

"They just did an EKG the other day, I know that."

"What happened? What could have happened?"

"Clots? He didn't say anything about clots—"

"His kidneys? But deVere White said he was making good water. That means his—"

"Dad was so scared of the surgery, maybe he just freaked out, maybe he—"

"You can't do that to yourself. Just kill yourself like that."

"But what happened, then? What could have happened?"

"DeVere White. He seemed strange this afternoon. Remember? You thought he was angry at us."

DeVere White *had* seemed odd when he came down from the OR at 1:45. Sweating profusely, not taking our hands and looking us in the eye, as he ordinarily would. I *had* thought he might have been angry at us for some inexplicable reason.

But no. He brought good news, remember?

"It's all out, it's in the bucket," he'd said. "It went as well as it could."

With prostate cancer, as with a number of other malignancies, surgery involves a two-step procedure. First the doctor "goes in," removes the lymph nodes surrounding the tumor, and sends them to a pathologist, who examines frozen sections to determine whether or not there has been metastasis. If there has been, the surgeon proceeds no further. He "closes." Since the worst has already happened, there would be no point in continuing. If there hasn't been metastasis, however, he begins the operation proper.

When we were told, as we waited in the lobby, that the surgery was "proceeding," we had practically wept with relief.

"He was just tired, that was all," I remind the girls now. "Exhausted. He'd been in the OR for five hours, for God's sake, probably on his *feet* for five hours."

"I don't know, Mom." Kathy is skeptical. "He was strange at six-fifteen too."

"Well, he didn't want to have to tell us about the blood. I guess he wasn't planning to tell us."

Returning to the hospital in the early evening, when we had been assured we'd at last be allowed to visit Elliot in the Intensive Care Unit, we'd run into deVere White standing on the steps with several other doctors. He was on his way out, apparently heading for the professional building.

"I just saw him," he told us. "He was woozy from the anesthesia and didn't want to chat. He said something like, 'I feel lousy.' "

Somebody remembered to ask him about the blood Elliot had donated. Had the surgery team needed to use any of it?

"Five units," deVere White said curtly.

I'd felt as if I'd been hit. "Five units?" I gasped. "He only donated two, so—"

"We always have backup units."

"But isn't that bad, that much blood?"

"It's neither bad nor good."

I close my eyes. I'm not ready to think about this conversation right now.

"Maybe he *did* have a bad heart, a heart attack, only we—"

"It doesn't make sense. He was so healthy. He always had so much energy."

"But then what happened?"

"The hospital. It was always a bad luck hospital. Think about the biopsy."

"And the failed intubation."

"And the *history* of this hospital. I told you to go somewhere else."

"Yes, but what could have happened this time? What happened?"

"Well, people *do* have heart attacks after just getting a clean bill of health. It happens all the time."

"And Dad's sixty. That's a bad age, that's just the age."

"But how? But why?"

"What happened? How did it happen?"

———

If you perceive the death to have been preventable, and assume responsibility for having failed to prevent it, your grief will be greater and you will experience more guilt, which will further complicate your mourning process.

—RANDO, *How to Go On Living*

The U. C. Davis Medical Center *has* been in several ways a "bad luck hospital," I silently concede, as I embark on a chain of thought into which I will be locked for months and months. Why was Elliot having his surgery here, not at Alta Bates in Berkeley or at Stanford or at U. C. San Francisco?

Through a haze of shock, I try to remember. Dr. Humphreys, the urologist in Berkeley? After we'd consulted with others, he didn't seem sophisticated enough to us, was that it? His nurse evidently told Elliot he didn't do the bowel cleanout that was, according to the Network, routine for most physicians before this surgery. If your doctor didn't do a cleanout and his scalpel slipped you could be in big trouble: peritonitis, septic shock, even colostomy.

And Dr. Stamey, at Stanford? He was the one our friend at NIH had recommended most highly. But when we met him, he terrified us, practically driving Elliot, ordinarily a cheerful and solidly sane human being, to the brink of a breakdown. Someone in the Network had had the same experience and warned us about it.

Stamey was an affable southern gentleman and a famous researcher, who claimed that even if a tumor in the prostate hadn't metastasized he could predict its course by measuring its size in cubic centimeters, which he translated into "sugar cubes" for laypersons. If a tumor was more than forty sugar cubes, the outlook was bad. Doing ultrasound on Elliot, he had exclaimed to a retinue of medical students, as Elliot lay ignominiously listening on the examining table, "Wha' this man has a huge cansuh!" Then, turning to Elliot, he had noted in his courteous southern voice, "Wha' it must be at least eighty suguh cubes!" He'd made no effort to soften the blow. He was courteous, yes, but not kind.

He'd advocated hormones and radiation, although he politely noted that of course he could *do* the surgery. By the time we left his office, Elliot was convinced he had only months to live.

But when we had reported Stamey's advice to Humphreys, deVere White, and yet another consultant—Carroll, a young specialist at U. C. San Francisco, with a cool, clipped manner and an air of restrained authority—they had all demurred. Humphreys still wanted to operate at once. Both Carroll and deVere White also favored surgery but had agreed upon a three-month course of preoperative hormone blockers, the procedure outlined in the article I had brought to our first meeting with deVere White at the UCDMC. And the special vividness of deVere White's personality, his optimism and enthusiasm, had won the day.

Then, too, he was our colleague. Elliot, who was a popular professor on campus and, as department chairman, a remarkably well-liked administrator, had developed a strong sense of institutional loyalty, a keen feeling, even, that his community couldn't and wouldn't let him down. "The chair of Urology can't kill the chair of English," he loved to joke to anyone who asked him about his upcoming surgery.

The chair of Urology. Can't kill. The chair of English. I laughed with the others. The idea of anyone killing anyone in surgery was obviously far-fetched. It was typical of Elliot's comic extravagance that he'd make such a joke. Still, I needed to believe something like that too, though (I told myself) for more cynical and "realistic" reasons.

"I'm sure academic medicine has its politics, doesn't it? Just the way regular academic life does?" I speculated on the phone to our friend at NIH.

A researcher, he deplored the pettiness and egotism found in some "star" doctors. "Absolutely," he agreed.

So then the bottom line was that *politically* the chair of Urology shouldn't "kill" (or, more realistically, injure) the chair of English, and therefore he couldn't and wouldn't.

On August 27, 1990, we had sat again in one of the small, bare examining rooms at the UCDMC where, after running a series of his own tests on Elliot, deVere White had repeated his urgent recommendation of surgery—"Ye're a young man, ye have twenty or thirty years left"—but qualified his argument with what was now a vigorous agreement that three months of combination hormone therapy would indeed make the tumor "easier to resect."

He administered a first injection of leupron, a substance that required monthly doses at the hospital, and handed us a prescription for pills containing flutamide, the other drug.

Gazing deeply at Elliot, "Ye should rejyce that ye're not havin' surgery next week," he said with an elfin Irish smile.

———

"What happened? What could have happened?"

"This is a bad luck hospital. I told you so."

"But what went wrong?"

The biopsy. The failed intubation.

Rejoicing, we had got back to normal life, at least as much as possible. I was so relieved at this turn of events, so heartened by the hope of twenty or thirty more years with my husband, that I even stopped smoking. He had always wanted me to do that, and though I had failed in the past, I was determined to succeed this time, if only to prove my love for him. And to survive to live with him.

And two-and-a-half smoke-free months went rather peacefully by. Elliot looked well, said he felt fine, and chaired the department with his usual verve. Even ordinarily dull committee meetings were jovial and full of laughter. The combination hormone therapy appeared to have no side effects other than the temporary and (we'd been told) completely reversible lowering of libido that was inevitable with testosterone blockers like leupron and flutamide.

We planted a new garden in Berkeley, we quarreled, we joked, we went to visit an old friend in Reno and spent a morning losing ten dollars in quarters to the slot machines at Harrah's. We talked on the phone with our kids, we started thinking about our Christmas shopping. I planned a surprise "Big Six-O" party for Elliot's birthday on December 1.

Then, in mid-November, Elliot had a routine bone scan in preparation for the radical prostatectomy that had now been scheduled for early December. When we went to get the results from deVere White, he was both ashen and flustered. "It's positive," he said.

Stupidly, I thought "positive" meant "good." Why was he distressed?

"That means there's a hot spot in one rib," he gently explained. A spot that suggested the prostate cancer had metastasized to the bone, which it frequently does if the patient's condition has worsened.

None of us looked at each other. DeVere White was gazing at

the Nuclear Medicine report on his lap. Elliot put one hand over his eyes. His face was unusually pink. I studied the floor, as if it might yield up some useful secret formula for survival.

"I'm so sorry," deVere White finally said. "Ye're such nice people."

"What do we do now?" I asked, still staring at the floor.

"He stays on the combination hormone therapy," deVere White replied flatly. "That's the treatment of choice when there's been metastasis."

"Indefinitely?"

"Indefinitely."

But after a minute he seemed to reconsider. Shuffling through the report again, he said he'd like to order a biopsy of the problematic rib. Metastasis directly (and only) to a rib, he observed, was unusual in prostate cancer. Ordinarily the cancer traveled first to some bone closer to the pelvic area—the pelvis, the hipbone, or the spine, for instance. Which was why sufferers from late-stage prostate cancer often complained of back pains.

On the way home, we stopped at a 7-Eleven so I could buy a pack of cigarettes.

The chief of Thoracic Surgery at the UCDMC, who turned out to be an old high school classmate of Elliot's, was to perform the biopsy on November 29, a few days before my husband's sixtieth birthday.

"That's not prostate cancer," said one of the technicians in Nuclear Medicine the morning of the twenty-ninth, as he inspected the hot spot on the screen so that he could mark Elliot's back in preparation for the surgery, which was fairly serious and would have to be carried out under general anesthesia.

"How do you know?" Elliot was awake and, of course, jumpy.

"It just doesn't look like it," the man said. "Not like what *I've* seen."

When the technician's marker touched skin, Elliot remembered that just there, on that spot, he'd had a bad cystic infection a few years ago. If anyone had pinpointed the troublesome area for him, maybe he could have explained. As he was being wheeled out of Nuclear Medicine, he called Kathy and me over to the gurney and urged us to have the biopsy postponed or cancelled, so he could discuss this with the doctors. But after investigating, deVere White's resident told us that, perhaps understandably, the urologist wanted the thoracic surgeon to certify that there was no metastasis before a radical prostatectomy was performed.

"The Lord knows I might be wrong, and of course we have to wait for the path. report," said Dr. Benfield, the tall quiet thoracic surgeon when he came down to see Kathy and me in the lobby after the biopsy was over, "but I've done hundreds of these, and it doesn't look like prostate cancer to me."

Our spirits rose a little as we packed to leave the hospital. Elliot trusted his old classmate and was in a particularly good mood, flirting with the nurses, who all called him "Professor" with jocular fondness.

As I was zipping up his overnight bag, a resident strolled in with a chart. "When you come back for the next surgery"—he means the prostatectomy, I thought with a surge of relief—"tell them to be sure to review these notes about the intubation," he said. "You were very difficult to intubate."

We must both have looked at him blankly. Difficult to intubate?

Something about Elliot's anatomy, he explained, the configuration of his mouth, neck, windpipe, made it especially hard to get a breathing tube down his throat. And a breathing tube is now considered essential with general anesthesia.

Oh, okay. The resident seemed unperturbed and so, then, were we. We would remind the doctors next time. It was wonderful that this young man was confident there would *be* a next time instead of merely an "indefinite" course of hormone treatment.

A week later the pathology report showed that Benfield and the resident weren't wrong. There was no metastasis.

Just before Elliot went under the anesthesia, said Dr. Benfield, the two of them had chatted about the senior play at their high school, of which Elliot was a coauthor.

Comforting. It had been curiously comforting, I realize now, to know that the two men had shared memories of high school when they encountered each other in the OR. As if the continuity of past and present guaranteed a continuity of the present into the future?

"What happened? What could have happened?" My daughters are still asking the same question, and I am still staring down at the little round table in the Davis kitchen, trying to reconstruct the events of the last two months.

We were going away to a professional meeting the week after Christmas. That was perfectly fine, deVere White said. There was no rush about the prostatectomy. As long as Elliot stayed on the combination hormone therapy. And no danger in doing *that*. If anything, the treatment would shrink the tumor further, make the resection even simpler, safer.

The operation was rescheduled for January 30. But as the date grew nearer, Elliot began to express increasing dread, perhaps even more, I thought, than is complained of by most people anticipating major surgery. He was worried about the anesthesia, fearful of unexpected side effects from the operation—paralysis, colostomy—and obviously anxious about its known side effects: incontinence, impotence.

Kathy and I had both had major surgery ourselves in the last few years, I, a hysterectomy, and she, what Elliot and I regarded as a truly serious procedure compared to ours: brain surgery for a tumor in the right parietal lobe. We both sympathized with Elliot and tried to reassure him.

"That moment when you're being wheeled into the OR," he said, "that moment when you think this might be your last moment of conscious life. . . . How does one . . ."

We told him we'd felt that too. Kathy had had death dreams for months before her operation; she and I had both made wills in preparation for our surgery. But now we recommended a sort of existential grin-and-bear-it insouciance. "You just say the hell with it, Dad," Kathy advised.

"Che será será," I added. "One entrusts oneself to the gods."

But did I really mean that, I who had awakened an hour after my hysterectomy to find Elliot at my bedside in the recovery room? I who had so soon been transferred to a cheerful private room that was quickly filled with friends and flowers?

I guess I believed we were all "working ourselves up" when we got so gloomily metaphysical.

"What if I'm in diapers for the rest of my life," Elliot muttered. "What if I'm an old man before my time, incontinent, impotent?"

I adduced statistics, percentages. I sang the praises of the Injection.

On the phone, Susan and I affirmed to each other the *emotional* reasons for following deVere White's advice to have surgery, reasons that seemed as crucial to us as the doctor's apparently unimpeachable medical logic.

"He has to get that thing out of him."

"I'd want to get it out, get it over with, wouldn't *you?"*

"He has to get it out, that's the only chance of a cure, too. *I'd* want to take that chance."

"I'd just want it out of me."

Nevertheless, Elliot and I arranged a last-ditch appointment with Dr. Bagshaw, a renowned radiologist at Stanford, who outlined the virtues of radiation treatment to us while admitting that surgery plus radiation might in Elliot's case be even more effective.

In the waiting room outside his office, we saw Alan Cranston, the senator from California whose prostate cancer had just hit the headlines and who was now probably Dr. Bagshaw's most famous patient. A thin, drawn man in his late seventies, he was leafing through a copy of *Newsweek*. He wore a stylishly youthful leather jacket and looked calm, indifferent, ill.

Elliot was not just younger, but healthier, I decided. Surgery was surely appropriate for *him*.

Of course deVere White agreed. "We've taken extraordinary steps to prove ye don't have metastatic disease," he said severely to my husband when we came back from Stanford. "Now, d'ye want a cure or don't ye?"

———

On the morning of January 29, Elliot checked into the UCDMC. As a faculty member, he'd been able to request a "special amenities room"—a private room with (unheard-of, I'd thought, in a hospital) carpeting, draperies, "French provincial" furniture, and a TV/VCR. He'd brought his blue and silver bathrobe, some videos, a Walkman, and tapes of Mozart and Wagner operas. I'd brought good luck tokens: Raggedy Andy, Orlando Furrioso, and a string of Puerto Rican "healing beads" given me by a Hispanic friend. I was to wear these while Elliot was in surgery, so the spirits would help the doctors along.

I didn't feel weird or self-conscious about planning to wear them, either. It turned out that some of our friends were engaging in similar gestures on Elliot's behalf. One colleague, an orthodox Jew, had asked fellow members of his congregation in Sacramento to mention my husband to God. A close friend of Susan's, in Indiana, had requested that an entire Carmelite nunnery in Indianapolis pray for Elliot at mass that day. And a famous poet who taught in our department was arranging a small Buddhist service in the foothills of the Sierras.

The bowel cleanout, facilitated by several gallons of a foul-tasting laxative water, took most of the day and left my husband tired and grim. He'd already spent forty-eight hours on a specially prescribed liquid diet, and he was a man who loved to cook and eat good meals.

Once, when I was away on a trip, he'd fixed himself an entire roast turkey dinner—stuffing, sweet potatoes, cranberry sauce, the works—just on a whim. Now, he supplemented the cans of something called Ensure, which constituted his liquid diet, with a superb broth that he made from roast turkey carcasses you could buy at a nearby Hofbrau.

When the anesthesiology resident came in for a preoperative interview that evening, we dutifully mentioned the difficult intubation at the biopsy. Blond, athletic-looking, and almost frenetically alert, the young man left the room and returned with Elliot's chart.

"It's true," he commented reassuringly, as if we'd be relieved to learn we hadn't made up the problem. "It says so right here."

But we weren't to worry, he told us. Anesthesiologists had remarkable techniques nowadays. In fact—he waxed notably enthusiastic—anesthesiology was *the* best and most interesting field in which to do a residency.

I was to spend the night in the room with Elliot, but our daughters and Liz were going to go back to the Davis condo, then return in the morning to have some time with us before the surgery.

As Kathy was saying goodnight, Elliot reminded her of their "deal." If he was on life support, paralyzed, or seemingly comatose, but his eyes were open, she was to ask him if he wanted to die. They had a signal. What was it? One blink meant yes, two meant no?

After the girls left, we settled into our side-by-side hospital beds. When this was all over, we decided, as we drifted, or tried to drift, off to sleep, we'd go to Hawaii. We'd never been there. At last we'd explore the beaches, the volcanoes, the coral reefs . . .

At eleven the next morning, an orderly in greens came up from the OR to get Elliot. Kathy, Susanna, Liz, and I were allowed to go down to the second floor in the elevator with him and walk as far as the locked entrance to the surgery suite. Each of us kissed him goodbye—I kissed him nine times, my magic number—and as the big doors swung open, and he was wheeled through, toward I didn't know what, I burst into tears.

"The doctor told us to go out for lunch, Mom," my daughters said, trying to comfort. "Let's go out for lunch."

Someone had recommended a surprisingly elegant Italian restaurant at a nearby shopping mall, where we gazed without appetite at exquisite platters of antipasti: artichoke salad, marinated roasted red, green, yellow, and purple peppers, stuffed mushrooms, *insalata di ceci*, tomatoes *caprese*—everything we usually loved to eat.

At two-thirty, we returned to the hospital, to be told that there was as yet no real news from the OR.

We settled ourselves on a window seat with books and magazines that we couldn't read.

At three-thirty, there was deVere White, looking chagrined. "They couldn't intubate," he said. "They were there with their fiber optics, but they couldn't intubate."

"What happened? What could have happened? What went wrong?"

Sitting in the kitchen of the Davis condo, we're all still saying the same stupid words over and over again.

Everything has happened wrong, I think now, everything has gone wrong.

"We should get him to another hospital, Mom," Susanna had said, as we gazed in amazement at deVere White's retreating white-coated back. "If they can't intubate after being *warned* that it's going to be hard, we should—"

I'd interrupted her impatiently. "You hear horror stories about every hospital," I said. "And anyway, it's too late now to get on someone else's surgery schedule fast enough."

I was becoming more and more nervous, too, but I couldn't think of an alternative to staying at the UCDMC. Why "fly to evils that we know not of?" I asked myself with, as it now seems, foolish grandiosity.

"Extraordinary steps," deVere White had said. "We've taken extraordinary steps. D'ye want a cure or don't ye?"

———

Because you were not prepared for the death and it had no understandable context, you will try to deal with your lack of anticipation by putting the loss into a series of events. You may find yourself looking back at the time leading up to the death and searching for clues that could have indicated what was to come.

—RANDO, *How to Go On Living*

A team of anesthesiologists, we learned on the evening of January 30, including the handsome, lively resident from the night before, had spent two-and-a-half hours trying to poke a breathing tube down Elliot's throat, until finally the membranes in the airway were so swollen that the procedure was plainly impossible, and deVere White had intervened, as surgeon, to call a halt. Afterwards, Elliot had to be given massive doses of steroids to reduce the swelling. The surgery would have to be postponed for at least three days, until he could recover and be examined by a pulmonary specialist.

Dr. deVere White was committed to running a urology conference at Lake Tahoe that week, however, so the next attempt at surgery would have to wait until he returned. He'd be back on February 10, he said; we could reschedule the surgery for February 11. That wasn't his usual operating day, but because the anesthesiologists had blundered so seriously, the hospital would make an OR available to him on a special emergency basis.

Elliot was flushed, hectic, and agitated from the steroids. So far as I could see, no one had made any effort to taper his dosage, as is usual with these strong drugs. When we left the hospital, two days later, I thought he was probably having a bad reaction to going off them too abruptly. The residents and nurses seemed undisturbed, though, and deVere White had already left for Tahoe.

"Do you know what?" Elliot asked me excitedly as we drove away. "They told me that when they had so much trouble intubating at the biopsy last month, I was exactly sixty seconds away from being brain dead!" Before the anesthesiologists had attempted to intubate on that occasion, he explained, they had "put him under" on the assumption that they'd be able to insert the respirator with dispatch. But they couldn't, and he wasn't breathing—his brain wasn't getting any oxygen—until they'd finally, blindly, jammed the tube down his throat. A fact no one had mentioned to him until now.

I believed him, but I was bothered by the feverishness in his voice. I decided I'd care for him myself, take him up the coast to our house at the Sea Ranch, an ocean-side community where we could stroll on the beach and lie in the sun, if there was any. There was no point in either of us going back to the department at this stage. An acting chairman had taken over Elliot's duties and someone else was covering my classes. Elliot was, after all, supposed to be hospitalized right now, and I was expected to be at his bedside.

That was our last week together. The steroids wore off, and Elliot calmed down, becoming, if anything, unusually quiet. We walked in the meadows near our house, in the woods, and on the beach. We watched movies on the VCR, built fires, fulminated—but somewhat resignedly—against the oafish anes-

thesiologists, and hardly spoke at all about the upcoming surgery.

Some of the time, I was, if anything, inexplicably harsh with
my husband. One night, for instance, he started to show me a
video of *Airplane II,* a film he'd thought hilarious, and I refused to
laugh.

"It's stupid, it's just too stupid," I said sullenly.

"Never mind then." He turned off the VCR the minute I complained.

"Why are you turning it off?" I asked querulously. "Don't you
want to watch it anyway?"

"I don't care." He was half whispering, his voice still hoarse
from the anesthesiologists' futile assault on his throat. "I just
want to sit here with you," he said. "I just want to sit here in this
room with you." For such a feisty man, he was suddenly surprisingly docile, even humble.

The living room felt cold and shadowy, even with the fire
blazing.

I scowled at him. Yes I did, I remember now with embarrassment, no, with pain, as I stare dry-eyed at the bright new
butcher-block cabinet that he just finished building for the
kitchen. I scowled at him that night, when he turned off *Airplane
II* and sat down beside me in front of the hearth.

Was I cross because I was frightened? Was Elliot docile because he was resigned? Was our dread, not just his but mine,
intensifying?

Or were we simply so determined that on the next try, on
February 11, the surgery had to happen, *had* to happen and be
over with, that we distracted ourselves by focusing on other
concerns?

That week seemed like time-out-of-time—or did it feel, somehow, posthumous, as though what was going to be had already
occurred?

When the short winter afternoons drew to a close, Elliot

would lie on the window seat in his old Irish sweater—a souvenir we bought in Dublin in 1970—half dozing, half watching the fading sunset leave its reddish trail over the icy glimpse of the Pacific that we get from our living room. I sat near him, not saying much but not wanting to be far away. I was trying to grade papers, write references for students, catch up on my work. I was sure I'd be too busy to get any professional stuff done in the hospital next week.

Every night at ten or eleven a family of raccoons visited our front deck, prowling around the picnic table and peering wistfully at us through the sliding glass doors. On the way back to Berkeley, our car hit a skunk, and we had to go straight to a carwash when we got home, to try to get rid of the stink.

An unusual number of animals had come down out of the hills this year, perhaps because of the drought in California. Even the house in Berkeley seemed to smell of skunk, and some creature was regularly toppling the trash cans. Our kids actually insisted that a skunk was living in our basement.

Were these omens, I ask myself now, gazing blankly at the copper pans on the wall. Should these *signs* have warned me that what has happened would happen?

On February 7, we had dinner with two old friends at a favorite Japanese restaurant in Berkeley. The Gulf War had begun. Three out of four of us argued about Saddam Hussein and the best way to "handle" him. I was animated, angry at the government. Again Elliot was uncharacteristically subdued. But he ordered the combination Bento box—sushi, shrimp tempura, chicken teriyaki—and ate well.

It was his last real meal. The next day he had to go back on the liquid diet and start making himself his special turkey broth again. Broth, Jell-O, fruit juice, tea, soda, and cans of Ensure. He never complained about it. He understood that it was supposed to be good for him.

"It's a bad luck hospital," both my daughters are still repeating. "We should have gotten him out of there."

"What happened? What could have happened?" Liz says it this time.

Are they right? Some fifteen years ago, there *were* rumors. The UCDMC had almost lost its accreditation because, we'd heard, of an excessively high mortality rate. But administrators had explained that since this was a teaching center, the staff admitted more difficult cases than surrounding institutions did. The rumors evaporated, the gossip petered out. In recent years, the reputation of the UCDMC had soared. Remember those emergency helicopters on the roof, carrying desperate patients from all over? And besides, there are terrible rumors about *every* hospital, there's always gossip. . . .

Involuntarily, I begin to rock, groan, cross myself again, and, hardly knowing what I'm saying, I resume my urgent question to my husband. "Elliot, why did you do it, baby, darling? What was wrong? Why did you do this stupid thing?"

My daughters put their arms around me and guide me gently from the table. "Go to bed, Mom," they're saying. "You've got to go to bed, you've got to get some sleep."

5

You may be confused and dazed, unable to comprehend
what has happened. You may feel bewildered and numb.
. . . The news may seem so overwhelming that you cannot
make any sense out of it. . . . You may quietly withdraw, act
mechanically without feeling, or feel as if you are outside of
your own body, looking from a distance at what is happen-
ing to you.

—RANDO, *How to Go On Living*

TUESDAY, FEBRUARY 12, 1991, 1:30 P.M.

I am sitting, again, at the kitchen table in the Davis condo. I've
been sitting here for hours, I think, with a cup of coffee in front of
me, but I'm not sure how I got here. How did I change out of my
nightgown and into the turtleneck, blue jeans, and sneakers I'm
wearing? How did I manage to shower and wash my hair?

I slept very late, I dimly recall. I didn't want to wake up, to
drag myself out of the bed where just two nights ago my husband had been beside me, comfortingly warm and well, his heart
beating steadily, his "pressure" normal, no "anastomosis," no
puffiness, no pallor, no small secret smile—if that *was* a smile—
no intubation, no pacemaker.

The Bereavement Packet lies open on the table. It is a large
blue and white folder. (Blue and white are the U. C. Davis school

colors.) It has pockets on either side. On the outside of one pocket there is a "checklist" for mourners:

  —*Have you notified Social Security?*
  —*Have you ordered enough copies of the Death Certificate?*
  —*Have you made funeral arrangements?*
  —*Have you obtained the Decedent's will?*
  —*Have you notified other insurance agents?*
  —*Have you been in touch with the Decedent's employer to ar-range for a final paycheck?*

Inside the pockets there are listings of churches, morticians, and cemeteries in the area, the telephone numbers of the local social security offices and of the county coroner, and the names of "skilled social workers" at the UCDMC who are available for counseling the bereaved.

I close the packet. I don't want to read it, in the same way that I didn't want to wake up.

Red-eyed and exhausted though she was, Kathy brought me orange juice and coffee in bed this morning. I huddled under the covers. She left the glass and the cup tactfully on the night table, so I'd have a chance to pull myself together, I guess. Then she came back ten minutes later, to sit with me while I swallowed the juice, sipped the coffee.

Swallowing is hard. For the next three months I'll have trouble swallowing. For six months I won't want to wake up. For at least four of those six months, people will rise above their own grief to take turns bringing me juice and coffee in bed, as if I were, after all, the one who had been hospitalized.

The phone has been ringing all day. The girls have been answering it. Unless I absolutely have to, I can't seem to talk to anyone. I've even stopped murmuring to Elliot.

Roger is en route from Ithaca, Susan from Indiana. My brother-in-law, Richard, and his wife, Joyce, are flying in from Georgia, where they were visiting their daughter. Somehow they're all scheduled to arrive at the Sacramento airport at around the same time. Kathy and Liz have gone to get them in two different cars. They can't all fit in the old Toyota.

Afternoon already. The Davis kitchen faces north, into a clear bright light. It's warm out. I can see people walking around in shirtsleeves. This is California, where it can be springlike in February. When Elliot and I left Berkeley two days ago, the plum trees were already flaunting plump rose-colored buds that were about to open into a haze of petals.

Elliot loved February, the month of plum blossoms, best of all the strangely skewed seasons in California. In New York City, where we both grew up, this was usually a period of icy desolation, and even in the so-called spring, in May for instance, we rarely saw any flowering fruit trees.

When I was teaching on the East Coast, Elliot would call on February evenings to tell me—half tauntingly, half irritably—that the plum blossoms were out, the streets were lined with feathery pink. He wanted badly for me to come back to California, and he was right, I'd muse, gazing out my office window at the frozen campus.

But I went back to California, and look what happened.

Maybe I should have stayed on the East Coast. Maybe then Elliot would have had the surgery at a hospital in New York, a really big, sophisticated hospital like Memorial or Mount Sinai, and he'd be alive right now.

Heart failure. A typed obituary for my husband lies on the table next to the Bereavement Packet. Someone from the English department brought it over just an hour ago. The university Public Affairs bureau had efficiently sent the draft out this morning. "Professor Elliot L. Gilbert, Chair of the English Department at U. C. Davis, died last night of heart failure following surgery at the U. C. Davis Medical Center," the release begins. I am supposed to check it for accuracy. Are the names of our children spelled properly? Have all his books been mentioned?

But of course I'm not supposed to check the diagnosis. Heart failure. Not a "heart attack." Who told the Public Affairs bureau to list this as the cause of death? And what does "heart failure," as opposed to "heart attack," mean anyway? I had thought I was a smart researcher and, for a layperson, comparatively knowledgeable about medicine. Consider how I found that article on preoperative hormone therapy! (And consider how much good *that* has done!) But it turns out that I understand nothing, nothing.

DeVere White on the phone this morning. "It seems they *don't* have to do a coroner's autopsy, luv," he'd confided. "But they *can*. So now ye have yer choice. We'd like to do an autopsy here at the hospital *or* ye can have the coroner's autopsy anyway *or* none at all." He pronounced these last words with particular Irish flair: "None ah *tall.*"

"But why don't they need to do a coroner's autopsy? I thought they . . ." I began.

He was noncommittal. "That's what they *tell* me, luv. I don't know about these things meself." His tone implied that *his* patients never died, or at least were never irresponsible enough to die so rapidly, unexpectedly, and mysteriously.

Kathy had immediately gotten on the phone to Dick Asofsky, our NIH friend. Although I was still blank, almost anesthetized, she and her sister were becoming increasingly suspicious of the hospital.

Their dad was a healthy man, Kathy and Susanna repeated over and over again. Why was his face so swollen, why was there blood on the pillow, what happened, what could have happened? Liz echoed their sentiments. She'd gotten to know and love Elliot in the last few years, when she and Kathy had been living in Oakland, not far from us.

Dick was shocked by the story Kathy told, but he collected himself at once to help.

"Wouldn't a coroner's autopsy be preferable?" Kathy asked

him. "Why should we trust the doctors at the UCDMC? Don't you think they might try a cover-up?"

As a pathologist, Dick said, he considered a cover-up unlikely, though not impossible. Every hospital has review mechanisms, checks and balances, he noted. The pathologists are really independent of the surgeons. In any case, a cover-up would be fraudulent, criminal. And besides, there was no doubt some simple and rational, if distressing, explanation for her father's death. Something like "silent heart disease" or an embolism, which would be uncovered by a thorough hospital autopsy and lay our doubts to rest even if it didn't console us for our loss.

"But wouldn't the coroner be more objective?" Kathy wanted to know.

More perfunctory, Dick assured her. If we really wanted answers, we would have to rely on the hospital, which was after all a major medical center, a research institution. And if the UCDMC didn't give us clear explanations, or if we couldn't understand what they told us, he'd be more than willing to review the materials himself—the autopsy report, the death certificate, even, should it seem necessary, the records from the OR and the recovery room. Although that last step almost certainly wouldn't be necessary.

I've known Dick since I was a sixteen-year-old freshman at Cornell and he was my college boyfriend's roommate. He later married *my* college roommate and, though we live on opposite coasts and don't see each other that often, he and his wife, Leah, are virtually family to us. Even if I couldn't bring myself to get on the phone with him, it was comforting to know that he was there to advise my daughters.

It only took a few minutes, after Kathy hung up, for us to decide on a hospital autopsy. Just before she left for the airport, Kathy called Carolyn from Decedent Services to tell her what we had chosen, and she was promised that we would have a rough idea of the results tomorrow. Soon after, my husband's body would be released to the funeral home we've selected.

I stare out the window, try to swallow some coffee.

Susanna comes into the kitchen. She's been upstairs making still more calls to friends, relatives, colleagues. What are we going to tell the grandmothers, she wants to know—Elliot's sickly eighty-five-year-old mother in Florida, my frail eighty-seven-year old mother in New York.

To the extent that I can notice anything, I can notice and be grateful for my daughters' solicitude and efficiency. What I don't quite realize, and won't be able to realize until almost a year from now, is just how devastated my kids are. Locked into my own astonishment at the calamity that's befallen us, I can barely see how, glazed with grief, wan and shocked, Kathy and Susanna have all day today been moving like robots through lists of chores that suddenly, inexplicably have to be done so that their father can be properly buried.

Perhaps, I'll speculate next year, our two daughters and our son have internalized my husband's fortitude, or whatever the quality was that got him through the demeaning rectal examinations, the unnerving diagnoses, the scary biopsy, the failed intubation, and all the other medical traumas of the last few months.

And we need to decide about further arrangements, Susanna points out now. To *which* funeral home will the body be released? And what about a service? And a cemetery plot, we don't have one, what are we going to do?

She pauses a minute, gazing at me with wide, strained eyes. "Your coffee is cold, Mom," she says. "Let me warm it up."

I glance toward the window again. There are the others, with their winter coats over their arms, walking toward our condo in the mild February air: Elliot's younger brother, Richard, and his wife, Joyce, looking exhausted and stunned; Susan, with dark circles under her eyes; and our son, Roger, his mouth set in a thin grim line.

Kathy and Liz lead the way, seeming, themselves, almost as dazed as the new arrivals.

WEDNESDAY, FEBRUARY 13, 1991, 7 P.M.

Everyone is setting the table for dinner. Even I have been somehow detached from the cane-backed chair in the kitchen where I sat all morning and much of the afternoon, staring out the big window into the northern light, and I, too, am setting the table.

We've just returned from the office of Rabbi Ronald, at the Davis Jewish Fellowship, where we made our final plans for Elliot's funeral tomorrow.

The service will be in the airy, high-ceilinged assembly room at the Jewish Center on Oak Avenue. The kids and I like the space; it reminds us of some of the open, shed-like spaces in the public buildings at the Sea Ranch.

And the service will be ecumenical. Neither Elliot, born Jewish, nor I, born Catholic, has been religious. But I think we must defer to his heritage, we must say the Kaddish for him. Yet I also want something of my own inheritance represented. So his coffin will be in the *schul*, as it would be in the church at a Catholic mass, and the rabbi will say prayers over it as a priest would. I believe the dead one should be in a sacred place for the mourners' last farewells, although, as I will later learn, this is completely contrary to Jewish custom.

We'll open with the "Cavatina" from Beethoven's Thirteenth Quartet, which Elliot regarded as perhaps the most transcendent piece of music ever written. Kathy, Susanna, and Liz will each read a psalm. Roger (who doesn't want to read from the Bible) and Susan and a few of Elliot's colleagues will make brief memorial speeches. I will be silent. I can't imagine being able to speak.

Except that I'll say the Kaddish with the rest, we'll all say the Kaddish, then end with the beautiful "sunset" music of "Im Abendrot," one of Richard Strauss's *Four Last Songs*, another piece that Elliot revered.

These arrangements have been emotionally exhausting, but at least we've made them. At least the others managed to get me out of the condo and all the way to Oak Avenue.

Rabbi Ronald wanted to know something about the "deceased" so he could say a few words too. Since Elliot was not a practicing Jew—and in any case, we spent most of our free time in Berkeley—he and Elliot had never met. For a minute, no one spoke, then everybody started talking at once.

"He loved music—opera, Wagner—and Beethoven, Mahler, you know, like the things we're going to play—"

The children spoke excitedly, heatedly, as if vehement invocations of their father's most special characteristics would bring him back to us in the flesh, full of energy and ebullience, laughing delightedly at his own comic insights into the world.

"He told wonderful jokes. He had a character named Rabinowitz. He told Rabinowitz jokes. He was famous for them. Some friends once phoned from the East Coast and asked him to tell a Rabinowitz joke while they got on all the extensions in the house they were calling from."

"He was a terrific Victorianist. And he did a dramatic reading of Dickens. He was asked to do it at conferences around the country. Got dressed as a nineteenth-century gentleman and read from *Bleak House*. We have a tape of it somewhere."

"I wish I could have met him," the rabbi said. Wistfully, I thought.

Roger and Kathy have opened our round pedestal table as far as it can go and put in both leaves. Now it has become a long gracious oval, and we're setting it for nine. Extended like this, it can accommodate ten, but the tenth person—my husband, who should be sitting at the head—is missing. Still, this will be the largest dinner party we've ever had in the Davis condo. Elliot and I really hadn't finished decorating the place until about a month ago, so we'd had very few guests. Until now.

Now the house is full of people, has been since yesterday. The kitchen counters are laden with food. Last night two of the English department staffers brought over a huge basket of delicacies: fruit, biscotti, Brie, smoked Edam, jams and jellies, sausages and special mustards. Susanna and Susan have arranged the cheeses and sausages on a platter for us to nibble with our drinks. And a colleague and his wife brought supper yesterday, a hearty stew. We probably have some of that left as well.

Flowers. My colleague and his wife came with a bunch of the first irises, too. Irises arrive early in California, along with plum blossoms.

Someone has put the irises in a vase at the center of the table. But will we be able to see each other over their bluish purple heads? All nine of us?

I sit down experimentally at one side of the table, to decide about this. Nine, we *are* nine, aren't we? Kathy, Susanna, Liz, and me—four. Plus Roger, Susan, Richard, and Joyce—eight. Yes, and plus my mother, that's nine.

The family decided that Elliot's mother is too ill herself to be told of her older son's death (my brother-in-law will travel to Florida in a few weeks to talk to her about it) but my mother arrived this afternoon. At eighty-seven, she rarely travels, but when Susanna called her yesterday to tell her what had happened, she became hysterical, began praying in Sicilian—a language to which she reverts only in the gravest crises—and said she had to be with her daughter. Susan's mother, who also lives in New York and who, at seventy-five, still prides herself on her competence and mobility, took her to JFK Airport this morning. Roger and Kathy picked her up in San Francisco this afternoon.

They had to be there anyway. They had to find a cemetery plot in Berkeley—I couldn't do it—and they had to bring back some black clothes for us to wear to the funeral tomorrow.

Roger changed the message on the answering machine at our house in Berkeley, too.

Elliot and I always loved recording joint messages.

Elliot: "Hi, this is Elliot Gilbert."

Me: "And this is Sandra Gilbert."

Elliot: "If you have a message for either of us, or for Roger, Kathy, or Susanna, please leave it when you hear the tone."

Me: "Messages sometimes get mixed up around here, so please tell us the time and date of your call. You may speak as long as you like."

For some reason, we usually cracked up while recording this message or a variant on it. Maybe it was the absurdity of the scene: the two of us hunched over a tiny mike in my study, solemnly reading from a script (we always prepared a script). No matter how often we re-did our performance, Elliot in particular was noisily struck by the hilarity of the enterprise. Even on the final product, his voice was just a little shaky with laughter.

Obviously Roger had to erase that. The voice of the dead man—the laughter of the decedent—doesn't belong on an answering machine. Roger soberly recorded a new, carefully neutral message: "Hello, this is 527-xxxx. If you have a message, please leave it when you hear the tone. Thank you."

If you're a woman alone, it's important to have a male voice on your answering machine, my mother advises. You don't want strange callers to *know* you're a Woman Alone.

That is what I am now. A Woman Alone. Like my mother, who has been a widow for a quarter of a century. This afternoon, when she got to Davis, she embraced me, weeping, and told me it's unpleasant, but I'll get used to it.

Unpleasant. Because she realizes her way of talking tends to be extravagant, theatrically Italian, my mother is trying to be calm and understated.

She too is setting the table, smoothing napkins, neatly aligning cutlery.

"It looks just great," I say to the others. "But the living room . . . Can we . . . ?"

The living room and the study, which, apart from the kitchen, make up almost the whole downstairs of the small condo, are strewn with mattresses and bedclothes. Because we suddenly have so many people staying over, friends have had to lend us rollaways, futons, sheets, towels.

Susanna and Susan begin folding linens and rolling beds into corners, so we can put more chairs around the table.

"Unpleasant." The word has an odd resonance.

DeVere White at Elliot's bedside. "For you this is unpleasant, awful, but for me it's *shattering.*"

What did he mean? Did he really mean that the doctor is even more pained than the "bereaved"?

All afternoon, while Roger and Kathy were back in Berkeley, Susanna and Susan were on the phone with Carolyn at Decedent Services, trying to track the progress of the autopsy. The funeral director we finally chose needed to know when the pathologists would release my husband's body, so he could prepare it for burial tomorrow. Kathy, Susanna, and Roger selected the coffin yesterday. I couldn't do that either.

"She says by three o'clock," I'd overheard Susanna murmuring to Susan at around one. "We should tell him to be there at three o'clock. But we have to call back to confirm it definitely."

Then, at two-thirty, they were told to call back again at three-thirty. Finally, I think, the funeral director decided just to set out for Sacramento in his van. An hour or so ago, he'd informed us that after a peculiar delay—what was the delay and why?—he'd been successful, he'd transported Elliot to Davis.

I shudder. Though I am still anesthetized, I know what I don't want to contemplate.

"Shattering. For me, it's *shattering.*"

Kathy and Roger brought a pile of black clothes back from Berkeley along with records and tapes for the service tomorrow. They dumped all the stuff on my bed upstairs. "Just grab everything you can find in Mom's closet," Susanna had suggested. Susan, Joyce, and my mother have packed black dresses, and Roger has somehow found a black tie. But none of the girls, of course, had been expecting to need such items. Susanna is in graduate school at Santa Barbara; there's no way she can get anything appropriate from her own apartment. And Kathy and Liz claim they don't *own* decent black garments. "We'll decide what to wear after we see what you can find in Mom's closet," Susanna had said sensibly.

Heaped on the bed: a quilted velvet jacket Susan had given me for Christmas this year. A silk blouse Elliot had bought me for my birthday. A velvet dress, now several sizes too small (but perhaps just right for Susanna) from when I lived in New York, more than twenty years ago. Several other skirts, dresses, blazers. All different shades of black. Black, I notice, does have different shades.

The funeral director needed clothes for Elliot, too. A jacket, shirt, tie—I could understand that, if we were going to "view" him in his coffin—but also, curiously, underwear, trousers, everything except a belt and shoes.

Just a few hours ago, I went bravely into the walk-in closet in our bedroom. He left a lot of his teaching outfits here. There are several dark tweed jackets, some striped shirts—the pseudo–Brooks Brothers kind he liked, or maybe these really are from Brooks—a tie I bought him not long ago at Liberty, in London, and a few other ties. Numbly I made my selection: the dark blue tweed, a blue-and-white shirt to match, gray flannel trousers, the Liberty tie. He would go to his grave as if he had dressed to give a lecture.

Then I began to scream. To weep and scream, standing in the closet, clinging to his clothes.

As soon as she arrived, Susan had rushed straight to the supermarket around the corner and bought two boxes of Kleenex. But this was the first time I had cried since deVere White and the resident and the Decedent Services woman stepped out of the elevator at 9 P.M. on February 11.

Pale and grim, my daughters took away Elliot's jacket, shirt, and trousers. I guess somebody drove over to the funeral home with them. Roger walked me downstairs. We sat on the sofa for a minute. Then I went back into the kitchen and looked out the window again. My mother brought me another cup of coffee.

Now Susan is offering drinks to everyone. It's time to nibble on the cheeses and sausages from the staff's gift basket. Susanna has centered the beautifully arranged platter on the glass coffee table in the living room.

My brother-in-law lowers himself into an armchair across from me. He is a stout, balding, sardonic man, three years younger than my husband. Last year he retired from a position as assistant principal in a New York City junior high school—a job that no doubt made him as sardonic as he is—but he was trained to be a musician, a flutist, and now he lives in Maine, where he spends much of his time building delicately crafted model airplanes.

If I don't look at him when he talks, I can believe I am hearing my husband's voice. They have the same intonations, the same New York accent, the same ironic timbre.

"Whenever you're ready," he says, "we can start rehearsing the Kaddish."

Although he is as nonreligious as Elliot was, they were both, of course, made bar mitzvah; both brothers learned Hebrew.

Richard actually had a *real* bar mitzvah celebration at a restaurant in the Bronx. Elliot had always comically resented that. Three years earlier, when Elliot was thirteen, his parents couldn't afford what was then called a "catered affair." His father, he'd always told me, brought little sandwiches, sponge cake, soda, and sweet wine, to the basement of the temple where Elliot "became a man." As the party drew to an end, the mish pocheh—the kids who were the pals of the bar mitzvah boy, the bar mitzvah bucher—exuberantly threw the little sandwiches at each other.

Maybe that's why Elliot always wrote funny stories featuring "little sandwiches." He'd produced a sequence of "one-page novels" about ten years ago. One of them ended, poignantly, "The little sandwiches would never be eaten now."

Susan, whose older daughter just had a bat mitzvah last year, has volunteered to help us learn the Kaddish too. She and Richard pass around copies of texts that they got from the rabbi at the Davis Jewish Fellowship.

Yis-ga-dal v'yis-ka-dash sh'may ra-bo. . . . My kids and I are stumbling over the unfamiliar Hebrew.

My sister-in-law, Joyce, is cooking dinner in the kitchen. She is making a recipe called "Captain's Chicken" that sounds as though it will be a real "down east" Maine dish. She and Richard are very happy with their new life in Maine, where, she tells us, she's done the whole house, a true Cape Codder, in colonial New England style. Elliot and I were supposed to visit them last fall, but then the prostate cancer intervened.

This afternoon, while Roger and Kathy were in Berkeley and Susanna and Susan were on the phone to Decedent Services, Richard and Joyce went to the supermarket and bought all the ingredients for Captain's Chicken, including special spices and garnishes. "I have to do *something*," Joyce said plaintively, "and Elliot loved my cooking."

An hour ago, as I sat looking out the window in the kitchen, she began assembling the meal. "Remember how Elliot used to love my stuffed cabbage?" she asked. "He used to say, 'Joyce, you're a great woman, Joyce,' whenever I made my stuffed cabbage."

In the middle of the second round of *Yis-ga-dal v'yis-ka-dash* Kathy interrupts. "Mom, the checkbook. We have to look at the checkbook."

She and Roger went with our old friend Bob to the Sunset View Cemetery in Berkeley. They toured the grounds, trying to find a plot that their father would like. When they found one, near a grove of pines overlooking San Francisco Bay, they asked if they could pay for it with a credit card.

No, the Sunset View Cemetery doesn't accept credit cards, not Visa, not MasterCard, not American Express.

I had signed a blank check for them, in case that should happen. But it looks as though there was actually no money in the bank to cover the check. Elliot always handled all our money, and he paid all our bills before he went into the hospital, leaving only a few hundred dollars in our regular account.

Now we have to figure out what to do. The kids have probably written a bad check to the Sunset View Cemetery.

"I think there might be overdraft protection in this other account," Kathy says. She's brought back a stack of unfamiliar-looking checkbooks and bank statements from Berkeley.

"Time for dinner." Joyce is in the doorway, waving a big serving spoon, and I'm relieved that we don't have to keep on talking about money.

Gathered around the long table, we look, I imagine, like any group of people at a family reunion. Perhaps a few of us show an unusual strain around the eyes, a redness, but otherwise we probably seem perfectly okay.

The Captain's Chicken steams invitingly in a big yellow casserole and Joyce begins to ladle it onto plates. Richard is passing around a bowl of salad. Kathy pours wine for everyone.

"Oh Mom." Roger pulls a cassette out of his pocket. "I found this when I was looking for the 'Cavatina.' Did you know about it?" He hands me the tape.

The label says: "D. Thomas Poems, E. G. Broadcast, June 1989."

Yes, I remember, I answer, although I'd forgotten it until this minute. My husband had recorded some poems by Dylan Thomas for the campus radio station. Elliot was a skillful performer; besides his popular Dickens reading, he now and then did other readings in classes or on KDVS.

I put down my knife and fork. I'm not hungry anyway. "Can we listen to it now?"

"Now?" The others are shocked. "It'll upset you, Mom. Anyway, we're having dinner."

"Just for a minute, just one poem." My greed for the sound of Elliot is urgent, infantile.

Roger goes quietly to the stereo tape deck. "Do you know which one?" he asks.

"Anything," I say. "Anything. Just play the first one."

Elliot's voice rises from the machine, full-bodied, poised, expert. Like his brother's but after all, I can tell, hearing it again tonight, not his brother's. He is reading "Fern Hill" almost as well, I think, as Dylan Thomas himself did.

While the great first stanza rings out, we all stare at our plates as if someone were saying grace.

> Now as I was young and easy under the apple boughs
> About the lilting house and happy as the grass was green,
> The night above the dingle starry,
> Time let me hail and climb
> Golden in the heydays of his eyes. . . .

Something is happening in the silence behind us. The telephone is ringing. Kathy rushes to answer it so its jangling won't disrupt her father's reading.

> ... In the sun that is young once only,
> Time let me play and be
> Golden in the mercy of his means. ...

"Mom." Kathy is standing over me, frowning. "It's Dr. deVere White. He wants to talk to you."

Roger goes to stop the tape.

"*You* talk to him," I say sullenly. "I don't want to talk to him."

"Mom." Kathy is adamant. "You've got to talk to him. Go talk to him, Mom. He wants to talk to *you*."

I rise slowly and walk into the kitchen, to the phone. Everyone at the table freezes.

"I'm callin' about the autopsy, luv," deVere White says.

"Yes? What did they find?" I can tell that my voice is unnaturally high, thin, constricted.

"Nothin' special, luv, nothin' that I know of. Ye'll get a report. But I wanted to tell ye that I specially asked Dr. Ruebner to look at the pelvic area, the surgery area. I was frightened meself. Afraid there'd be a quart of clots or somethin'. But there was nothin'. Nothin'. The operation was successful. As I told ye. We made the right decision."

"But then what happened? What happened?"

"That I don't know, luv," he replies in a conspiratorial tone. "Ye'll get a report. They're still runnin' some lab tests. They still have to figger it out. A lot of the physicians here are workin' on it. Everyone's talkin' about it. But *I* wanted ye to know we made the right decision."

"Oh." I hesitate, then plunge ahead. "We're having a small

private service tomorrow at the Davis Jewish Center. Maybe you'd like to come."

"Ah, alas." I can imagine him closing his eyes, looking pained. "Alas. I'll be on a plane tomorrow, on me way to a conference where a whole audience is goin' to be waitin' for me words of wisdom." He interjects a short ironic laugh. "Such as they are."

"I see." Good night. Thank you. Goodbye. Good night.

Everyone swerves to face me as I return to the table. "Nothing," I say. "They didn't find anything yet."

Roger starts the tape again.

Nothing I cared, in the lamb white days, that time would take me
Up to the swallow thronged loft by the shadow of my hand. . . .

The Captain's Chicken seems to be preening itself on my plate. It is generously doused in tomatoes, currants, mushrooms, and what looks like grated orange peel.

My husband's voice soars toward the big finish.

Oh as I was young and easy in the mercy of his means,
Time held me green and dying
Though I sang in my chains like the sea.

6

In an effort to gain some control and understanding over what often appears to be a meaningless, unmanageable event, you may repeatedly review the death, trying to make sense of it. Also, you may attempt to restructure the situation so that it seems that you had some inkling that it was going to happen. . . . This is especially important in circumstances of sudden death, when you must come to some cognitive understanding of what happened so suddenly to your loved one.

—RANDO, *How to Go On Living*

WEDNESDAY, FEBRUARY 13, 1991, MIDNIGHT

Tomorrow is Elliot's funeral. The "Cavatina," the psalms, Strauss's "Im Abendrot." Everyone else in the condo has gone to bed. Are they sleeping? I hope they are, they all had such smudges around their eyes. I want to sleep, too, but I can't. I lie here rigid with wakefulness.

The bed seems much too large for one person. A queen-sized bed. I don't feel queenly. I'm a married woman. This is what the French call a *lit matrimonial,* a marital bed. Elliot belongs in this bed beside me.

If he were here, that would mean we don't have to go to the

funeral tomorrow: the coffin, the "Cavatina," the rabbi, the autopsy would be only a set of bad dreams. If he were here, I might be awake like this, but I could be holding him, he could be holding me. We'd snuggle warmly together, and if we couldn't sleep we'd tell jokes or gossip about people in our department— or even about the doctors at the UCDMC, for God's sake, even about *them.* And I wouldn't be remembering the scenes in the hospital over and over again. Remembering them as if a fluorescent light had gone on in my skull and couldn't be turned off, the searing blue-white light of total recall.

———

MONDAY, FEBRUARY 11, 1991, 1:45 P.M.

We're sitting in the lobby. I'm eating a dry and tasteless turkey sandwich that Kathy and Liz have just brought me from the hospital cafeteria. Kathy, Liz, and Susanna have finished their lunch and are sipping coffee from the vending machine around the corner. I'm drinking a Diet Coke and looking at (but not reading) a copy of *Newsweek.*

DeVere White is walking across the lobby toward us. I'm putting down my half-eaten sandwich, my Coke, my magazine, and struggling to my feet.

He's wearing surgical greens, the sort of short-sleeved V-necked jumpsuit they don in the OR. The outfit reminds me of the summer pajamas my children used to have. He has on green booties over his shoes.

We've been here since about nine-thirty. A dour nurse with a German accent came up from the OR to get Elliot this morning at five-thirty. Kathy, Susanna, and Liz had arrived in the dark at four-forty-five. How did they manage to drag themselves out of bed that early?

Elliot and I were awakened at four by a floor nurse who

turned on all the lights in our room. I lay there half asleep in my hospital bed while Elliot got up and took a shower, no mean feat since he was tethered to an IV pole.

I decided I would take my shower later. I didn't want to leave the safe nest of my bed yet.

Elliot and the nurse began discussing the enemas he'd had. Were his bowels sufficiently cleaned out? Last night someone said "it had to run clear" when he went to the bathroom, but was "it" in fact "running clear enough"? He was worried. The night nurse had made him nervous about the "cleanout."

The morning nurse was reassuring. Jean, the night nurse, was a novice, she said. Jean didn't understand that "it" most likely would never "run absolutely clear." There's always a little something left in the stomach.

Elliot was relieved. He began joking around, acting more "normal." I started getting dressed. When the girls arrived at four-forty-five, I was just tying my shoelaces.

Someone turned on the TV. Voices and music swelled in the room; images flashed on the screen. I'm not a morning person and was amazed that all this was happening, must be happening every day, at what seemed to me to be such an ungodly hour.

When the German nurse appeared, wearing not only a green jumpsuit and booties but also the sort of green shower cap I guess they issue to everyone on the surgery floor, we milled around in confusion. Wasn't she a little early?

No, it's time now, she told us.

As usual, Elliot had more energy than anyone else. He stood up with alacrity, dragging his IV pole behind him, and walked almost eagerly to the gurney.

The rest of us must have seemed tired, dazed, and slow-witted by comparison.

Elliot lay down on the gurney and the nurse tucked a white

coverlet around him. Then she put a heated blanket over his legs.

He lay down on the gurney. We watched him lie down on the gurney. We didn't know that he would never stand up again.

We all swarmed into the elevator, struggling to be cheerful, to keep on joking, laughing. The OR nurse gazed at us sourly. Her frown let us know that she was busy and preoccupied. Elliot was biting his lip.

Once more unto the surgery floor, the blank white hallway just outside the locked suite where the "procedures" happen.

We all kissed Elliot goodbye again, the way we did twelve days ago. I, as I had last time, offered my magic nine kisses, but more perfunctorily than before.

The last kisses on his living lips.

I was in a trance, I just wanted this to be over with, I wasn't going to burst into tears this time.

I fingered the Puerto Rican healing beads I was wearing again.

Once more the big doors swung open. My husband was being wheeled away, into the unknown corridors beyond.

"Go *for* it, Elliot!" Liz shouted as the gurney and the IV pole passed slowly through the doorway.

Flat on his back, Elliot silently raised an arm, silently waved. He wanted to tell us he was going to go *for* it.

The last sight of his living hand.

Before I manage to get to my feet, my daughters and Liz are standing next to deVere White. He looks drawn and tired. His face is glazed with sweat, even the front of his jumpsuit is wet with perspiration, and the part of his neck and chest that you can see under the V is shiny.

"How did it go, how did it go, what happened?" Kathy, Susanna, and Liz are all talking at once.

"It went as well as it could," he says.

As well as it could?

I want to know if he "got it all out."

"It's in the bucket." His eyes rove around the room as if he were looking for someone else to discuss the surgery with. As if we were somehow inadequate or inappropriate interlocutors.

"And the nodes?" I ask. "How much could you tell about the nodes?"

"They're all out," he says. "There doesn't seem to be any metastasis. But they were hard to get out. They were fatty, fatty."

"Fatty?" What are fatty nodes? We all stare at each other.

"From the hormones. I warned ye." Warned us? He'd never warned us that there might be such a side effect from the hormone therapy. He'd agreed with the article: preoperative combination hormone therapy makes resection easier, simpler, faster, less "bloody."

"How is he now? Is he okay?"

"Still in surgery. They're closin' now. He should be in the recovery room by two, though." DeVere White is motionless but still covertly surveying the lobby. Perhaps he's searching for a colleague, someone he's supposed to have lunch with.

Suddenly he seems to collect himself, to remember that he still needs to deliver the "prostate cancer talk—part 2." He smiles rather mechanically. "Ye can't see him yet. Ye'll be able to see him when they move him to Intensive Care, around five this afternoon. Go out and have some lunch, there's no point in sittin' around here all day."

He hasn't noticed my half-eaten sandwich. Obviously he's hungry himself. That's probably why he's behaving so oddly. He turns slightly toward me, speaking rapidly, reciting what are clearly familiar directions. "Ye'll see him later this afternoon. Ye'll take him home in six or seven days. Two weeks from then ye'll bring him back to have the catheter removed."

Before we can think of more questions to ask, he's off, hurrying toward the revolving doors to the parking lot.

"Do you think he was angry at us?" I ask the girls. "Did we do something wrong?"

"Of course not, Mom," Kathy says vehemently.

"I don't know." Susanna frowns. "He *did* seem strange, as if he might be annoyed with us. But what could we have done?"

(*And why should we have been too shy or scared to* ask *him what was wrong?*)

"Oh well," I say. "He was probably tired. I mean, the surgery seems to have taken more than five hours. Anybody would be tired from that!"

At eight this morning, Dr. Reitan, the anesthesiologist, had come upstairs to Elliot's room, where we were all sharing a breakfast I'd been given, to tell us the intubation had been completed satisfactorily—although he'd had to use a bronchoscope instead of the usual instruments—and the surgery had begun. Which meant the operation had lasted almost six hours. More than six, considering that Elliot still wasn't out of the OR. According to my researches into prostate cancer surgery, and the testimony of the Network, a radical prostatectomy usually takes about four hours. The authors of the preoperative hormone therapy article had said that the treatment they advocated could reduce the patient's time in surgery to under three hours.

But perhaps the difficulty of the intubation meant that the OR team had to go more slowly?

After Reitan left, a nurse advised us to pack Elliot's things up and take them home for the time being. We couldn't bring his robe, his videos, his walkman, his tapes, Orlando Furrioso and Raggedy Andy, to the ICU for him.

We'd dumped everything in the back of the car, then returned to the lobby to wait. Now we think with relief that we can deposit it all at the condo. We'll go call Roger, my mother, Susan, the English department, and a few friends in Berkeley. Have a drink, relax, then come see Elliot in the ICU. We'll take his belongings back when he reenters his "special amenities room," tomorrow or the next day.

———

MONDAY, FEBRUARY 11, 1991, 6:15 P.M.

We're late returning to the hospital. We were all so exhausted that we slept too long after making our phone calls. Elliot is probably already in the ICU. He's probably enraged at us, at *me*, for being late. I'm always late, and he hates it. I can imagine him saying groggily, "You're always late for everything, sem. You'll be late for your own funeral—or mine." ("Sem," a girlhood nickname made up of my then-initials, was what he called me at intimate moments.)

As the car pulls into the parking lot, I sneak a glance at my watch. It's after six already. "Oh my God," I say guiltily to the girls, "we're *so damn late!* He's going to just kill us!"

"We were tired, Mom," Susanna begins, "he'll understand that we—"

Before she can finish talking, almost before Kathy has finished parking, Liz is leaping out of the car. "There's Dr. deVere White," she cries. "Over there. I want to ask him about the blood."

On the way over here, we'd remembered that we hadn't asked him if he'd had to use any of the blood Elliot had donated. That was an important question, we told each other.

We're all crowding around deVere White, who is standing on the steps talking to some other doctors. He's back in his starched white coat and appears refreshed, rejuvenated—a lot better than he'd looked this afternoon.

"The blood? Did you have to use any of the blood?"

"Five units."

"Five units!" I gasp. "But he only donated two—"

"We always have backup units."

"My God, but isn't that bad?"

"It's neither bad nor good." His inflection is neutral.

"But why, why did you have to use so much blood?"

Suddenly he's almost shouting. "It was stock, stock!" he seems to me to be saying in an angry Irish tenor.

"Stock?" I turn helplessly to my daughters. I have a strange vision of bouillon, broth, soup stock. "Stock? What does he mean?"

"Stuck, Mom, he's saying it was *stuck*," Kathy explains patiently.

"Stuck? What was stuck? Why would it be *stuck*?"

DeVere White still sounds angry. "The hormones, I told ye, the hormones. I warned ye."

We're all silent, frowning. We must look very frightened because he becomes quieter, kinder. "I just saw him," he volunteers. "He was fine but he didn't want to chat. He was woozy from the anesthetic, the way he was after the biopsy. He said somethin' like 'I feel lousy.' "

Oh. We are placated, we exchange reassuring glances. It's easy for us to imagine Elliot being cross and uncomfortable. "I feel lousy." He'd hate pain, be angry at it. That's just the sort of thing he *would* say. Reproachfully. "I feel lousy. Look what you did to me, you creeps!"

I light a cigarette. You can't smoke in the hospital so I'll have a puff before going up to the ICU. The grayish twilight is pleasantly cool, with lights winking on all around the parking lot and in the windows of the hospital above me.

"So we can see him now in the ICU?" somebody asks.

"No, not yet, luv." DeVere White's tone is regretful. "They're still waiting' for a bed in Intensive Care. They're very busy tonight. Probably won't have one till around eight. Why don't ye go out and have a good dinner? No sense hangin' around here some more."

"Well . . ." I hesitate. But we *do* have to eat sometime. Perhaps it would be efficient to eat now. There's a Chinese restaurant a few blocks away that a friend who lives in Sacramento recommended. Maybe we should try it out. We're going to be needing a supply of good restaurants next week, so we might as well start our investigations right away.

One of the girls has thought of another question, though. "Do you think he's going to need radiation, Dr. deVere White?"

He looks at us enigmatically. "Now, now, let's not get away from ourselves," he says. "It's only the day of the surgery, y'know. We have to take things one day at a time right now. One day at a time."

"One day at a time?" Just this afternoon, he'd told us we'd come back in three weeks to have the catheter removed.

One day at a time? What can he mean? And why don't we ask him what he means?

THURSDAY, FEBRUARY 14, 1991, 12:30 A.M.

"Oh my God, oh my God." I'm sitting up in bed, rocking back and forth. "What happened? What could have happened?"

One day at a time! What did deVere White know? Did he *know* something I don't understand?

The bed. The bed with the white coverlet in the room outside the recovery room. Elliot's frost-bitten cheeks, his smile. DeVere White's dark suit. "For me it's *shattering*!"

And the night before the surgery. The girls were fighting over what to watch on TV. As if they *were* "girls," not the young women they really are. Then we went down to the cafeteria to eat a bad dinner while Elliot was having more enemas.

The doctors had decided not to make him drink the disgusting laxative water this time. They were giving him enemas instead. He had already had three or four when I left for dinner. Every time a nurse would come in with another enema, Kathy, Susanna, Liz, and I would go out into the hall and feel sorry for him.

We sat in the cafeteria complaining about the food. "It has no taste," Kathy said, vigorously salting something indefinable on her plate.

"I'll treat you to a meal at Biba's when this is all over," I offered. Biba's is the fanciest restaurant in Sacramento. Not far down the road from the hospital. Elliot loved it: we used to go there, sometimes, after his leupron injections, just to prove to ourselves that we were in a real city.

While the girls were desultorily sampling flavorless desserts, I went back up to Elliot's room. But the curtain was drawn around his bed. He was having yet another enema.

He heard me come in. "Sem," he said wistfully. "It's so demeaning, sem."

His small, secret smile, his chilling lips. "So demeaning."

I can't stop rocking and groaning. I'll have to take a Halcion. The way we did two nights ago.

While Elliot never takes sleeping pills, I do sometimes. When the nurse came in with, in one hand, a tiny paper cup containing two Halcions, and, in the other, a bigger cup of water, he didn't want to touch them. "Try them," I urged. "You need a good night's sleep. You have a big day tomorrow."

A big day. I'd have a big day too, I reflected. I convinced him to take two Halcions and I took two myself. I didn't want us to "drift" off to sleep the way we had last time. I didn't want to think about Hawaii and its coral reefs. I wanted to be slammed into sleep, plunged into it, drowned in it. So tomorrow would come, February 11 would be here, and the surgery would happen, and it would be over, and everything would be all right again.

Sweating—sweating the way deVere White was sweating, no, sweating more intensely, more passionately—I toss off the covers, get out of bed and tiptoe to the bathroom. I'll take two Halcions right now. Plunge into sleep. Stop thinking about February 11 and February 14. The surgery and the funeral.

I stand in the bathroom gazing at myself in the mirror. My face seems perfectly normal, doesn't it?

Bloated. Elliot was bloated. That's what my daughters said.

Heart failure? The U.C. Davis obituary had named that as the cause of death. If your heart failed, that made you bloated. My father had died of heart failure, and when he was in the hospital they tried to get him down to "dry weight" so his body wouldn't keep retaining all that dangerous water for his heart to have to pump.

Strangely enough, just before we left for Davis on Saturday, February 9, fathers became thematic. We were going to spend the night at the condo so Elliot could get to the hospital early the next morning and start drinking the awful laxative water. He didn't know they were going to give him all those enemas. But before we left, he wanted to show me part of a new videodisc recording of Wagner's *Die Walküre* that he'd just bought.

In fact, he'd spent his last day in Berkeley hunting for that recording and writing down some music he'd composed long ago. A setting of Keats's poem "I had a dove and the sweet dove died."

I was already nervous, anesthetized, almost unconscious from anxiety. I went downstairs reluctantly and sat sulkily in front of the VCR. Elliot put on "The Ride of the Valkyries." Ordinarily I'd love this music, this scene, but now the whole business seemed grotesque to me. Like a bunch of big black buzzards, *soprano* buzzards, the supernatural sisters were carrying dead heroes up the mountainside, whooping and yipping as they staggered onto the stage, dragging their prizes behind them. Then they all cowered behind a rock as Wotan, the angry father god, approached to punish Brunhilde, the rebellious daughter.

They were so stupid, such stupid Teutonic women. So absurdly terrified of the father god. For some reason they made me think of Katherine Mansfield's short story "The Daughters of the Late Colonel," whose protagonists are consumed with fear and guilt because they've had to bury their father.

" 'Buried!' " Mansfield's heroines imagine their dead father howling. " 'You girls had me buried!' "

I began to laugh. "Just like Katherine Mansfield," I said. " 'The Daughters of the Late Colonel'! Buried, you girls had me buried!"

Elliot was offended, angry. "That's idiotic. Just shut up about that."

We carried our bags to the car in silence. But almost all the way to Davis I kept giggling under my breath. "Buried, you girls had me buried!"

"Shut up about that."

Buried. We're going to have him buried tomorrow.

Furtively, hastily, I gulp down two Halcions, just the way I did the other night. I want to slam into sleep, not wake up again.

7

Participation in the funeral ritual—standing at a wake and repeatedly looking at your loved one in the casket, attending the funeral service, accepting the condolences of others, seeing the casket at the grave—graphically illustrates to you that the death has indeed occurred.

—RANDO, *How to Go On Living*

THURSDAY, FEBRUARY 14, 1991, 2 P.M.

Valentine's day. I'm standing beside my husband's grave, looking down at his coffin. A long gleaming oak box with brass handles—my daughters chose the one they thought their father would like the best—it vaguely resembles an expensive linen chest or sideboard, though now it's blanketed with flowers. A linen chest or a sideboard wouldn't have wreaths and chains of blue, white, and purple blossoms all over it.

It's warm in the cemetery, almost hot. I'm sweating in my black silk blouse, black wool skirt, quilted black velvet jacket.

But, I reflect, Roger, Kathy, and Bob did find a beautiful spot—or do I mean "plot"? Elliot would love the small stand of pines just off to the right of his grave, the gentle green hillside unobtrusively dotted with flat gray markers, the blue slice of San Francisco Bay below him in the distance.

Everyone is gazing at me expectantly. I am supposed to be

reading something now. I am the last speaker. Then we'll say the Kaddish and the funeral will be over, and Elliot's coffin will be lowered into the ground.

Keats. Susan put the book in my hands, open to the page I have to read from. I am going to read "I had a dove and the sweet dove died," the poem whose musical setting my husband transcribed during his last afternoon in Berkeley, before we left for the hospital.

I begin in a high, tight voice. The audience, a crowd of friends, relatives, and colleagues grouped together across from me, on the other side of the grave, looks nervous, probably afraid I'll break down. My mother tucked a wad of Kleenex in my pocket as we were getting out of the car, but I know I can't, won't cry. Not now, not here. I focus on the coffin and tell myself I'm talking to Elliot.

> I had a dove and the sweet dove died;
> And I have thought it died of grieving.

The words are almost uncannily appropriate. Elliot was grieving for his health, his youth, his potency. Did he die of grieving? Did he have a premonition that he might die of grieving? Is that why he spent that afternoon of February 9 writing the music down?

> O, what could it grieve for? Its feet were tied,
> With a silken thread of my own hand's weaving.

Did *I* weave a silken thread, tie my husband up so that he felt he *had* to have the surgery he dreaded, the surgery that killed him?

For a second I hesitate, and nervousness mounts to anxiety in some of the faces turned toward me.

There are so many of them, so many other mourners here. Quite a few have followed the funeral party sixty miles down the freeway from Davis, where we had the service. Others have come from Berkeley, San Francisco, and Marin to meet us here. When we arrived, I was shocked by the mass of people assembled at the grave. I thought maybe we'd stopped in the wrong "unit" of the cemetery.

One of Elliot's oldest California friends is half-hiding behind a pine tree, wiping his eyes.

I bite down hard on the inside of my lip and resolve to get through the rest of the poem without weeping myself. I imagine Elliot listening to me, singing his own melody in his head.

> Sweet little red feet! why should you die—
> Why should you leave me, sweet bird! why?
> You liv'd alone in the forest-tree,
> Why, pretty thing! would you not live with me?
> I kissed you oft and gave you white peas;
> Why not live sweetly, as in the green trees?

Everyone is visibly relieved when I sit down again in one of the six folding chairs that have been placed at the graveside for members of the immediate family.

But now I am told I have to get up once more. Two Jewish colleagues have volunteered to take charge of the burial ceremony, since we don't have a rabbi in Berkeley and are completely ignorant about how to proceed with a Jewish or semi-Jewish burial. Looking solemn and rabbinical in their dark suits, *yarmulkes* and *talithim*, Michael Kramer and Michael Hoffman explain that at this point anyone who wants to participate directly in the traditional ritual should drop a bit of earth on the coffin, as a sign that the dead man has been lovingly buried by his friends and family. The widow is supposed to go first. Others should then line up behind her.

I rise unsteadily and walk slowly back to the graveside. A deep hole has been dug below the coffin, which is temporarily suspended by a kind of sling. A pile of dirt, half covered with more flowers, lines the site. Someone hands me a trowel, an ordinary-looking garden tool, the kind I've used countless times for transplanting geraniums and marigolds. Now, I think bizarrely, I'm using it to transplant Elliot.

As I look down, the hole in the earth seems to widen and deepen. I'm afraid for a minute that I'll topple in. Or do I mean that I *want* to?

But I don't, don't topple, don't pitch forward into the pit. I let a little dirt fall on the coffin. It makes a surrealistic thump, as if a clot of earth had dropped on a sideboard.

Thump after thump. The procession of mourners seems endless, winding around the grave. Then at last it's over—*yis-ga-dal v'yis-ka-dash*—and we're all saying the Kaddish again, the way we did three hours ago at the Jewish Center in Davis.

As we finish speaking, several women detach themselves from the group and hurry toward their cars. They are going back to my house, where they'll put out food and drink for the mourners. "The funeral baked meats." Years ago, Elliot set that passage from *Hamlet* to a jazzy accompaniment. "The funeral baked meats / Did coldly furnish forth the marriage tables." I always thought it one of his funniest creations. Now a few of our friends are going to load our dining room table with funeral baked meats in his honor; Michael Kramer and Michael Hoffman are inviting everyone back to my house.

Roger has taken my mother's arm. He's guiding her down the hill, away from the grave, toward our car. My daughters are on either side of me. Although they themselves are tense with the effort of holding on and holding grief in, they're supporting me as if I were an invalid who might collapse at any minute. The other mourners are gathering solicitously around us. A few are blowing their noses or patting their eyes with tissues, but most have the same blank, shocked stare that I guess I must have. Nobody expected anything like this. Everyone was ready for postoperative congratulations rather than postmortem condolences. One of them sent the "GET WELL" balloon; another ordered the potted plant.

What happened? What could have happened?

Behind us, a bulldozer or tractor, some piece of earth-moving equipment, is slowly grinding toward Elliot's grave.

"Come on, Mom, let's go," Kathy says urgently. Her eyes are wide and panicky. "You don't want to see this."

Now they're really going to bury him. This is the way they do it. With a bulldozer.

Inside the shiny, expensive oak coffin, he is wearing his dark blue tweed jacket, his blue-and-white striped shirt, his Liberty tie. They will lower him into the earth in these clothes. I will never see the jacket, the shirt, and the tie again. Neither will he.

I envision him lying there patiently, waiting for the next procedure to begin. My own eyes begin to smart.

At the funeral home we actually did see him lying there, patiently, so patiently, with a wry, oddly jaunty expression on his face. Roger, Richard, and Joyce refused to go into the "viewing room," where a last private "visit" for the family had been arranged. But the rest of us went in to say goodbye. First, though, the funeral director took Susan aside to explain something to her.

Something about the bloating. Elliot's body was very bloated—"marked by severe edema"—when he picked it up at the UCDMC. The man said he'd tried to "do the best" he could, whatever that was, in preparing Elliot, but there was only so much he could do. He wondered if there had been kidney failure.

Susan said we hadn't been informed of any kidney failure. DeVere White had told us, on the contrary, that Elliot was "making good water."

The funeral director said he'd actually had to take two trips to the hospital before he could get the body. There was a peculiar delay, he said, because the pathologists wanted to "look at the liver again."

Susan said we hadn't been told anything about that either.

Then she came out of the office and the funeral director took us into the room where we said goodbye to Elliot. This time, even I could see that his face looked swollen. But patient and sardonic, wry and rueful, too.

And this time he was icy and adamant as granite.

The roar of the bulldozer has come closer. My daughters are practically pushing me down the hill toward the car. The ground is uneven, hard to walk on. I'm afraid of tripping. It would be humiliating, wouldn't it, to fall down here, right in front of the whole burial party.

Everyone is getting into cars, revving engines, driving away fast. A few are carrying flowers in tall vases, bringing them back to the house for us. But the coverlet of white and blue and purple blossoms has been left there on the coffin.

The coffin that is now adrift, alone, on the hillside.

———

THURSDAY, FEBRUARY 14, 1991, 4 P.M.

A weird sort of cocktail party appears to be underway by the time we get home. People are milling around the dining room table, shaking hands, sipping wine, carrying paper plates heaped with elegant salads and crudités, cheeses, breads, and charcuterie from an assortment of classy delis in Berkeley and Tiburon. I wander through the room, smiling and kissing my guests, thanking them for being here. Someone puts a paper plate of food in my hand. I set it back down on the table. I am a hostess. I have to do my job.

In the living room, I introduce a well-known radical sociologist, who was interviewed on *MacNeil-Lehrer* about the Gulf War last week, to a conservative economist, who has been interviewed about the war on several other programs. I am pleased, and a little surprised, to note that they appear to get along very well together.

Out on the deck, Michael Kramer, one of my two rabbinical colleagues, is telling Susan a story about the funeral service this morning. "Did you see the small piece of wood in front of the Torah?" he asks her, grinning. "Those Talmudic scholars have their ways!"

She confesses that she hadn't noticed the wood.

A dead body, he explains, isn't actually allowed in a synagogue. But, he reminds her, if you put a piece of wood or some other divider, no matter how small, in front of the Torah, the screening of the holy book changes the room from a *schul* or temple, a sacred space, into an ordinary profane place. So Elliot's funeral hadn't really taken place in something resembling a church after all.

The ingenuity of rabbis charms Michael Kramer. Susan is amused too.

From the Jewish point of view, someone else interjects, a dead body is unclean. Judaism celebrates life while Christianity, especially Catholicism, is more death-oriented.

I roam back into the house. In a corner of the dining room, my brother-in-law and a cousin of his and Elliot's are telling jokes. My husband and his brother have always been brilliant raconteurs. I feel it incumbent on me to carry on Elliot's tradition, so I parrot one of his latest stories, a joke neither of them has heard yet. Are they studying me strangely? Is it odd for the widow to tell jokes while offering funeral baked meats to the other mourners?

A colleague from another U.C. campus zeroes in on me. He and his wife want to know exactly what happened, they're frowning with concern. Last night, they say, they talked to a lawyer friend who thinks we might have a "case."

Why did Elliot die anyway? If he had a heart attack or heart failure, shouldn't the hospital staff have been able to do something more for him than what they did? Might the failed intubation on January 30 have been a contributory factor? What happened, what could have happened? Would I like the name of their lawyer friend?

"I don't know." I shake my head in what feels like hopeless confusion. "The doctor said the surgery was successful. The right decision! I don't know what to do."

Others crowd around. Don't worry, don't think about it now, they advise. Wait and see. Wait for the death certificate, the autopsy report. There's bound to be an explanation.

"I don't know," I repeat. "I don't know what to do." My eyes are beginning to smart again. It's so crowded, smoky, and stuffy in here. Unusually hot for February, even February in California.

I make my way into the kitchen, then out the back door, just for a minute, onto the street. A little air might help, a breath of fresh air.

The last time I walked out this door, I was with Elliot. We were carrying our bags for the UCDMC. We'd forgotten Orlando Furrioso and Raggedy Andy—was that a bad omen?—so Kathy and Liz had had to bring them the next day.

When we got into the car, I was still chuckling about the Katherine Mansfield story. "Buried, you girls had me buried!" But when we reached the entrance to the freeway, I turned to Elliot and said censoriously, "Now don't tell me that this might be the last time you'll ever drive on this road."

He'd said those words—melodramatically, I thought—as we drove up Route 80 to the hospital on January 29, before the failed intubation. "Think, sem, this might be the last time I ever drive on this road."

Such gloom infuriated me. "Now don't tell me that," I reiterated. "You have to have a positive attitude."

He was obediently silent. But maybe that was what he was thinking.

And he would have been right.

I survey my street. It's jammed with cars. Behind me lights are going on in the house. A buzz of voices, even a muted cacophony of laughter, spills out the open windows and doors.

The sky is bluing, darkening. It's nearly six. The only brightness, now, radiates from the plum blossoms, exploding into their annual blur of wounded, sore-looking pink.

PART TWO

IN

DISCOVERY

It should be noted that the plaintiffs have not fully completed their investigation of the facts relating to this case, have not completed their discovery in this action and have not completed their preparations for trial.

—Walkup, Shelby, Bastian, Melodia, Kelly, Echevarria and Link, Response to Written Interrogatories, *Gilbert* v. *Regents*, November 1991

8

The following physical symptoms are not unusual in grief:
Loss of pleasure
Anorexia and other gastrointestinal disturbances
Apathy
Decreased energy
Decreased initiative
Decreased motivation
Decreased sexual desire or hypersexuality
Physical exhaustion
Lack of strength
Lethargy
Sleep difficulties (too much or too little; interrupted
   sleep)
Tearfulness and crying
Weight loss or weight gain
The tendency to sigh
Feelings of emptiness and heaviness
Feeling that something is stuck in your throat
Heart palpitations, trembling shaking, hot flashes, and
   other indications of anxiety
Nervousness, tension, agitation, irritability
Restlessness and searching for something to do
Shortness of breath
Smothering sensations
Dizziness, unsteady feelings
Chest pain, pressure, or discomfort

—Rando, *How to Go On Living*

THURSDAY, FEBRUARY 21, 1991, 2 P.M.

Gray and chilly. Kathy, Susanna, Liz, and I are sitting at the dining room table in Berkeley. I am in my usual position, the chair that faces two very large drawings of Elliot and of me that were done more than ten years ago by a talented local artist.

During the day now, there are only a few places where I can bear to put my body. Most of the time I remain virtually motionless in "my" chair in the living room. It is a swiveling tub chair covered in dark brown velour, and it has a footstool in front of it so I can sit with my feet up if I want to. I have many visitors— my children, my friends, even relatively distant acquaintances— but by general consent the people who come in and out of my house give this chair a wide berth, even when I'm not in it. Everyone understands that it's my place, where I have to sit for something like ten hours a day.

When I am in my living room chair, I can see the portraits on the dining room wall almost as well as I can see them from my dining room chair.

Carole Peel, the woman who did the pictures, is widely admired in Berkeley for a kind of stylized verisimilitude that she achieves through her meticulous use of a precisely sharpened, hard graphite pencil. The background details of her portraits— intricately flowered wallpaper, complex fabrics, and textures— have always engaged me. Now I wonder why I never paid much attention to the expressions Elliot and I are wearing in these two side-by-side pieces.

How prophetic they are! Surely someone ought to have been able to decipher them before this! I am, as is quite plain, looking astonished and frightened. My eyes are wide, I'm half-frowning and staring in alarm at something I don't want to see. And Elliot—as for Elliot, he has exactly the same look of rueful resignation that he had in the terrible white room at the medical center where we saw him just after he died, the patient, resigned, almost ironic or even sardonically apologetic look he had, too, in his coffin. Except here his eyes are open. His darkly thinking eyes follow me around the public spaces of the house, from living room to dining room, seeking my attention, reminding me that he'd been trying for ten years, ever since this picture was made, to warn me of what was going to happen.

I can even see his face reflected in the hall mirror, just as if he still had a living image that could be trapped in glass.

"I'm so sorry, darling," he wants to say, quietly, tenderly, "but this is the way it has to be. I'll just have to die. There's nothing I can do about it."

But my portrait talks back. My portrait begs him to stay alive, explaining that if he is so stupid and stubborn as to die, I'll never again be able to budge from my living room chair. As if I were indeed Jewish, but almost excessively so—a grieving widow who sits shivah forever and a day, until even her children and best friends give up on her.

"We *have* to open it now, Mom," Kathy says sternly.

In front of her on the dining room table, next to a stack of bills and benefits materials, is a brown envelope that arrived today from Sacramento. In it are the ten copies of Elliot's death certificate that we ordered the day of his funeral.

I look away from Elliot. "Okay, *you* do it," I say.

As she picks up the envelope and begins to tear at the flap, we all breathe in sharply. None of us has ever seen a death certificate before.

Each of the pieces of paper that emerge from the envelope has an embossed seal on it. Across the bottom of every page is written:

THIS IS TO CERTIFY THAT IF BEARING THE SEAL OF THE SACRAMENTO COUNTY HEALTH OFFICER, THIS IS A TRUE COPY OF A RECORD ON FILE IN THE VITAL STATISTICS SEC-

TION, SACRAMENTO COUNTY DEPARTMENT OF HEALTH, SACRAMENTO, CALIFORNIA.

Betty G. Hinton, M.D., Registrar
Bonnie York, Deputy

We're all silent for a moment, then we huddle around Kathy, reading the first copy together, as if it were the only one.

The information at the top is poignantly routine, the same set of facts that would appear on a passport or on an application for a credit card, although even amid the ordinary phrases the context requires dark interpolations here and there.

Name *of Deceased*, First, Middle, Last.
Date of Birth. Full Name of Father.
Full Maiden Name of Mother.
Military Service.
Name *of Surviving* Spouse.
Usual Occupation, Kind of Business, Employer.
Usual Residence.

We skim over most of this stuff fast, ignoring the little black box in the upper right-hand corner which makes it quite clear that this is not an application for credit:

Date of Death—mo., day, year: *February 11, 1991*; hour: *2015.*

Then we get to the part we're looking for but afraid to see:

Section 21. Death Was Caused By: (enter only one cause per line for A. B. & C.)
Immediate Cause: A. *Cardiopulmonary arrest* (Time Interval Between Onset and Death: *60 min.* Was Biopsy Performed? *No.*)

Due to: B. *Probable liver failure* (Time Interval Between Onset and Death: *60 min.* Was Autopsy Performed? *Yes.*)

Due to: C. *Prostate cancer* (Time Interval Between Onset and Death: *7 mos.* Was It Used in Determining Cause of Death? *Yes.*)

25. Other Significant Conditions Contributing to Death But Not Related to Cause Given in 21: *splenomegaly, fatty liver.*

These causes of death are certified—sworn to and signed by—U. Poonamallee, M.D. (Certifier's License #G059055), Dr. deVere White's chief resident.

Liver failure? We're staring at each other in bewilderment. *Splenomegaly? Fatty liver?* What do these words mean? No one from the hospital had ever mentioned them to us. A heart attack was what deVere White had talked about. "We've had a problem, a big problem, Dad's had a heart attack," he said as he strode out of the elevator, as he guided me down the hall, as the Decedent Services woman hurried along beside us. "Dad's had a heart attack." As Poonamallee stood beside my girls, watching Susanna fling her shoulder bag across the hospital lobby, listening to the screams of all three. "A heart attack." As I began compulsively crossing myself and murmuring the Hail Mary under my breath.

———

THURSDAY, FEBRUARY 21, 1991, 5:30 P.M.

"I can't understand it, it doesn't make any sense, it's a very strange clinical determination."

Kathy and I are on the phone with Dick, our friend the NIH pathologist, and he's thinking out loud about "cardiopulmonary arrest due to liver failure due to prostate cancer" and about "splenomegaly, fatty liver."

"A liver doesn't fail in sixty minutes," Dick says, "unless some toxic substance is introduced into the system or unless there's serious liver disease to begin with."

"And splenomegaly—?" Kathy begins.

"Enlarged spleen, probably not relevant here. As for fatty liver—" Dick pauses. "I just don't get it.

I'm silent, feeling oddly like an eavesdropper. What has this conversation to do with me and Elliot, the couple who sat so innocently for those portraits in 1981?

"But this must be what they found at the autopsy, wouldn't you say?" Kathy ventures. "They've never told us *anything* about the autopsy."

Dick's tone is definitive. "This doesn't make sense to me."

I pick up Elliot's Raggedy Andy and hold him tight. "Why not?" I finally blurt out.

Raggedy Andy and his pal, the orangutan Orlando Furrioso— the cheery stuffed pair my husband called "the boys" and took to the hospital with him—are living intimately with me now. Day and night, they sit on Elliot's side of the bed. One of the many grief books I've been reading advised a surrogate object to make sleep easier—"a pair of your husband's old pajamas or maybe a soft toy."

"Why not? Because there's a logical contradiction here." Dick is calm and teacherly. "If the routine blood work that they *have* to have done before surgery revealed any kind of serious liver problem, they wouldn't have gone into the OR. But if the liver was healthy, it couldn't have failed in sixty minutes."

"But you said a toxic substance—?"

"Very unlikely. It would have involved other consequences and they'd have—" He hesitates. "They'd have had to tell you, I'd think."

"But then why, why is this on the death certificate?" Kathy insists.

"I don't know, that's what puzzles me," Dick admits.

There is a brief silence. I hug Raggedy Andy tighter and pat Orlando Furrioso.

"Tell you what," Dick says. "You have a legal right to see all the medical records. Why don't you write a formal letter requesting them and then send copies of them to me. Since the people at the medical center don't seem to be very helpful, I'll try to figure them out and see what I can come up with." He pauses, then adds, "Just to reassure you, you understand. Just to reassure you."

Kathy and I are almost tearfully grateful. He'd offered help earlier, we remember. Why didn't we do this sooner?

But then for the last ten days we've been hoping for a phone call or a letter from deVere White or from someone, anyone, at the hospital. Surely the medical center is eventually going to have to give us an official explanation of Elliot's death, or so we keep telling ourselves.

"Be sure and get *all* the records," Dick warns. "I believe that under California law you're entitled to see everything, everything from his first visit to the UCDMC until his death, including the autopsy report, pathology reports, and so on."

We promise that we'll ask for everything and thank Dick again.

After we hang up, I settle Raggedy Andy back into his place on the bed. He regularly sits on the right of Orlando, closest to the side where I sleep, so Orlando can put a big hairy arm around him in a chummy brotherly way. Just like Elliot in the portrait and in the coffin, Orlando always wears an expression of ironic forbearance. With his painted smile and gleaming shoe-button eyes, on the other hand, Raggedy Andy is always relentlessly cheerful.

That's why he was Elliot's favorite storybook character when my husband was a little boy. Elliot knew it was best to get through life by being cheerful, no matter what horrible things were going to happen.

But of course now Elliot is Orlando, and I am a clone of Raggedy Andy. Orlando waits patiently on the bed, clinging to his buddy, while I impersonate a rag doll in the living room, sitting quietly in "my" chair and smiling fixedly at the kindly visitors who file in and out.

FRIDAY, FEBRUARY 22, 1991, 3 P.M.

Our letter to the medical records department at the UCDMC is brief and, I am pleased to see, quite official-looking. I type it into the computer while Kathy, Susanna, and Liz collaboratively dictate.

> TO WHOM IT MAY CONCERN:
> Please release all medical records, including a complete autopsy report, for Elliot L. Gilbert, to myself, Sandra M. Gilbert. I do not want any materials withheld, including recovery room notes, doctors' notes and charts, nurses' notes, psychiatric records or HIV test results. I would like, in other words, to have a copy of his complete UCDMC medical file beginning in August of 1990 and ending on the day when he was autopsied in February 1991.
> I enclose herewith a check in payment for the first twenty pages. Thank you for your swift cooperation.

I can't think clearly enough to formulate most of these sentences myself, but luckily I can still type and spell, and I remember how to save files on my computer.

While we're printing out several copies—one for us, one for Dick, one for the UCDMC—the trapper shows up at the kitchen door.

Like some demonic incubus (or so I tell myself), the skunk whose presence my kids had first noticed in January has continued to haunt our house. In fact, the skunk smell has gotten so awful that Kathy has called a trapper in Oakland, because no local exterminators are willing to "handle skunks, raccoons, and other wild animals." Rats seem to be the largest pests they're ready to deal with.

The trapper—a handsome, bearded, black man who's got an endless fund of zoological lore about the ways of skunks in the Berkeley hills—has just developed a theory about our problem, something about an adversarial relationship between our skunk and an opossum who also, in his view, inhabits the premises.

I imagine that the basement of my house is full of scuffles, snarls, buried bones, and little streaks of blood. I imagine that, as in Parkinson's law, the animal stench will expand to fill the space available.

The trapper chuckles benignly. He has a plan. First he'll catch the opossum, after which the skunk. . . . But I can't follow the details. My daughters and Liz, though, volunteer to go downstairs with him so he can explain to them where he wants to put bait for which creature and what we should do if either of the combatants gets caught in the cage into which he intends to lure one of them.

As soon as I'm alone in the kitchen, the phone rings. Although I usually can't bear to pick it up these days, I force myself to do so this time, and there is deVere White's benevolent brogue at the other end of the line.

"Just thought I'd call to tell ye the surgery was a complete success," he says bizarrely.

"A success?" I seem to have to talk in a whisper.

"The pathology reports have come back and all the nodes were negative for prostate cancer," he explains. "We got it all out. I wanted ye to know we did the right thing."

"But then—but then why did he—?" I begin.

"You were worried that surgery wasn't the right thing," he interrupts briskly. "I wanted ye to know it was the right thing. We did the right thing, made the right decision."

To my own surprise, I recover some measure of poise. "In that case, why did he die?" I murmur ironically. "Perhaps the right thing wasn't done in the right way?"

"Ah, that I don't know, luv," he says almost tenderly. "That I don't know."

I envision him sitting in his office at the medical center. He's wearing chinos and a sport shirt—maybe a striped sport shirt, maybe a plaid one—under his crisp white coat. Perhaps there's a stethoscope hanging out of one pocket, to reinforce the doctorly look. Maybe he has his feet up on the desk. He's probably tired from a long day in the OR, probably wearing comfortable old brown loafers.

"According to the death certificate," I remark with some severity, "my husband died of cardiac arrest due to liver failure, and he died in sixty minutes. How can that be?"

"That I don't know, luv," he reiterates gently, regretfully.

"But the death certificate was signed by your resident, Dr. Poonamallee," I remind him.

"Oh he didn't know anything about it, he knew nothing about it," deVere White replies. "He just signed what the pathologists told him to sign."

"I see." I can't think what else to say so I say goodbye and hang up.

The kitchen is very quiet. I go out into the dining room and look at Elliot's portrait again.

"What in the world did you—do you—expect?" Elliot asks me.

"I don't know," I answer.

From downstairs, I can hear the voices of the girls and the trappers. They're animatedly discussing something, no doubt the fate of the skunk.

I decide to unload the dishwasher. I seem to be pretty good at cleaning up in the kitchen. It's one of the few normal things I can do. Which is lucky, since my friend Bob has constructed an elaborate dinner schedule that he rather unnervingly calls "the duty roster." Tonight, for instance, he and two other friends are coming over with a fancy cassoulet.

I won't be able to swallow much of it, of course, but the table has to look nice. We'll eat in the dining room, under the portraits, and I'll keep on trying to smile like Raggedy Andy.

9

―

So far as it fits their particular purposes, for surgeons death ends their action. It is not unfair to recognize that there is a gladiator dimension to surgery and surgeons. Surgeons take up scalpels against disease; they resist with force its invasion on the body. When death comes, the struggle is ended. Little is said to the patient's family.

—Charles L. Bosk,
Forgive and Remember:
Managing Medical Failure

Monday, March 4, 1991, noon

Rain, rain, rain. I can hear it seething and hissing on the roof, gurgling in the gutters. It's been making headlines in the Bay area this week.

To our surprise, Elliot's records have already arrived from the medical center. Kathy just brought them into my bedroom with the other mail. I am as usual propped up on the pillows, next to Raggedy Andy and Orlando, smoking, sipping coffee, and pretending to read the newspaper. Everyone understands, now, that most days I can't get out of bed before twelve or one—or sometimes even two. I sit here with "the boys" and turn the pages of the paper, trying but failing to focus on the war that is evidently still raging in Saudi Arabia, Kuwait, and Iraq.

Sometimes I gaze out the window at all the blossoms that are gradually giving way to tiny new leaves. Or, as now, I stare at the rain that's seriously pelting the deck and the treetops.

The rain terrifies me.

Everyone else is delighted by it, after five years of drought in California. People come into the house wet and rosy, with smiling, uncontrollable exclamations of pleasure.

"Thank God for this rain!"

"At last it's *really* raining!"

Then they glance furtively at me and fall silent.

My children and friends have found out that I'm very worried about Elliot being out in the rain by himself, with only a few shiny wooden boards between him and a ton of wet dirt. They all understand that I can't stop believing he knows about the rain and wants to come in out of it.

Elliot never liked rain. He was sensual and sensitive. Loved basking in the sun. Sleeping in the comforting heat of the September beach at the Sea Ranch. Hated running to the car through streaming sheets of water when we'd forgotten an umbrella.

Some mornings I lie down and try to go back to sleep, in case I might then wake up and discover that I've really just been dreaming all this.

Elliot hardly ever appears in my sleep, though according to my grief books a number of widows regularly encounter their lost husbands that way. I'm just as glad I haven't seen him much. The two times he did show up were frightening.

A few days after his funeral, he spoke very distinctly and sorrowfully from behind some blurry barrier.

"It's cold here, sem," he complained, "so cold."

I knew I was supposed to help him, to warm him, but I wasn't sure how. When I woke up, I was gasping, trembling, my heart racing as in an episode of tachycardia I once had, and I needed to take a pill to make it beat normally again.

The other time wasn't so scary but almost as sad. Elliot walked into the room and stood next to the bed. He was looking jaunty and wearing the light blue parka I gave him one Christmas.

"Always here for *you*, babe," he said reassuringly.

I've hardly cried at all since February 11, but that time I woke with a prickling sensation in my eyes and a funny tightness in my throat. My self-help books, I thought, might consider that I was making progress in my "grief work."

The package from the medical center is surprisingly thick and heavy. Can there have been so many records about one man? Kathy begins to open it but I'm afraid to look. Instead, I start tearing at today's pile of condolence letters.

These have been arriving with bleak regularity ever since February 13 or so. They come from everywhere, not just from relatives, friends, and colleagues of Elliot's and mine but from former students, distant professional acquaintances, even carpenters, dentists, and rental agents who've taken care of us in the past.

My daughters and I read them, then carefully put them back into their envelopes because my friends Leah and Susan have admonished me that I will eventually have to answer them all. In fact, both Leah and Susan have been urging me to go out and order mournful thank-you cards in preparation for that task. They tell me these cards should say something like "The family of Elliot Lewis Gilbert is sincerely grateful for your words of consolation and kindness."

But another friend says that according to Miss Manners, printed notes are tacky in this situation. You're supposed to write personally to everyone who took the trouble to write to you, even if there are more than three hundred of them.

The question seems to me to be moot, since I am on compassionate leave from my teaching duties and never leave the house these days except twice a week, when somebody drives me to

Oakland to see my shrink. A trip to the stationery store sounds as unlikely as a trip to the moon.

Kathy has split open the mailer from Sacramento, and a thick, cryptic-looking stack of medical records is weighing down the blankets on my bed, just next to the newspaper. The sight and size of the pile are nauseating. And how could we begin to decipher them? Kathy seems tempted to read, but as she riffles through the pages, with their tiny black annotations and mysterious technical squiggles, I can see her becoming discouraged.

"Dick has to do it," she sighs. "Obviously *he* has to do it."

I agree and tell her, somewhat peremptorily, to take them away, hide them someplace where I won't have to see them.

Actually, my dread of reading them doesn't come mainly from my fear of not understanding them; it comes, rather, from my fear that I *might* understand them. Suppose there's a page noting, quite plainly, in ordinary English, that deVere White mistakenly operated in the wrong place on Elliot, or clumsily cut off some perfectly healthy part of his body? Suppose there's a page recording an early visit in which deVere White comments that this patient is obviously doomed?

A number of my friends, along with all three of my children and some of my children's friends, are getting increasingly suspicious about the circumstances of Elliot's death. A few have begun, carefully, tentatively, to relate medical horror stories.

A college classmate called from Minnesota to report that she has a neighbor who is a surgery nurse. She said her neighbor told her that when something terrible happens in the OR, the doctors often hustle the mortally wounded patient into the recovery room so he or she can die *there* instead of on the table. Recovery room deaths, the neighbor explained, are not as bad for the hospital as deaths on the table.

The mother of one of Susanna's friends is also a surgery nurse. *She* confides that the hospital is supposed to notify the family to stand by if something has gone wrong in the OR or the recovery room. Medical ethics require that the staff notify the relatives if a patient is in critical condition.

Kathy comes back into my room. "I've turned every page and I can't seem to find anything that's called an autopsy report," she snaps. Even in my state of misery and panic I can see that she is tense with frustration, flushed with anger, maybe even despair.

"Well, how would *you* know what an autopsy report looks like," I answer in a tone as cross as hers. "Why don't you just Xerox everything and send it all to Dick the way you're supposed to?"

I look at my watch—twelve-thirty—and toy with the idea of going back to sleep, but then realize that in fact I must get up. The burglar alarm man will be here at two, and the trapper may also show up a little later on.

And now the rain is beginning to falter and thin to a faint drizzle. Just northeast of my deck, in the direction of the Sunset View Cemetery, the sky is clearing. Maybe Elliot will feel safer soon.

———

MONDAY, MARCH 4, 1991, 7 P.M.

Tonight we are six at dinner. Four of my closest friends from Davis have come bearing paella, salad, Italian white wine, and chocolate decadence. Kathy is eating with us too. It's pouring again as we sit down in the dining room: brutal needles of rain batter the skylight over the table, and there are even flashes of lightning, rumbles of thunder. Kathy glances toward me nervously, but I assume my fixed rag-doll smile and start refilling wine glasses.

This afternoon Kathy called another colleague of mine to ask him to put some pressure on his friend the associate dean of the medical school, so we could find out whether Elliot's autopsy report really was missing from the materials we received and, if so, why.

Then, later, as we all sipped our first glasses of wine before dinner, everybody trooped into my study to listen to the second poison call, the one that was recorded on my answering machine. The two calls came on Saturday night, just after that evening's companions had departed, and my reaction to them has inspired my friends to advise me that I must get in touch with a burglar alarm company.

The phone rang at almost twelve, a minute after the gate swung shut behind my guests, and a breathy young female voice asked for Elliot.

As always, I didn't know what to say. None of us has been able to figure out what to say when phone calls come for him. Evidently no one wants to articulate the simple truth: *Sorry, he can't come to the phone right now (any more? ever again?) because he's dead.*

This time, for some odd reason I asked who was calling.

"Lisa," replied the breathy voice.

"Lisa? Lisa?" Standing next to a stack of dirty dishes, I felt a curious pang of dread. "Lisa? Who *are* you?"

"I'm his girlfriend," said the voice.

And I hung up.

A minute later the phone rang again, but this time I let the answering machine take over, with Roger reading the careful greeting he'd recorded two days after Elliot died.

"Lisa" left a long melodramatic message. "Oh, Elliot, I guess I was just talking to your wife. Oh, Elliot, why did you do me like you did that last weekend?" Oh"—breaking down in theatrical sobs—"Oh, Elliot, I love you, love you, love you."

Barely audible in the background were the mutterings of an enigmatic male voice.

When "Lisa" finished her monologue, I stumbled frantically into the kitchen. At last, I thought, the walls of my house were really falling down around me: I was living alone and naked in the middle of the street. And Elliot was no longer here to protect me.

Why had I—he—been targeted for this assault?

Irrationally, I picked up the kitchen phone and dialed Susanna, who had just two days ago gone back to graduate school in Santa Barbara, three hundred miles away, and screamed my anxieties into the receiver.

Very rationally, Susanna pointed out that it would be hours, perhaps even a day or two, before she could get here to help me.

Then I called Bob, who was a mere five miles away. My house was being watched, I told him. Behind one of the neighborly looking windows on my street lurked a Peeping Tom and his sidekick "Lisa." Their next step was—was what?

Or maybe it was worse. Maybe "Lisa" and the man in the background were calling from the UCDMC to taunt and torment me. Because it was completely obvious that they knew Elliot was dead.

It never occurred to me that my husband might have actually had a girlfriend named "Lisa." Elliot was too bourgeois, too shy, and indeed too uxorious. And besides, we hadn't been apart on a weekend in almost a year.

As rationally as Susanna, Bob observed that he too was pretty far away. It would be fifteen or twenty minutes before he could get to my house. He urged me to call 911, then call some friends who live down the street from me, and then phone him back in case I needed more help.

Later, standing in the study with my neighbors, a large, mustached policeman, and Kathy and Liz, who came in from a movie just as the police car drew up outside the door, I had to listen several more times to the message on the answering machine, in case I might be able to identify "Lisa's" voice.

After some discussion about its timbre, the policeman turned to me and bluntly, shockingly, asked if Elliot might have had a girlfriend.

"Of course not, officer," I replied without hesitation. "Why, my husband was a *professor!*"

Nor could I understand why everyone in the room began to laugh.

But that was two days ago. Two whole days. Now my favorite colleagues are here, and I'm okay. Although a huge clap of thunder splits the quiet, and the lights flicker as we dig into our paella. Someone inquires politely about the cost of a burglar alarm system, and we start discussing the efficacy of such systems, then turn to literary topics.

But I see that, at the other end of the table, Kathy—my staunch, rock-like Kathy—is rubbing her eyes and staring apprehensively at the ceiling, at the flickering lights, and the lightning flashing above the skylight.

"Daddy's angry," she suddenly says, and, looking up as another crash of thunder hits the sky, she adds "Stop that, Dad!"

WEDNESDAY, MARCH 6, 1991, 4:30 P.M.

The trapper came again this morning. Both the opossum and the skunk continue to elude him, so he decided to move his baited cage from downstairs near the basement to upstairs just under the deck off the kitchen. I worry that this means the smell of skunk, which so far has mostly arisen like some dreadful smoke from the cellar, will now permanently disfigure the kitchen. For their part, Kathy and Liz increasingly worry about the sufferings of any animal that gets caught in the trapper's cage.

But the trapper says that none of us should worry. If the skunk gets locked in, it'll end up, paradoxically, feeling safe, so it won't be scared and it won't stink up the house. He assures us that it's cosy in the trap. Womblike. Most animals enjoy being there.

I wonder if that's how the dead feel in their coffins, comfy and secure in a padding of satin.

I'm sitting at the dining room table, trying to fill out a claims form for one of our insurance companies but really interrogating Elliot's portrait about death and coffins, animals and cages and darkness, when Kathy and Liz get back from their trip to the Xerox place and the Fed Ex box. They mainly went to copy the medical records and express-mail them to Dick, but they were also copying some materials for Elliot's public memorial service at the university, which has been scheduled for this coming Sunday, March 10.

Kathy and Susanna are going to sing three of Elliot's songs, including his setting of "I had a dove," and we'll end the service by playing the "Hostias" from the Verdi *Requiem*, a piece he loved. I want everyone in the audience (the congregation?) to have copies of all the lyrics, especially the ones to the *Hostias*, which comes from a Catholic liturgy but talks specifically about Israel, so it's an appropriate lament for a lapsed Jew who had been married for thirty-four years to a lapsed Catholic.

While I sat here at the table, waiting for Kathy and Liz, I reread the words from the *Requiem*, to reassure myself that I'd made, as Dr. deVere White put it, "the right decision."

> Hostias in preces tibi, Domine,
> laudis offerimus.
> Tu suscipe pro animabus illis,
> quarum hodie memoriam facimus.
> Fac eas, Domine, de morte transire ad vitam,
> quam olim Abrahae promisistic et semini ejus.

A sacrifice of praise and prayer, O Lord,
we offer Thee.
Accept it in behalf of those souls
we commemorate this day;
let them, O Lord, pass from death to life,
as you promised Abraham and his seed.

Kathy and Liz come in looking grim. Kathy puts the mailer with the first set of records down on the sideboard. Liz hands me a sheaf of song lyrics for the memorial service and a pink Fed Ex slip.

"What a mess," Kathy says bitterly, "They were a mess. It looked to us as though everything was out of order—and some stuff didn't seem to have come out right on the hospital's copies—"

"And there definitely was no autopsy report," Liz interrupts.

"Goddamnit," Kathy says. "My dad's been dead for almost a month. They should have sent us the goddamn autopsy report by now, shouldn't they? Wasn't that why that stupid goddamn doctor was calling you the other day? Because *he'd* seen it and—and anyway, I'm really going to call them *now!*"

"Oh I don't know." I gaze up at Elliot's portrait for guidance. "I don't know whether you should call them right away, Kathy. Maybe they'll get suspicious, hostile. Maybe they'll—"

But Kathy has already left the room, and Liz is noisily making coffee in the kitchen, grinding beans and banging pots around.

"What are you afraid of?" Elliot studies me patiently, wryly. "Hasn't the worst already happened?"

I know what I'm afraid of. I'm afraid of what the autopsy report might or might not tell me.

"I actually got to speak to the goddamn director." Kathy is standing in the doorway. "How do you like that? They actually let me talk to the director of the medical center," she says with heavy sarcasm. "And you know what he told me?"

"No. What?" I stare down at the table, not wanting to hear.

"He told me they've had the autopsy report for a week or so but they have to *retype* it!"

"Retype it?"

"Yeah, something about its being too hard to read. They'll send it to us as soon as they *retype* it."

"Oh, well. So what?"

Kathy looks at me pityingly. "For God's sake, Mom, don't be so stupid. What if they're doctoring the records? That's probably the best kind of doctoring they do!"

10

---

*Hospitals have a duty to inform the patient or the patient's
survivors when it is aware of a deviation from the standard
of care that causes an injury. . . . Strong policies support
imposing the fiduciary duty to disclose on the modern day
hospital. When patients enter a hospital, they place their
confidence and trust in the hospital as an entity; they rely
upon the nurses, technicians, laboratory reports, and physicians . . . and expect that the hospital will see to their best
interests.*

—J. Douglas Peters and Jeanette C. Peraino,
"Malpractice in Hospitals:
Ten Theories for Direct Liability,"
in *Law, Medicine, and Health Care* (October 1984)

Sunday, March 10, 1991, 3:15 p.m.

We've arrived at the U. C. Davis Faculty Club for Elliot's memorial service almost an hour early, but some of the department
secretaries and a few of my colleagues are already here, helping
with last-minute preparations: flower arrangements, stacks of
programs, and platters of cookies for the public reception that
will be held afterwards. Later still, there will be a private gathering at our Davis condo—a weird sort of cocktail party, I suppose,
not unlike the one that followed the funeral last month—and yet

125

another staff member is right now busy overseeing the arrangements for that.

My children and Liz and Susan cluster around me like secret service agents as we enter the building. I seem to have to walk very slowly, leaning heavily on Roger's arm, as though I were years older than I am, and I feel absurdly conspicuous in the almost parodic widow's weeds I've chosen for the occasion: a black dress with tiny white polka dots, a black jacket, a long black chiffon scarf.

The acting chair of my department—Elliot's replacement—and the department administrative assistant appear to be moving toward me just as slowly as I move toward them, as though we are all traveling underwater, and they speak in hushed voices.

Someone ushers me and the girls into a small side parlor. Someone else brings a cup of coffee and a set of programs. Roger and Susan go into the room where the service will take place to get our primitive sound system set up. It turns out that the faculty club doesn't have any audio facilities of its own, so we'll have to play the "Hostias" (and, again, the "Cavatina") on the same little boom box that we used for the "Cavatina" and "Im Abendrot" at Elliot's funeral last month.

Kathy, Susanna, Liz, and I study the program, which is, we tell each other, gratifyingly professional looking. Because Elliot loved the ocean and the cliffs, meadow, beaches at the Sea Ranch, someone decided that it should have a photograph of a beach with the tide going out and a path of light across the water, with next to it the words

IN MEMORIAM
Elliot L. Gilbert
December 1, 1930–February 11, 1991

Inside, the names of the principal speakers, close professional or graduate school friends of Elliot's, along with the other participants in the program (my kids, me, and my daughters' accompanist) are decorously listed. I guess everything looks okay, just like a regular memorial service, whatever that's supposed to look like, although Roger worries that—what with the girls singing their father's songs, him reading an excerpt from one of his father's essays, and me reading a poem I once wrote for Elliot—the whole event will seem too much like a Gilbert family talent show.

Although she's had a lot of professional training, even Kathy is a bit nervous about having to sing. As for Susanna, who also has some professional training and, like her sister, a good deal of experience, she dreads the prospect; she's sure she'll break down the way she did at the funeral, when she read from the Psalms and started weeping so hard that Susan had to get up and help her finish. For her part, their accompanist is fretting about her outfit—a red sweater and gray slacks. The rest of us are wearing lugubriously dark clothes, so she is afraid she looks disrespectful.

"I always think of memorial services as celebrations," she explains, "life-affirming events, so I guess I didn't *expect* you guys to wear black."

We try to reassure her, but she wanders off, shrugging uncomfortably, to test the piano that has been wheeled into the faculty club dining room.

When we, too, follow her, we are unnerved by the size of the group that has already assembled in this makeshift space. Three hundred people? Four hundred? I don't know how to count crowds, but I know I'm overwhelmed by the number of students, colleagues, and friends assembled here. Some have flown in from out of town—from Iowa, Texas, L.A., and I don't know where else. Others have driven long distances—from Nevada, southern California, Marin, Sonoma, San Francisco.

Roger just arrived from Ithaca yesterday and Susan from Indiana. At least they got here in time for dinner and a quick review of the plans for the memorial service. Roger found some of the extra turkey stuffing that Elliot had frozen in December, just after Christmas. It is a Genovese stuffing, with spinach and sausage, that everyone calls "Grandpa's stuffing" because my grandfather taught Elliot how to make it. Roger, an accomplished pasta chef, decided to use it in home-made ravioli, just the way my grandparents always did in the first week of January. So in a sense I guess Elliot and his son collaborated in preparing a special memorial meal for us last night.

Then I played the "Hostias" for Roger and Susan, to make sure that they agreed it was an appropriate choice. But when the sombre, soaring notes began—*Hostias in preces tibi, Domine, laudis offerimus*, "A sacrifice of praise and prayer, O Lord, we offer thee"—I began to scream. "Not for *you*, Elliot, no, not for *you*."

Not surprisingly, everyone is pretty worried about me today. But, flanked by my family, I make my slow underwater way into the memorial service room, toward the front center chair. Standing alone in the aisle, at the edge of the first row, the chancellor of the U. C. Davis campus is waiting to greet me, looking solemn and sympathetic. I shake his hand, accept his murmured condolences, and try to scan the audience over his dark shoulder. Might there be anyone here from the UCDMC? They too were Elliot's colleagues, after all, and this man is *their* chancellor too: deVere White's chancellor, Reitan's chancellor, Poonamallee's chancellor.

What will I do if I see them? Will I rush up to them, begging them to explain about "liver failure," about "splenomegaly," while the "Hostias" rises in the background and the chancellor frowns?

Dick's wife, Leah, called two days ago to assure us that the bulky package of medical records we FedExed on Wednesday had just arrived in Bethesda. She said that Dick was going to spend the weekend studying them. He's probably reading them right now, as I furtively look around the faculty club for UCDMC physicians.

And what about "Lisa" and her coach, the enigmatic man-in-the-background on the answering machine? Might *they* be here? A few colleagues have advanced the theory that "Lisa" & Co. may be a pair of disaffected students, even though I can't think of any students who hated Elliot enough to torment me (him?) now that he is in his grave—or even of any who might hate *me* so much, for that matter.

I keep on searching the crowd for doctorly figures and sour young faces. But everyone blurs into everyone else. I can't seem to distinguish one expectant, sympathetic countenance from another, and now my children are bearing me along, as if I were a black barge riding a slow tide, toward the center of the front row. They're attentively settling me into one of the folding chairs, handing me a program and a handkerchief along with the book that contains the poem I'm supposed to read near the end of the service. And once more, as in a grimly recycled dream, the opening chords of the "Cavatina" are sounding their bleak alarm.

———

SUNDAY, MARCH 10, 1991, 5:15 P.M.

A mild drizzle coats the asphalt of the parking lot as we drift toward our car after the memorial service. A "small rain," I think; this is what the anonymous medieval poet meant by a "small rain."

When I first began to teach, Elliot advised me to use the poem in which that phrase appears when I did Introduction to Literature courses. Students, he explained, need to be told the difference between what they *think* is a poem (often, anything that rhymes, he warned) and what really *is* a poem. Consider, he noted, the difference between "Roses are red, violets are blue," and "O western wind." He sat companionably in the study, grading papers from his own classes, while I typed the ditto masters for handouts I'd give my students, urging them to "compare" and "contrast" these two verses:

> Roses are red,
> Violets are blue,
> Sugar is sweet,
> And so are you.

> Oh western wind,
> When wilt thou blow,
> That the small rain down shall rain?
> Christ that my love
> Were in my arms,
> And I in my bed again!

But the first poet was probably smarter than the second one, I muse, as we make our way across the parking lot, shaking hands with compassionate students and colleagues. Roses, violets, and sugar are a lot less dangerous to one's love than even the smallest rain.

I stood in front of the three or four hundred people who sighed and creaked on folding chairs. I addressed my love. All the other speakers were witty, charming, elegant. Several told a few of Elliot's Rabinowitz jokes. Some discussed his cooking, his fondness for Jewish deli food, his love of music, his sometimes combative—even curmudgeonly—commitment to his own ideas about education. Susanna *did* begin to weep, or at least her voice quavered, as she sang her father's setting of Housman's "When I Was One and Twenty." Dry-eyed but impassioned, Kathy sang his settings of "The River"—a poem Susanna and I wrote together, to go with his melody, when she was ten years old—and of Keats's "I had a dove." Our acting chair read tributes from a range of other friends and students.

A group of my former colleagues from Princeton celebrated his humor—"infectious and probably also addictive"—and confessed that "Once when he was away in Davis, we organized a conference call to get him to tell us more Rabinowitz jokes." From as far back as twenty or thirty years ago, a range of former students remembered his love for Hopkins, his "joy in Dickens," and his energetic readings of various other writers; a number declared that he was the best professor they'd ever had.

Then Roger read from a short, unfinished essay—"Speculations on Time"—that he'd found on one of his father's floppy disks when he went through them after the funeral.

All day, for several days, Roger had scrolled through Elliot's files, printing out everything that looked remotely significant, backing up copies of essays, articles, notes, letters, as if by preserving what was on the computer he could keep his father from dying into the past.

"We are all, therefore, cripples in eternity, the name of our disability being 'time,' " Elliot had observed, adding, "(This is specifically the Eden punishment, the fall from eternity into time, the fall from immortality into death.)"

And then I spoke to my husband, trying to make myself believe that he really was there, at the back of the room, just beyond the silent, blurry, straining faces.

I read him a poem of mine called "Anniversary Waltz." When I wrote it, it was about our life. Now it was about how we *once* were alive together. Near the end, I said—how strange it seemed now—

Your beard begins to get gray,
but not your eyebrows.

We're stuck in the thick of it, we smile wryly,
we fatten, we grow dumb.

And then, in front of all those people, I had to confess my embarrassing need:

Once in a while
I have to hang on to your hand.
I cannot imagine
who else we might have become.

But Elliot probably wasn't listening. I can tell that he very likely wasn't listening because here I am in the rainy parking lot, pulling my black chiffon scarf tighter around my neck, and climbing into the car to set out for yet another funereal party, even while I realize how right the medieval poet was, after all, about what it means to be "cripples in eternity."

"Christ that my love were in my arms, and I in my bed again!"

———

MONDAY, MARCH 11, 1991, 6 P.M.

I'm sitting in "my" chair in the living room, having pre-dinner drinks and discussing the memorial service with Bob and Moneera, who have brought tonight's meal over. Bob's *choucroute garni* is warming up on the stove in the kitchen, but we're already nibbling crudités dipped in Moneera's hummus. Moneera is Egyptian and makes hummus better than anyone else I know.

Although I have visitors, the house seems depressingly empty. Exhausted and subdued, Roger and Susanna left this morning—both had to get back to school—and Kathy is working late tonight.

Yesterday, on the way home from the memorial service, we

picked up a custard pie, Elliot's favorite, at a bakery he especially liked, so that we could have an impromptu slapdash "celebration" for Susanna, whose birthday is tomorrow, March 12. Smiling determinedly, anyway *trying* to smile determinedly, the six of us sat around the breakfast room table, toying with a few leftovers from the post–memorial service party. Then Susanna opened her presents.

We hadn't even thought of getting her any gifts, but it had been surprisingly easy to find things for her.

First she got an alabaster egg from a set Elliot and I had bought on our very last trip to Europe, in the little Tuscan town of Volterra, known for its pre-Roman Etruscan tombs.

The ancient Etruscans believed that an egg, even an alabaster one, was a symbol of rebirth, of potential resurrection from the dead.

Then she got CDs with the *Four Last Songs* of Strauss (including "Im Abendrot"), the late quartets of Beethoven (including the "Cavatina"), and the Verdi *Requiem* (including the "Hostias")—the ones we'd played at her father's funeral and his memorial service.

We were all silent as she tore at the old birthday paper Susan had found in the back of the hall closet. The pool of light in which we sat suddenly seemed shrunken; shadows gnawed at the edge of the table.

The presents were just what she wanted, Susanna assured us. Especially the music. Especially all the ceremonial music.

Suddenly I'm a little frightened without the kids, maybe because the memorial service *was* such a family affair.

But Susan is still here. Right now she's in the kitchen keeping an eye on the *choucroute* and talking on the phone to Dick. I'm staying put in the living room because I'm not sure I want to overhear any part of the conversation.

Monday the 11th: exactly one month to the day since my

husband died. But that night it was cool, clear, breezy, while tonight it's raining again, a "small rain" so far, like yesterday's, but steadily gathering in force.

I swivel toward the big living room windows and stare out at the deck, glistening with wetness in the cocktail-hour light. I wonder if it might help to pray for more drought. Or perhaps I'd feel better if I *did* go into the kitchen and listen to what Susan is saying. Even out here I can hear her voice rising and falling. She's been on the phone for almost forty minutes now. First she talked to Leah for a while, and then Dick got on. She had a pretty long list of questions when she called—about "liver failure" and toxic substances and the possibility of another intubation problem—but by now she must be mostly learning Dick's interpretation of the records.

Bob and Moneera clearly sense my jumpiness and try to distract me with chat about the burglar alarm man, who came this morning to give me an estimate on a security system.

He figured out, I tell them, that my house is quite vulnerable because it has an unusual number of outside doors along with two or three problematic windows through which even the least athletic of intruders might climb.

It's a wonder we haven't had any break-ins, Moneera remarks.

But Elliot was my security system, I reply.

She and Bob look pained; they change the subject to the trapper, who still hasn't had any luck catching either the skunk or the opossum.

Urban trapping evidently isn't easy, I comment. No doubt wild animals become wily animals in the city, just like the rest of us.

Rain slants against the windowpanes. I decide to brave the kitchen and get another drink.

Susan is hunched over the little desk in the corner of the

breakfast room, taking notes, but she hears me come in and motions for more paper. As I leave to find some, I hear her saying, *"Her*matocrit? *H*ematocrit?"

I don't understand what she's talking about but it's plainly some technical hospital term.

Susan is getting quite a medical education, I reflect. This morning she called Joe Tupin, M.D., the UCDMC director to whom Kathy spoke last week. Although she's a scrupulously polite person, she was really aggressive with him. I stood behind her in my study as she snapped questions into the phone on my desk.

"It's been a month today since my collaborator's husband died, and she still hasn't been given any satisfactory explanation of what happened," she said sternly. "What's going on there anyway?"

Dr. Tupin said he now had a typed copy of the autopsy report and promised to FedEx it to us right away, but when Susan asked him if it said anything that would help us understand what killed my husband, he was studiously neutral. He'd "reviewed" the report himself, he admitted, but—although pathology wasn't his field—he had to inform her that in his view its "findings" were "inconclusive."

"Inconclusive! He says the findings are inconclusive. What can 'inconclusive' *mean?*" she exclaimed to me, slamming down the receiver.

In front of her on my desk was one of the few pictures I have of my husband as a baby: my "baby Elliot pictures," I call them. Elliot looks like a Campbell Soup kid in this particular shot, round-faced and rosy cheeked, with blond curls, wide eyes, and eyebrows raised in an innocent question.

"What now? What's all the fuss about *this* time?" he seemed to be wondering as Susan shoved the phone away in disgust.

Now I can hear her hanging up in the kitchen, going over to the stove to stir the *choucroute,* moving back to the counter to pour herself a drink.

We fall silent in the living room, waiting for her to report on her conversation.

But when she appears in the doorway, she's silent, grim.

"Well, what *did* Dick have to say?" I ask with an effort at joviality.

Susan motions toward me with one hand. "Come in the kitchen for a minute, Sandra," she answers quietly.

"That's ridiculous," I reply. "Why don't you just tell *all* of us about it? Anything you can tell *me* you can tell Bob and Moneera. I'm obviously going to talk to them about it anyway so—"

"Just come in the kitchen a minute, please, Sandra," she repeats.

I glance from her to Bob to Moneera with mock disgust and follow her reluctantly.

For some odd reason, we stand facing away from the rest of the house, looking out the kitchen door at the rain that's slashing, now, into the rhododendron blossoms. Susan puts an arm around me.

"Dick isn't one hundred percent sure what happened," she says, "but Elliot was given a lot of blood. He must have been bleeding a lot."

"Well, I know they had to give five units in the OR," I assure her.

"No." She lowers her voice. "It's worse than that. And Dick thinks it's strange that they didn't tell you. They gave seven more units of blood in the recovery room. By the time he died, Elliot had been given *twelve* transfusions."

"Twelve units!" I'm finding it hard to breathe.

"Twelve units."

"Twelve? Why would they give that much?"

"Bleeding," she murmurs. "Hemorrhaging."

"But why—?"

"Dick isn't sure. He's still having trouble putting it all together, and he seems pretty upset himself. But he'll call back tomorrow."

I'm silent for a minute. And then I'm kicking the kitchen door and screaming and cursing. "The bastards, the *bastards*! Why didn't they tell me? What happened? What did they do to my husband?"

And I'm weeping and cursing and kicking, and Bob and Moneera are standing in the kitchen behind me, trying, like Susan to hold me. Trying to comfort me and stop me from kicking so hard because, even if I don't break my toe, I may well do some permanent damage to the door.

11

---

*It may seem a strange principle to enunciate as the very
first requirement in a hospital that it should do the sick no
harm. It is quite necessary, nevertheless, to lay down such a
principle.*

—FLORENCE NIGHTINGALE,
Preface, *Notes on Hospitals* (1863)

TUESDAY MARCH 12, 1991, 11 A.M.

I'm in bed, half dozing beside Raggedy Andy and Orlando Furrioso, with an untouched mug of coffee on the table next to me,
when Susan comes in carrying another official-looking envelope
from the UCDMC. As Tupin had promised, the autopsy report
has arrived.

Who is going to read it, and when, and how?

"Have you ever seen an autopsy report?" Dick asked me when
we called him back, briefly, last night. "It's got a very standard
format. The pathologist describes all the organs in the body—
their size, weight, condition—and so forth, then summarizes his
conclusions on the last page." He pauses, sighs. "I don't think
you want to read it, I don't think you should look at it—except,
maybe, for that last page. Although even *that*—"

"No, I don't want to read it at all," I whispered. "I'll tell Susan
to look at it, if she can stand it, but we may just FedEx it to you
right away, without any of us looking at it." My voice was still

hoarse from screaming, and I *was* wondering whether I'd broken my toe, kicking the door.

We'd called back so Dick could help the others calm me down by pointing out that he still hadn't put all the pieces of the puzzle together, and therefore we shouldn't jump to any extravagant conclusions.

"Just get it out of here," I tell Susan now. "I don't want to see it, I don't want to know about it, I want it *out of here.*"

I take one sip of cold coffee, then lie back down with my arms around "the boys" and my head almost under the covers. The simmering sound of steady rain on the roof would ordinarily be soothing, but of course I'm still trying to escape from it.

"And the rain went RUMMA RUMMA RUMMA on the rhubarb leaves," Elliot used to laugh. It was a line from a story, I can't imagine what story, that he'd loved when he was a little boy. When he was "baby Elliot," with his ignorant curls and his naively questioning eyebrows, knowing nothing of prostate cancer, of surgeons and ORs, and blood transfusions.

I sit up with a start, dragging Raggedy Andy out from under the covers along with me. Andy's pointy blue-and-white cap is askew, and I adjust it carefully, so it rests neatly on his smiling cotton head. Just outside my bedroom door, I hear voices in earnest discussion. Kathy and Susan.

"Mom." Kathy comes in looking vaguely anxious. "The basement is flooding and water is backing up in the downstairs bathrooms. I'm going to call Roto-Rooter, okay?"

Our basement often floods toward the end of the rainy season. The roots of the oak trees begin to grow rapidly as spring arrives; they reach out and suck voraciously at the water table, then slither into pipes and other objects buried in the garden. They have a whole weird life underground, a life I don't want to think about, considering that Elliot is down there too, in his tweed jacket and his Liberty tie.

"Just call them, then, just call them," I tell her impatiently, turning away and fiddling with my cup of cold coffee.

But Susan comes in behind her, frowning. "I read it," she says. "I mean, I tried to read it. I turned the pages and looked at most of what they said."

I close my eyes and hold onto the coffee cup. "Well? So?"

Kathy sits down heavily on the edge of the bed. "Can you tell us?"

"Well, nothing much. It keeps on saying that everything is 'grossly unremarkable.' All the organs 'grossly unremarkable.' In other words, it looks to me as though everything in his body was just fine. No heart problems, no lung problems, no liver problems, no nothing." Susan pauses. "It seems to me that we'd all be lucky to have such a good autopsy report," she adds sardonically.

"Could it be a cover-up?" Kathy wants to know.

"How can I tell?"

I get out of bed and start pacing around the room, lighting a cigarette and gulping my icy coffee. I'm wide awake now. "What does it say on the last page?" I ask. "That's where Dick says the pathologists give their main conclusions."

Susan lights a cigarette too. Her frown modulates into a scowl. "It's kind of bizarre," she answers. "It says 'No anatomical cause of death.' Whatever *that* means."

———

TUESDAY MARCH 12, 1991, 6 P.M.

Sunset, and thank God, no rain. A reddish glow filters through the skylight, and in its mild glisten my portrait and Elliot's stare down, bemused, at a dining room table littered with papers. All afternoon, Susan and I have been trying to work "normally." We're revising and proofing the first part of a parody of a TV script entitled "Masterpiece Theatre," which is scheduled for publication this summer. The piece is all about what happens to "texts"—as academics in our field now tend to call most written works—in a "post-structuralist," semi-literate age like our own.

Elliot loved this little project, which actually summarized many of his own skeptical ideas about the state of literary criticism today. When we first read (or, more accurately, performed) it at a professional convention, he came and sat on the floor, in a surprisingly crowded Washington, D.C., ballroom, wearing his light blue parka and beaming encouragement at us.

We'd been nervous about the jokes. Would people understand we *meant* to be funny? Elliot obligingly punctuated our reading with theatrical laughter, in case it was necessary to show other members of the audience that our comedy was intentional. Afterwards, he told us that we should really expand "Masterpiece Theatre" into a book. "Like *The Pooh Perplex*," he said. "Or *1066 and All That*."

Today, we decided that we'd honor his suggestion and also that we'd dedicate this first published installment of "Masterpiece Theatre" to his memory. So this will be the first *in memoriam* publication, other than the program from the service at Davis.

But sitting side by side in front of my computer, Susan and I were both unusually inarticulate. Although we've coauthored three books and coedited a number of anthologies, we debated— even quarreled over—nearly every word as if we'd never worked together before. In the end, it took us almost an hour to write two sentences: " 'Masterpiece Theatre' was written with the advice, support, and encouragement of Elliot L. Gilbert, whose wit and humor were matched by his passionate commitment to the life of letters. This episode and the two others that will complete the work are dedicated, with love and gratitude, to his memory."

An hour or two ago, we faxed this statement to our editor in Chicago, asking him to place it prominently on the first page of the piece. Now Susan is on the phone with Dick again, and I'm

shuffling through the papers on the table, half-heartedly arranging them into piles: manuscripts, editorial comments, lists of
things to do, estimates from the burglar alarm man, copies of the
dinner schedule (a.k.a. "duty roster"), bills (from the trapper
and Roto-Rooter, among many others), insurance forms, medical notes.

Medical notes. These are from yesterday's telephone conversations, and Susan shouldn't have left them around, she really
shouldn't have. I don't want to see them just the way I didn't
want to see the autopsy report, which Kathy and Liz have already FedExed to Dick.

Presumably that's what he's discussing with Susan now.
Among other things.

I glance up at Elliot, whose expression in the portrait suddenly
seems curiously scornful.

All right, I tell him. I can do it. I can take it.

I pull the first page of the medical notes toward me. Written
across the top, in Susan's hasty handwriting:

Leah—March 11.
 "Dick thinks disturbing,
 doesn't think E managed
 optimally. Leah is saying he wouldn't
 give her this info. if alone or not in
 good shape.
 Very troubling news—
 given lots of blood—
 Dick has feeling he was bleeding &
  not on top; & loss of blood
  precipitated heart attack.
 He's been going through it all
  weekend—hard to read
  not legible
  missing papers—"

"Wouldn't give her this info. if alone or not in good shape?"
"Her" must be me. "Her" = me, *Elliot! Not in good shape, either.*
But, biting my lip, I push on to the next page:

Dick—March 11.
"Sometimes reports *are* inconclusive—
a couple of bad heart episodes = ?
Review in brief—w/out papers before
him
Pages are disordered
Certain details missing
At least one paper missing that
may or may not exist—
Only looked at last admission—
What transpired—
Top sheet—2nd sheet, printed
called Coding Summary
About Diagnoses—
Diagnoses—in order—Prostate
Asthma
A/C-acute
anemia
Why is asthma on there—intubation
not issue
issue is acute posthemorrhagic *anemia*—
inadequate oxygenation was case w/ Elliot—"

Acute posthemorrhagic anemia?

Something hot is happening inside my eyes, something wet.
Tears. Pooling and spilling.
Through a film of salt, I gaze up at Elliot, who gazes back at
me ruefully.

———

WEDNESDAY, MARCH 13, 1991, 10 A.M.

"Remember how angry I said he was when he came out of the anesthesia after the biopsy?" I'm still in bed, but bolt upright, pushing today's stack of condolence letters impatiently out of the way. "Well, what if *that's* what happened?"

Susan, sitting at the foot of the bed, looks puzzled. She reaches toward Orlando and idly pats his shaggy head. "If *what's* what happened?"

I'm eagerly, feverishly alert, certain that I'm at last onto something. "Oh *you* remember, you must remember. I told you he was really angry and mean coming out of the anesthesia, after the biopsy. After the failed intubation too, as a matter of fact. He told me he got like that when he was a kid, too. After he had an appendectomy when he was in high school, he told me he was screaming curse words nobody knew he knew, not even *him*, and so—"

"And so?"

"So, I've got it." As much to my own surprise as Susan's, I swing myself out of bed—disregarding the condolence letters that scatter wildly onto the floor behind me—fling on my bathrobe, and head for the kitchen, coffee cup in hand.

Susan is mild and patient. "Got what?" she asks, following me.

"They were horrible to him, horrible, horrible, after the biopsy." I pour myself more coffee with unusual vigor and slam the pot down on the counter. "He was in pain and cross and a nurse and an orderly were trying to get him from the gurney to the bed, but he kept complaining so they just sort of dumped him on the bed and left him there in the wrong position and said to me—to *me*—to help him get comfortable, and then they just walked out of the room and left him there, and what was *I* supposed to do with this large man who was in such bad pain, and I wasn't strong enough to move him by myself, and besides I don't know what's the *right* way to move a patient after surgery—"

"Well, but what's your point?" Susan pours herself some more coffee too, then carefully replaces the pot on its electric burner.

"You're being *stupid*," I say irascibly. "God, you're being so stupid." Irritable energy surges through me. "Dick said the other day that he might have been bleeding because a suture came undone, right?"

"Right."

"Well, *why* would a suture come undone?" I'm almost shouting. "Elliot must have been tossing and turning on his bed, poor baby, he must have been angry coming out of the anesthesia. And he was so mean and angry that they left him alone—they just left him alone the way they did after the biopsy—and *I* wasn't there to help him, the kids and I weren't there—" And now my voice is breaking. "And so he was tossing and turning and a suture came undone and he started to bleed, to hemorrhage, but they left him alone because they were mad at him—and—and so he died."

Susan looks at the floor, on which, in my agitation, I've spilled a good part of my coffee. "Well, I guess that's one story," she says.

———

THURSDAY, MARCH 14, 1991, 1 P.M.

I'm at the dining room table again. Heat is pouring through the skylight as though trying to cook the papers piled in front of me. Susan is in the kitchen, chatting with the trapper, who has come to rebait his cage. Kathy is in my study, looking for my 1990 engagement book.

In Bethesda, right now, Dick is working on a time line of what happened to Elliot in the OR and the recovery room, in case such a document would be useful to a lawyer. When Leah comes to stay with me next week—she's going to be the friend "on duty" after Susan has to go back to Indiana and start teaching again—she'll bring Dick's time line with her. So in a few minutes, Kathy and Susan are going to help me make a similar record of my own, a personal narrative of Elliot's medical history between August 1990, when he was first diagnosed, and February 11, 1991, when he was pronounced dead in the recovery room at the UCDMC. My time line, too, is intended for a lawyer.

We don't actually *have* a lawyer yet, but the phrase "you'll have to talk to a lawyer" or, more magisterially, "you'd better consult an attorney" is becoming increasingly common in my living room. We don't say too much about Dick's suspicions—he has warned us to be circumspect—but we've said enough so that a number of the friends who drift in and out of the house have begun offering us the names of lawyers and law firms specializing in medical malpractice.

In Dick's opinion, much of the case turns on 1) the issue of the hematocrits, and 2) the timing of transfusions. He says that at around 3:00 P.M., when Elliot had been in the recovery room for forty minutes or so, his blood pressure dropped very radically. ("What happened?" Susanna had asked deVere White that night, in the white room. "I don't know, luv, I don't know. His pressure just dropped—" the doctor had said.) This probably happened, Dick speculates, because Elliot had been bleeding internally. It's a well-known fact that internal bleeding causes a drastic drop in blood pressure. ("Why did his pressure drop? Why?" Susanna had asked. "I don't know, luv, I don't know," the doctor had shrugged.)

Someone in the recovery room drew blood for a hematocrit, a test that measures the percentage of red blood cells in the body and can therefore help diagnose internal bleeding. The sample was sent to the hospital lab at 3:05, but Dick can find no record of a hematocrit having been returned. By 3:20, Elliot's blood pressure had been raised through fluids (not blood) administered intravenously.

Then the pressure dropped again at 6:00. Another blood sample was evidently taken, and this time the hematocrit showed that my husband's red blood count was dangerously low. A normal hematocrit should be in the thirties, Dick says. Elliot's was seventeen. But "curiously," Dick tells us, nothing much was done about this problem for a while.

For a dangerous while.

Orders to "type" and "cross-match" blood for transfusion apparently weren't given until 6:50. And Dick doesn't think much blood was given until 7:30, after the "code team"—the emergency team that's supposed to try to resuscitate dying patients—had been called in.

Elliot was pronounced dead at 8:15. They had transfused the blood much too late. Dick thinks his heart failed because, as a result of a hemorrhage or a "slow leak," his red blood cell count dropped so dramatically that he wasn't getting enough oxygen and the heart couldn't work properly.

Dick seems to think, too, that one or two units of blood on hand in the recovery room were overlooked or misplaced, which was why there was a delay in transfusing after 6:00 P.M. He says, understatedly, that he's puzzled about the missing results of the 3:05 P.M. hematocrit, and adds, dryly, that it's odd we weren't told anything about bleeding, about transfusions and hematocrits.

Of course, he notes, we have to understand that some of his points are still just hypotheses, just speculative, since the records are so messy and chaotic. Nevertheless, he's afraid we'll have to find a lawyer.

Afraid. He's afraid. Afraid because he'd set out to *reassure us.*

And nothing that anyone tells us about lawyers and lawsuits is reassuring, either.

This morning Susan called her brother-in-law, who is a partner in a prestigious New York firm. Of course he could help us, he said. Of course he could come up with the name of an excellent malpractice attorney in San Francisco. But, "Does she realize what this might do to her?" he asked. "The strain? The horror of having to relive what happened over and over again? It's very debilitating."

Leah said the same sort of thing to me on the phone a few minutes ago. "Do you think you and the kids could take it, Sandy?" she wondered. "A malpractice suit can be pretty awful. You can't get the death behind you. You have to keep thinking about it all the time."

"That's all I do anyway," I said.

Both Susanna and my shrink made a different point. In a situation like this, they observed, as long as you're suing you live with the illusion that a positive outcome to the lawsuit might resurrect the dead person. If we could get the doctors and nurses at the UCDMC to admit that they did something wrong, then maybe we could get them to go back and do the *right* thing. Like running the film of the Kennedy assassination again so that the fatal bullet *doesn't* hit the president.

This problem doesn't bother me, since in any case I live with the illusion—only I don't think it's an illusion—that Elliot is really still alive. When my shrink said something about my "dead husband" the other day, I stared at her indignantly. "Don't you dare tell me that my husband is dead!" I exclaimed with hauteur.

In a funny way, the kids have the same feeling.

On the surface, they seem far more convinced than I am that their father is actually dead, but every once in a while, especially when we're discussing the possibility of litigation, one or another of them slips and uses the wrong verb tense: "Dad *wants* us to sue. I *know* he does."

Anyway, we're all in complete agreement on *that* point. *Dad wants us to sue. Dad will be—I mean would be—in a rage if we* don't *sue.*

Now Susan emerges from the kitchen. "He's had no luck yet," she sighs, standing in the doorway of the dining room. "But this time he thinks—"

"Here's the calendar," Kathy says, coming in from the study. "Thinks what?"

"Thinks maybe there are several of them. Several skunks. One opossum," Susan says.

"Oh my God, what's he going to—?"

"Never mind." She sits down across from me at the table, next to Kathy, and pushes a notebook toward me. "Let's begin. What was the day of the diagnosis, who gave it, etcetera, etcetera."

And I begin to write.

"July 31, 1990: Prostate cancer diagnosed by Dr. Humphreys, Elliot's Berkeley urologist. August 23, 1990: First visit to UCDMC. First meeting with R. W. deVere White."

———

FRIDAY, MARCH 15, 1991, 6 P.M.

Once more Susan is on the phone with Dick, who wanted to make a few last points to her before she leaves tomorrow. I'm in a half daze, typing *my* time line into the computer. Images of scowling death masks, demonic ritual figures, African goddesses, bloody Hispanic Christs lurk at the edge of my mind.

Last night I left the house in the evening for the first time. I decided that I wanted to "go to the gods."

The "gods" are a collection of primitive statues and other art objects belonging to Erle, an octogenarian painter and art critic who is a good friend of Bob's. When I said that I wanted to go see them, Erle and the woman he lives with were kind enough to invite me, Susan, Kathy, and Liz to dinner there, along with Bob and Moneera.

The vast living room of Erle's modernistic Berkeley hills house is like a museum. The "gods" are beautifully lighted, arranged in different sections according to whether they come from Africa, Latin America, or someplace else.

Most of them are dark polished wood or burnished stone. Unlike a guard at a normal museum, Erle let us touch them, pick them up, caress them.

The largest bloody—*bleeding*—Christ, contorted on his cross, hangs over the fireplace. I think he's a seventeenth-century piece, maybe from the American Southwest, maybe from Mexico. All day and all night, he has to look straight at a pair of grimacing Polynesian death masks fixed on the wall behind the dining room table. No wonder he seems to be tossing and turning the way I imagine Elliot must have.

I wanted to see the gods. I thought the gods might help me. But I should have understood that they'd scare me, too. Help me with their out-of-the-forest mystery. Scare me with their scowls, their stony breath, their terrible complaints.

My fingers rattle on the keyboard of the computer. I type fast so I won't have to think about what I'm typing. "January 29, 1991: Elliot enters the UCDMC for a radical prostatectomy. January 30, 1991: Failed intubation. February 10, 1991: Elliot enters the UCDMC for second attempt at radical prostatectomy."

"Dick says you should tell whatever lawyer you contact that he'd better get the records for himself." Susan is standing behind me, with yet another sheaf of notes in her hand. "He says there are two important items missing. One is something called an 'intake/output' record, a record of all the stuff that goes into the patient's body (medicines and IV fluids and so on) and everything that comes out. It should be there but it isn't. The other is something called a 'Death Summary Dictated,' the attending physician's note on cause of death. That's supposed to be an account produced after the death of any patient and it *must* by law be there, but it isn't."

"Oh." I keep on typing fast. "February 11, 1991: at 5:30 A.M. a nurse comes to take Elliot down to the OR." I swivel to face her. "What else did he tell you?"

"Not much. Except—"

"Except?"

Susan hesitates, looking ill. "I asked him how he'd feel if what happened to Elliot had happened to Leah? Would *he* be litigious?"

"And he said?"

"He said, these were his exact words, 'if this had happened to Leah, I wouldn't be litigious, I'd be homicidal.' "

12

Life is short
And the art long;
The occasion instant,
Experiment perilous,
Decision difficult.

—Hippocrates

Physicians acquire their knowledge from our dangers,
making experiments at the cost of our lives. Only a
physician can commit homicide with complete impunity.

—Pliny the Elder

Monday, March 18, 1991, 1:30 p.m.

A break in the rains, so it's quiet, sunny. Washed in light, the house looks startlingly clean and unusually empty. No papers strewn all over the dining room table and piled up in the living room. No dishes in the sink. Kitchen counters scrubbed so they almost shine. Even my bed is made: Raggedy Andy and Orlando, arms around each other's waists, are tidily propped against puffed-up flowery pillows.

And I too am washed, dressed, combed, brushed, sitting at the round oak breakfast table with a sandwich and a Diet Coke in front of me. Soft white bread, mayo, thin-sliced turkey—baby food, just what I tell everybody I need and want!—and ice cubes bobbing among the soda bubbles.

Of course all this is because Kathy is here. She came by so we could call the lawyer, but first she decided to straighten things up because the place was such a mess. Ruthlessly, she routed me out of bed and into the shower. The sun was blazing over the oak trees, the sky a vacant blue—maybe that's why I was able to follow her orders.

Not that I feel like eating the sandwich. I stare at it and listen to her soothing chatter. She's in the kitchen making herself an elaborate burrito. How can she dream up such a concoction!

"I'll do it, Mom," she's saying, "I'll *do* it, all right? It's just got to be done!"

"I don't know whether it's time yet, I don't know whether I can talk to anybody about Daddy, I can't decide if . . ." I mutter, more to myself than to her as I begin tearing the crusts off the sandwich. Soft as it is, the bread still isn't soft enough, not with that brownish semblance of crust around its bland center.

Kathy brings her burrito over to the table. It seems to be filled with all kinds of things I'd ordinarily love—refried beans, ground beef, cilantro, salsa, shredded Monterey Jack—but which now smell unpleasantly exotic to me.

"Look," she says, pushing the annotated lawyer list across the table, "this is the one, this is the guy, there's no point in putting it off, we've got to call him."

Susan assembled the lawyer list before she left the other day. From her brother-in-law who's a Park Avenue attorney, from the lawyer who's handling Elliot's estate, from my friend Joanne's ex-husband—and from a whole bunch of other people around the country—she put together something like fifteen names and addresses of malpractice specialists in the Bay area. Several names were mentioned by more than one informant, but only one was (as we put it to ourselves) "triangulated": Dan

Kelly was highly recommended by Susan's brother-in-law, by Jeanne the estate attorney, and by Joanne's ex-husband.

Kelly is, we're told, a partner in a law firm called "Walkup and Downing." Even the allegorically resonant name, *Walk*up and *Down*ing, we're told, strikes terror into the hearts of otherwise arrogant medical defendants. Negligent doctors, says Joanne's ex with a mirthless laugh, begin anxiously walking up and down at the mere receipt of a letter from someone at Walkup and Downing. No wonder Kathy is eager to call Dan Kelly.

"Eat your sandwich, Mom," she urges, biting into her burrito. "You've *got* to eat."

"I'm not hungry." I shove the plate away. "Okay, *you* call them. Call them now. What are you going to say?"

"I'll say we're all very concerned, my mother is extremely concerned and confused, my father died in the hospital under mysterious circumstances, and a friend who's an important pathologist believes there's reason to suspect malpractice or negligence—"

"Be sure to tell them we got the records, and he's making a time line, and tell them we've made one too," I interrupt. "Because otherwise they'll probably think—*you* know—" I take a sip of the Coke, which has gotten watery and flat from standing so long with a lot of ice cubes in it—"What they always think. I mean, they always think the family is crazy, don't they?"

"Not *this* family," Kathy sounds stern. "Not *us*." She too shoves her plate aside. "I'll call right now."

"Okay," I answer calmly. Then I jump up in a kind of panic. "I'll be in the bedroom. I'll just go lie down in the bedroom while you call. If you need me for any reason, I can get on the extension."

But even from three rooms away I can hear her making the call, asking for Dan Kelly, explaining her business to some secretary or receptionist.

I lie motionless on the freshly made bed. I focus on the afternoon sunlight haloing "the boys." I think about what Kathy is
explaining to a no doubt perfectly indifferent legal stranger.
What if he says that even on the face of it the case has no merit?

"Mom." Kathy is in the doorway. "He says he's got to talk to
you. He says he can't work with you if you won't talk to him."

"Oh, of course, of course I'll get on the phone."

I tell myself that sitting up straight, sitting on the edge of the
bed with my feet on the floor, will force me into a grownup
professional mode I've forgotten since February 11. I remind
myself that I'm not "just" a widow, I'm a professor, an intellectual, a writer, a *feminist*.

Dan Kelly's voice is deep, brisk, authoritative. Somewhat censoriously, he repeats what he'd just told Kathy, that I *must* talk
to him if I want to work with him.

To placate him, I explain that he's been recommended by
three different people and drop a few names. He relents, laughs,
and remarks that he's flattered.

Trying to hang on to my sense of myself as a "professional," I
outline what we know of our story—or, rather, Elliot's story.

Kelly neutrally notes that the procedure at his firm is to do an
in-house review of the records, then, if the case seems viable, to
solicit opinions from outside consultants, medical experts who
will read and interpret the UCDMC materials for themselves. He
adds that all of this investigation will be done at no cost to us,
since, by law, malpractice specialists operate on a contingency
basis: if they win, they get a percentage of the settlement; if they
lose, they get nothing and are even out of pocket for their own
expenses.

The first in-house review is done by a "physician-attorney,"
he tells me.

"A physician-attorney?" I'm bemused.

"A doctor-lawyer, if you like," Kelly explains. "We have a

fellow on our staff—Wes Sokolosky—who was a doctor for twenty years and then went back to law school to get a J.D. He does the initial review of all our malpractice cases."

I puzzle over the existence of this oddly hybrid professional, then, beginning to get panicky again, I protest that, after all, the records have already been reviewed by Dick, so . . .

"A family friend," Kelly interjects ironically. "And not a specialist in prostate cancer."

But how long will all these further reviews take? And isn't there a statute of limitations?

"It'll take three or four months for us to decide whether or not to accept this case," Kelly replies. "But when you're suing the Regents of the University of California, you have a year from the date of death."

Three or four months! And what if the decision is negative? And time is running out already, already it's nearly the end of March! I'm getting breathless. Can we "multiple-submit," I wonder, the way writers sometimes do—send the records to more than one law firm?

"If you do that," Kelly says severely, "we'd still undertake our in-house procedure but wouldn't be inclined to expend any monies on outside consultants, so I have to advise you that it's not in your interest."

And what about the fact that we'd be suing the Regents, I exclaim. I thought we'd be suing the doctors or the hospital. As a professor at U. C. Davis, I'm an employee of the Regents myself. Is it even possible for me to sue them—and how would it look if I did that?

"Of course it's possible for you to sue the Regents, Ms. Gilbert," Dan Kelly answers calmly. "Your own position at the university has nothing to do with the matter."

But what will the chancellor say, I ask myself irrationally. There he was at the memorial service in his somber suit, looking administrative. Will he put pressure on me to drop the case?

I was a black barge, laden with grief. Susan and the children towed me toward him. The chancellor took my hand, said he was sorry. I looked over his dark shoulder for doctorly faces.

Elliot had been so pleased when deVere White impulsively embraced him at a chairmen's meeting the chancellor convened in the faculty club last fall.

The chair of urology. Can't kill. The chair of English.

I thank Dan Kelly for his attention. I tell him we'll FedEx the records and both time lines, Dick's and mine, by this weekend. He'll have all the materials on Monday morning.

What else is there to do?

———

THURSDAY, MARCH 21, 8:30 P.M.

"Are you sure you don't want to wait till the morning?" Leah is sitting beside me at the table in the breakfast room. Dick's time line is in front of me. "It really may upset you, Sandy. It really may."

"I think she's right, Mom, I think we should all wait till tomorrow," Susanna comments from the kitchen, where she's loading the dishwasher.

"*Really*, Sandy," Leah repeats.

"Sandy." It's curiously moving to hear Leah call me "Sandy" the way just about everybody did when I was in high school and college. No one except my very oldest friends calls me that anymore. Even Elliot, whom I started going out with in my junior year, called me something different: "sem," after the initials with which I signed my poems in those days.

Why is it so refreshing—such a *relief*—to be "Sandy"? Ah, if I'm *Sandy*, I'm neither sem nor Sandra, and none of this has happened. I haven't even met Elliot yet, we haven't yet made the mysterious and dire choices that led us to the UCDMC on February 11. Maybe, if I'm *Sandy*, I can meet him all over again and then we can apply for different jobs, jobs in another state where he might not even develop prostate cancer, and even if he does he'll have better doctors and live to be ninety.

Another thirty years. Suppose you turn the clock backward. Thirty years ago he was thirty. Ninety to sixty is like sixty to thirty. So because I stopped being "Sandy," Elliot had to die at what is at least analogously the age of thirty.

"I'm sorry, but I just *have* to read it now," I tell Leah and Susanna.

"Well, okay, if you have to I can understand it, but just let me sit next to you, and if you need me to explain anything, I can explain it as we go along. And also, Dick will still be awake in Bethesda for another hour at least. We can call him if we need him."

Leah arrived from Washington this afternoon, with the time line tucked into her shoulder bag like a contraband weapon. Emerging from her plane, wearing black slacks and a snappy white windbreaker, with a raincoat over her arm, she looked like any other pleasant suburban housewife, rosy-cheeked, smiling, her gray-brown hair cut in a stylish shag. Who could have known what was secreted in her purse or, for that matter, in the back of her mind!

"It's in a lot of different sections, Sandy," she says. "It begins with a general outline of the case, including Dick's interpretations and questions. But then he's also excerpted key points from the chart notes and highlighted major clinical events from the most important pages of the records. It's kind of complicated, so maybe—" She hesitates. "Maybe it'll be best if for now you just look at the outline in the beginning."

Susanna comes over to the table, wiping her hands on a dishtowel and looking vaguely ill. She, too, just arrived; she's going to spend her spring break at home in Berkeley. "I'm going to read it along with you, Mom," she says. "I have to read it too."

"Of course," Leah says, nervously reassuring. "We'll all read it together. We'll all sit right here together and look at it together."

I light a cigarette and open the file folder in front of me, which contains several copies of a manuscript that looks thick enough to be somebody's master's thesis.

The top copy has a cover page with the word ORIGINAL on it in large black letters.

The first page is headed "PUTTING IT TOGETHER: SUMMARY OF CLINICAL EVENTS."

Dick's prose, I notice, is impressively detached and scientific. I guess this is the way doctors present cases to each other at pathology conferences and other important meetings.

Dr. Elliot Gilbert was a 60 year old Professor of English admitted to the hospital on 2/10/91 to undergo radical retropubic prostatectomy for carcinoma of the prostate. He was in good health at the time of admission.

Dr. Elliot Gilbert was. Was. Was in good health.

The prostatectomy was begun the morning of 2/11/91, and apart from a somewhat large loss of blood, replaced by transfusion of PRBC (5 units; 2 autologous, 3 from the blood bank), the operation appeared to go well, judging from the OR record. Vital signs were all in the stable range throughout.

The morning of 2/11/91. The operation appeared to go well. That's right, Elliot. We sat in the lobby. I tried to read *Newsweek.* Liz and Susanna were studying, or pretending to study. Kathy had some stuff that she was trying to do for her job. Every now and then one of the girls went over to the receptionist and asked what was happening in the OR, and the receptionist said she didn't know. Then they called down from the OR, Elliot, and that's right, they said it was going well. I ate half a turkey sandwich. Somebody came up to us and delivered a silver Get Well balloon. Then somebody else came and brought a potted plant with some flowers. One of the flowers had a blue blossom, I think.

Dr. Gilbert was admitted to the recovery room around 2:00 P.M. or a little later. At this time his vital signs were good, and remained so for the next 45–60 minutes. A hematocrit obtained around the time of admission to the recovery room was 32. The hematocrits in the OR had been: 32 at 10:08; 29 at 11:42; and 25 at 2:01. The hematocrit of 32 at 2:45 indicated that the transfusions had returned the red cells about to normal levels.

Normal. The transfusions. Normal levels. Everything was normal, darling. Dr. deVere White was wearing his greens because he'd just come from the OR, where everything was up to *normal levels* even though he was sweating, yes, he was sweating, but he told us to go home, he must have been tired and hungry so he wanted us to go home and have lunch and take a nap. We put your balloon and your flowers in the back of the car so we could bring them back to you later in the afternoon. We were tired, too, Elliot, so we went home to start our telephone tree, tell everyone that things were normal, and then take our naps.

Orders written on admission to the recovery room appear to require that 2 units of PRBC (Packed Red Blood Cells) be at hand, and that a transfusion be done if the hematocrit had not returned to normal. There was at this time 1 unit of PRBC on hand; no further cross-matching was done until later (6:50 P.M.).

At 3:05 there was a sharp drop in blood pressure to 72/48

from a level of 132/98. This hypotension was treated vigorously with fluids and plasma expanders, and the blood pressure was restored to acceptable levels (98/60) by 3:15, and to normal levels (113/67) 5 minutes later. The notes indicate that a hematocrit was sent to the laboratory at 3:05; there is no report of this hematocrit in the record. Note that a 'Critical Lab Report' dated 2/11/91 lists no hematocrits between 2:45 and 6:30 P.M. (This report was reviewed by someone on 2/12/91.)

Vital signs were recorded every 15 minutes until 4:00, and every 30 minutes from then until 6:00 P.M.

At 6:00 P.M. a blood pressure of 54/0 was recorded. Treatment with fluids and plasma expanders was again accelerated, with a transient rise in blood pressure to 99/41 at 6:21, but normal blood pressure was never restored thereafter.

Normal blood pressure. Never restored. "What happened, doctor, what happened?" Susanna screamed. "I don't know, luv, his pressure dropped."

A hematocrit of 17 was recorded at 6:30. It is not clear when this sample was obtained since there was no order for one and no notation of 'hematocrit sent' as there was at 3:05. I presume the sample was obtained at 6:00, since the drop in blood pressure would essentially have required it. Under the circumstances I would have wanted to know the hematocrit as soon as possible.

To know. To know as soon as possible. What does Hippocrates say? *The occasion instant, Experiment perilous.*

Orders to 'transfuse 2 U PRBC now', and to type and cross-match 4 more were written at 6:50 P.M. It is possible that this order is recorded after the fact, since the cross-match report also shows a time of 6:50. However, I think that the 6:50 on the lab report actually indicates 'ordered at 6:50, sample received at 6:59'. There is also an order 'hold heparin.' Heparin is an anticoagulant used to prevent clots from forming, and was being given here to prevent clots in the veins from forming. Embolism (the breaking off of such a clot, and its lodging in a large blood vessel in the lung) is an important potential complication of this type of surgery, and the use of heparin as a prophylactic measure is advocated by some. These orders indicate that the physicians are concerned that the patient may be bleeding.

Bleeding. Bleeding secretly. Bleeding uncontrollably. "Come here a minute, Sandra," Susan said. "Come into the kitchen for a minute." "Why do I have to get up? Anything you can tell *me* you can tell Bob and Moneera." "Come into the kitchen, Sandra, just for a minute." Rain on the deck. "Sandra, they gave him 12 units." "12 units!" Kicking the door. Screaming. Rain on the deck. That's what I was doing, Elliot, kicking and screaming.

"The nurse's notes indicate that a unit of PRBC was given at 7:12; the intake and output records show . . . 55, presumably 6:55 as the time of administration. There are a number of possibilities here: (1) the unit given recorded in the nurse's notes at 7:12 and the one shown on the intake record at . . . 55 are the same, just recorded at different times; (2) they are different, and the nurse's note fails to record a PRBC unit number; the recorded number may not be reliable, since FC71715, the unit recorded in the intake record is also recorded by the code team at 7:41. (Note here that the blood bank summaries indicate that 2 units were transfused that appear nowhere in the chart.)

A pulse of 36 was recorded at 7:20; code team notes began at 7:30. They found severe metabolic acidosis and a hematocrit of

13. Despite their vigorous efforts to revive the heart (there was a very severe arrhythmia, 'ventricular tachycardia'), and the administration of 5 units of PRBC from 7:31 to 7:52 in order to correct the anemia, there was no response. Dr. Gilbert was pronounced dead at 8:15. It should be noted that at 7:52 the surgical drains (? I surmise—I don't know what a 'JP' drain is) were attached to suction, and that at 8:05 'JP drains 2450 red blood' was recorded.

8:15. Pronounced dead. I was in the parking lot, I think, smoking a cigarette, naive and hopeful. We'd come back from the Chinese restaurant. Stuffed with wontons, tired.

The doctor is coming down to see you, the receptionist told the girls.

Liz came out to the parking lot. *Sandra,* she called, *the receptionist said the doctor is coming down to see us.* She had a strange, blank look on her face. *Doctor?* I said. I was curiously irritated. *WHICH doctor?* I wanted to know. Why couldn't she just *explain* that to me, I wondered.

CONCLUSION

There is little doubt that the major clinical problem was bleeding. Loss of blood is the most reasonable explanation for the simultaneous sharp drop both in the blood pressure and the hematocrit. If I've read the code team's note correctly concerning the drains, this bleeding was massive—2450 cc is a little less than half the blood in the body. Probably the 450 cc of bloody fluid found in the paracolic gutters described in the autopsy should be added to the 2450 cc obtained by suction. In addition, the 670 gm. clot found in the lesser sac probably represents 600 cc or more of original blood. I believe, therefore, that the CODING SUMMARY is correct. 'Acute posthemorrhagic anemia' which can dispose to acidosis when the hematocrit is low enough, and to heart problems because of poor oxygen supply to the heart, was likely the major clinical problem.

Half the blood in the body. Half the blood. Heart problems. Poor oxygen supply. "What if this is the last time I'm driving down this road?" "Don't be stupid, don't say that again." *Probably the 450 cc should be added. The 670 gm. clot. Probably represents 600 cc or more of original blood.*

QUESTIONS AND COMMENTS

1. Why wasn't a second unit of PRBC cross-matched and kept on hand as ordered at 2:15?

2. What happened to the hematocrit sent at 3:05? If it were low, say below 29, then the delay until 6:00 was probably fatal. If it were high, then that suggests that the blood loss was even more acute than I suppose. Why was nobody curious about the whereabouts of this hematocrit? The episode of hypotension at 3:05 is an unexplained 'loose end.'

3. I think the change to the recording of vital signs every half hour (instead of every 15 minutes) after 4:00 was a mistake, since there had been that unexplained hypotensive episode, but I don't know how often such things are seen.

4. Things seem to have moved very slowly after 6:00.

a. Why was there a thirty minute delay until the hematocrit was reported?

b. Why was there a further 20 minute delay in writing the orders for PRBC, and why wasn't the unit on hand started at 6:30 at the latest?

c. Why was the blood cross-matched at 6:50 held until the code team arrived? It could have been given from 6:55 to 7:20, using the same schedule that the code team used.

d. Why wasn't more blood cross-matched?

e. Since bleeding was such a likely possibility, and since the site of surgery was the likely place it was happening, why was suction not applied to the drains earlier? The amount of 'red blood' found by the code team suggests that surgical intervention to find a bleeding blood vessel, or to pack the surgical bed tightly if such a vessel couldn't be found, might have been needed.

Surgical intervention. Dick thinks surgical intervention might have been needed. He thinks they should have taken Elliot back into the operating room and "gone in" again. Opened him up again, tried to figure out what was wrong, tried to correct it. *Since bleeding was such a likely possibility. And since the site of surgery was the likely place.*

February 11, 6:15. Lights going on in the hospital. "How *is* he, doctor?" "He's woozy, woozy from the anesthetic. *I just saw him.* He said something like 'I feel lousy.' " "When can we see him, doctor?" "They're waitin' for a bed in Intensive Care. Go to dinner." "Will he need radiation, doctor?" "Now, now, this is only the day of the surgery. We have to take it a day at a time, now. Only the day of the surgery." Dinner, okay, dinner. We tried that Chinese restaurant, Elliot. We took the silver Get Well balloon and the blue flower and put them back in the car.

"Sandy, are you okay, Sandy?" Leah has her hand on my arm. My cigarette has expired in the ashtray. Susanna is staring at the "Questions and Comments" in front of her as if her gaze were a burning glass, as if she might incinerate the page if she just stared hard enough.

"Let's put it away for now, Sandy," Leah says gently.

"All right, all right," I tell her. "I'm all right." I put my arm around Susanna. "We'll read more of this tomorrow, okay? Now maybe we'll just sit in the living room for a while. Listen to music or something."

A little less than half the blood in the body. Surgical intervention might have been needed.

———

SATURDAY, MARCH 23, 1991, 4:15 P.M.

Susanna, Leah, and I are plunging through the rain, speeding on the dark slick backstreets from Emeryville to Oakland, Susanna hunched over the wheel like a racing driver in the movies, Leah cradling the thick medical packet—records, time lines, notes—that we have to get to the FedEx place by 5:00 if it's going to reach Dan Kelly on Monday morning as I'd promised it would.

Although I was told on the phone that it would be open, the pick-up station in Emeryville was closed, and we lost fifteen or twenty minutes trying to figure out where to go because it's Saturday and only a few depots are accepting materials, and now look how late it is!

I don't know why it matters so much to us to send this packet off. What difference would it make if the lawyer got it on Tuesday instead of Monday?

Probably we just irrationally want the stuff out of the house. Irrationally because of course we'll still have our own copies. But probably we want someone else, someone *official*, to have a record, a token of our pain, so he can share the burden of reading the time line, studying the charts. Maybe then this someone else, this fantasy Man of Law, will help bear witness to what Dick has witnessed and told us about.

The charts.

The questions about the charts. The annotations.

The coding summary: "Acute Posthemorrhagic Anemia."

"What could have caused it?" I asked Dick on the phone last night. "What could have made him *bleed* that much?"

"Probably what I said before," Dick answered cautiously. "Maybe a suture came undone. Then there could be a massive hemorrhage—or maybe . . ."

"Maybe?"

"Maybe it started in the OR, maybe a slow leak, which would account for the drop in pressure at three . . ."

"And then they didn't, they didn't—" I could barely get the words out. "Didn't monitor him properly so . . . ?"

Dick is still cautious. "We can't be sure, of course, until an attorney investigates further, deposes them and so forth. But they certainly seem to have moved very slowly. As if they were walking through molasses. Or underwater, anyway."

Underwater. Well, that's where we are. The car nosedives into a huge puddle, practically a pond, and Susanna steers it across the intersection as if it were a motorboat.

"I think you made a good choice, Sandy," Leah says from the backseat as we pull up in front of the sharply lighted FedEx office. 4:25. We're here with time to spare. "I think they'll look very dignified."

I can tell that she's trying to cheer me up by reminding me that we've accomplished *something* beyond our broodings on the records. This morning we ordered printed thank-you notes to send to the three hundred or so writers of condolence letters. Despite various invocations of Miss Manners, we decided I just couldn't reply by hand to that many people.

Hanging on to the edge of the counter at the fancy stationery store in downtown Berkeley as if I were seasick, I rejected a host of flowery formulations while Susanna and Leah nodded approvingly at me, and the saleswoman, soothing as a funeral director, reminded me that I could say anything *I* wanted to say.

Our card will read:

**The family
of Elliot Lewis Gilbert
thanks you sincerely
for your expression of sympathy.**

And because Elliot was an editor and a lifelong fan of good printing jobs, our words won't appear in what he considered vulgar sans serif or pretentious italics or in any weird colors but in regular, straightforward, black roman letters.

"I hope so, I hope we got the right thing. I mean I hope he'll—he'd—like it," I tell Leah as we all step out into the tidal rush of the parking lot.

———

SUNDAY, MARCH 31, 1991, 11:45 P.M.

I'm alone in the breakfast room, staring at a basket of colored eggs, a wind-up bunny, and—because I can't stop myself—the records from the UCDMC. Easter Sunday.

At least the sun was shining today for a change and there were flowers everywhere and all the kids were at the table along with some of our closest friends—Bob, Dorrie, Moneera—and we had our traditional family dinner: leg of lamb, asparagus, risotto, strawberry shortcake, the paradigmatic spring meal. And the centerpiece was two dozen Easter eggs in all the usual pastels.

Kathy, Susanna, and I dyed them yesterday afternoon, dipping them into the little cups of color the way we always have, cracking a few the way we always have, arguing about the depths of purple and blue the way we always have.

Then I rubbed them lightly with olive oil on a paper towel, the way I always do, the way my aunt and grandmother taught me to.

When you rub them like that, you feel how cold they are, how cold and hard, like oval stones.

"Don't they look great?" we said to each other, the way we always have, as we arranged them in the long slim breadbasket lined as usual with shiny cellophane "grass."

And we fixed up an Easter basket for my grandson, Val, too. It was crammed with enough goodies to delight any four-and-a-half-year-old boy: jelly beans, chocolate eggs, marshmallow chicks, and the windup bunny I'm staring at right now because Val left it in the kitchen when he went to bed.

If you wind the bunny really hard, it'll hop across the dining room, all the way from the living room doorway to the wall where Elliot and I are hanging looking scared (me) and wistful (him).

Roger and his wife, Gina, and Val, their little boy, arrived from Ithaca early this afternoon. Roger is on his first sabbatical—he's an assistant professor at Cornell—so they're going to stay with me for the next few months. Susanna went back to Santa Barbara right after dinner, and Leah had to leave three days ago because she was hosting a seder in Bethesda on Friday night. But I won't be alone in the house.

As soon as Roger got here, we went straight to the cemetery to visit Elliot. Roger wanted Gina and Val to see "Grandpa Elliot's" grave because they couldn't come to the funeral or the memorial service.

It's lucky that it was such a sunny day, lucky not just for us but for all the other people who were also visiting Sunset View, trimming the grass on the graves, putting calla lilies in the flower holders, gently brushing and patting the headstones as if they had mastered some sort of Morse code through which they could communicate with their husbands or mothers or children down there underneath the epitaphs.

Even on a nice day, though, we've learned that Sunset View is disappointing. One of the kids will say, "We should go see Daddy," but then what happens when we get there? Nothing. Just the grass and the stand of trees where Elliot's oldest Berkeley friend paced around, weeping, while two of my colleagues said the Kaddish, and the bulldozer rampaged toward us.

When we got back, we helped Roger and Gina and Val settle

in downstairs. Roger is going to help me edit the unfinished book manuscript that his father left behind, so he and his wife and son are going to have the whole lower floor of the house, including the music room that Elliot and I furnished with a baby grand, a convertible sofa, a TV/VCR and his ever-growing collection of videotapes. Roger will like that because, besides working on Elliot's book, he's been trying to reconstruct all the songs his father made up for him and his sisters when they were little, and also he's a film buff—a Hitchcock, Fellini, Kurosawa, Laurel-and-Hardy buff—just as his dad was.

Of course the kids don't realize I have the records in front of me right now, along with the Easter eggs and the windup bunny. Kathy and Liz went home about half an hour ago. Roger and Gina and Val went to bed even earlier. They all probably think I'm trying to sleep too.

Although they know I have trouble sleeping. They know I stay up half the night reading grief books and then can't get up in the morning.

My favorite grief book at the moment is *Widowed* by Dr. Joyce Brothers. I like it because her husband was just about Elliot's age—well, maybe a few years older—and they had been married for more than thirty years, just like me and Elliot, and after Milt Brothers died, Dr. Joyce suffered from loneliness, confusion, and anxiety the same way I do.

Of course, her husband died of a *disease*—he had terminal cancer of the liver I think—whereas Elliot was still pretty healthy, all his organs "grossly unremarkable" according to the autopsy report.

Dr. Joyce Brothers's husband was dying when they brought him into the hospital, whereas Elliot had no symptoms of illness when he went in, but he was dead when they brought him out.

It's very quiet in here this late at night. Only a minor humming from the refrigerator, a faint buzz of fluorescent lights, the creak of my bentwood chair as I shift from side to side, studying the eggs, the bunny, the records. All the Easter dinner leftovers have been neatly stashed in the refrigerator: a quarter of a leg of lamb and lots of other stuff.

Without Elliot around, no one knew how to carve the roast— not even Roger or Bob would volunteer, not even Kathy—until Gina said she'd just *do* it for God's sake and attacked the lamb with one of the knives we'd forgotten to sharpen.

I slide the records toward me, push the bunny away so fast that it falls off the table and lands with a feeble hop next to the chair where Elliot used to sit.

On top of the pile is one of the charts that Dick summarized in his time line: *Nursing Notes.* He's highlighted parts of it, I guess for the lawyers.

The writing is a little clearer on this chart than on some of the others, but even when I squint through my reading glasses I still can't decipher most of it, and what I can see I don't want to see.

14:30. BP: 142/104. Pulse: 132. Problem/Focus: D: restless and uncoop. Ch 7, CBC, PT/PT. Observations/Treatments: TEDS/Sequentials on. Palat restraints. Rung pain. Warm Bts on, CXR held. Restlessness.

15:05. BP: 72/48. Problem/Focus: Hct sent.

16:00. BP: 112/61. Pulse: 123. Problem/Focus: Pain. Observations/Treatments: R: Quiet w/ int. periods of wakefulness.

16:30. BP: 99/62. Pulse: 117. Problem/Focus: CXR done. Observations/Treatments: Awake and coop. Denies pain. Restraints off.

17:30. BP: 114/70. Pulse: 126. Observations/Treatments: D: C/d Feeling "Awful." Loc Pale. Rare PVC noted. A: Dr. Storer apprised of condition. Team.

18:00. BP: 54/0. Pulse: 113. Observations/Treatments: Dr. Jones & Storer At Bedside. Loc—Arouse—Shaking.

19:20. BP: 56/0. Pulse: 36. Observations/Treatments: Dr. Jones to bedside. Unresponsive, BP. Attempting to intubate. BP non palp—code blue started———

20:15. Code called. Per Dr. Jones.

22:35. To morgue.

I shove the chart aside, light a cigarette, pick up the fallen bunny and wind it tight, then let it go so it doesn't just hop, it leaps across the table and back down to the floor.

17:30. Feeling "Awful." Loc Pale.

Dick's comment, scrawled across the chart: "I'd have wanted to know more about this."

DeVere White, outside the hospital. Six-fifteen. *18:15 hospital time.* Blue, windy. "I just saw him. He was woozy, woozy from the anesthetic. Said something like 'I feel lousy.' "

Then we went to the Chinese restaurant.

I pick the bunny up, wind it even tighter than before, wind it so hard that the metal key digs a furrow in my right index finger, then let the thing go again.

I think I may keep on doing this all night.

13

*Sudden hemorrhage . . . may present itself as a finding, it
can result in a feeling, but . . . perhaps one should simply
regard it as an eruption—something which bursts upon the
scene, creating anxiety and terror.*

—Jonathan Miller,
The Body in Question

*The surgeon cuts. And all at once there leaps a mighty
blood. As when from the hidden mountain ledge a pebble is
dislodged, a pebble behind whose small slippage the whole
of the avalanche is pulled.*

—Richard Selzer,
Mortal Lessons: Notes on the Art of Surgery

Tuesday, April 9, 1991, 3 p.m.

"What we'll be asking' them is whether or unduh what circumstances the blood loss should have been treated before he died of
it." Wesley Sokolosky, M.D., J.D., the physician-attorney who is
"of counsel" in Dan Kelly's law firm has a soft, pleasant, slightly
diffident southern voice. Standing in the breakfast room, clutching the receiver as if it might magically transport me to his
deskside, I imagine him as a thin, worn-looking man in a gray
suit and wire-rimmed glasses. A man in his late forties or early

fifties who's been prematurely aged by all the medical and legal troubles he's seen. A man who's very quiet because he knows it would be pointless to shout.

"Ah have two urologists in mind," he continues, "both very experienced with this type of surgery."

Wes Sokolosky has been reviewing the UCDMC records for the past few weeks, and he just phoned to outline the next steps the firm will take. My heart is pounding, and I'm breathless the way I was when I first spoke to Dan Kelly, because I'm aware that Sokolosky is the medical-legal dragon at the gate of Walkup, Shelby, Melodia, Bastian, Kelly, Echevarria and Link.

No, it turns out, to our sorrow, that the firm is not called *Walkup* and *Down*ing, though their reputation does seem to warrant such a name.

If Sokolosky decides the case has merit, he goes before a committee which authorizes him to investigate further by hiring outside consultants, as many as necessary. If Sokolosky decides against the case, there's no appeal, no matter how aggrieved the would-be plaintiffs are. If Wes Sokolosky thinks the case can't be won, it's on to the next law firm, and the next and the next and the next, for the hapless victims.

"What do you—when do you—" I'm so breathless my words jostle and stumble.

He's cool and tolerant, obviously experienced with incoherent survivors. "We'll be sendin' a legal copyin' service up to Sacramento in the next week or two, so they can recopy all the records as accurately as possible," he explains. "We can't rely solely on the materials the hospital forwarded to you. We have our own people go in there with their own Xerox machine, and then—"

"So no one can fiddle with the charts? So they might find the stuff Dick thought was missing?" I interject excitedly.

"If possible," he agrees. "And then we'll be sendin' the new records to the consultants and expectin' to hear from them within a few more weeks." He pauses a moment, then adds, "This should all take about four to six weeks."

"And do you—I mean I know you can't commit yourself—but how do you personally think the consultants may respond? I mean, given your *own* review of the records and so forth."

He pauses again, and when he answers his tone seems to me even dryer and cooler than it was a minute ago. "Mah gut reaction," he says in what I think is a sardonic drawl, "mah gut reaction is that someone will say your husband shouldn't have bled to death followin' this procedure."

"Oh, I see." I suddenly feel as if I've been hit with a two-by-four or a nightstick. Why should I feel this way? We all knew Elliot "bled to death," didn't we? That's the whole point about "acute posthemorrhagic anemia," isn't it? The point of consulting Walkup, the knife point that keeps *us* walking up and down all day and all night.

Sokolosky is silent, probably because he's so used to this sort of thing that he knows he has to give me time to assimilate his remark.

I sit down heavily at the breakfast table and stare at the tiny scratches in the oak and the crayons Val has strewn around his Ninja Turtle coloring book.

Val has been working hard on Leonardo today. Leonardo is his favorite among the Ninja Turtles because he's "the leader of the gang."

Obviously there was a part of me that desperately wanted Wes Sokolosky, M.D., J.D., to say, "Nonsense. There was nothin' wrong at all with the way they took care of your husband." Obviously I wanted the fantasy Man of Law to say, "All that could be done was done, he died because he had to die, because he was fated to die."

The fault, dear Brutus, is in our stars, not in the UCDMC.

"Bled to death—" I've finally found my voice again. "Bled to death? Won't they say how *could* someone bleed to death in the middle of a modern American medical center in the middle of a modern American city?"

"They could say it happens every day in American hospitals," he answers, still oh-so dryly.

And we say goodbye, and we hang up.

"Well? What was *that*? What was *that* all about?" Kathy is standing in the doorway, holding a bag of groceries. I don't know how long she's been there, I didn't hear her come in.

"That was Sokolosky," I tell her.

"Sokolosky! He *called* you! And what did he say, what does he think?" She drops the bag on the counter and begins absently unloading cans and boxes.

"He said he was sending the records to outside consultants, and he thinks they'll say your dad shouldn't have bled to death following the procedure. Shouldn't have *bled to death*, that's how he put it."

"Bled to death," Kathy says slowly, as she folds the grocery bag. "Shouldn't have bled to death."

And she bursts into tears.

———

WEDNESDAY, APRIL 10, 1991, 2 A.M./Monday, February 11, 1991

Dick put it in writing: "Surgical intervention might have been needed."

And Sokolosky said it out loud: "He shouldn't have bled to death following this procedure."

Shouldn't have.

Three ice cubes sway in my glass. A large scotch and water in a French jelly jar. Exactly three ice cubes, all melting fast.

It's already two A.M., and I can't sleep, probably because I've been reading a bunch of medical books, trying to understand about hemorrhages and heparin, clots and PRBCs. The fluorescent lights are buzzing again, buzzing like a headache, and the refrigerator is humming too.

And here are the records and here is the Ninja Turtle coloring book. Val moved on to Donatello after supper. Donatello is supposed to wear red, while Leonardo wears purple.

"Grandpa Elliot" liked the idea of the Ninja Turtles. He was very amused by the wittiness of their names—Donatello, Leonardo, Raphael, and Michelangelo—when Roger, explaining Val's new passion, told him the story at Christmas.

I covered the thick stack of records and Dick's time line and his comments with the coloring book when I came in here half an hour ago. But the records seem to keep sliding out from under the Turtles, as if Leonardo and the others want me to read them again.

Don't look at them. Don't. Light a cigarette instead. Maybe turn on the radio. KDFC-FM, San Francisco and Palo Alto, plays lots of classical music "to help you through the night."

To help you through the recovery. The recovery room.

14:30. BP: 142/104. Pulse 132. Problem/Focus: restless and uncoop. . . . Palat restraints. Rung pain. . . . Restlessness.

The clicking. The white clicking. There is a thickness. A thickness he knows about. Arms, legs, not moving, strapped down.

He's turning, trying to turn. Wants to get up. Wants to pee.

Did you need to pee, darling? You needed to pee after the biopsy. You were cursing, and they just dumped you on the bed, and I couldn't move you, and you needed to pee.

And thin things. Thin things coming out of him. Tubes, clickings. Stuck to the thickness, the arms, the legs.

Where is he? Where is sem? He tries to move, can't, what are these straps, these fastenings? What is clicking and buzzing, making that pale noise, that hissing?

I'm on my way back to the condo, darling. We're going to tell everyone you're fine. We're going to take a nap, too. But rest easy, rest quietly, we'll be back in a few hours with the blue flower and the silver Get Well balloon.

Pain. One of the things pressing up and out from inside, low down inside him, is pain. And there is a tube for that, a tube with a button on it.

Rung pain. Warm Bts on, CXR held. Restlessness.

He wants to get up, get up and leave, but the tubes are holding him down, growing out of him everywhere, as if he were tangled in a net of tubes.

Dearest, remember Art B., who told us how he exulted when he woke up in the recovery room after his prostatectomy and discovered the catheter in his penis and the drains in his abdomen? He knew that meant they were able to operate, to get it all out. Darling, they got it out, they operated! That's why I went back to Davis: to call everyone up and tell them the good news.

There are two tall white shapes beside the bed. Talking, bending. They put warm things on the legs, move the tubes, fiddle with the straps.

He's moving, trying to get up, get rid of the tubes and straps. Where is sem? Why isn't she here to help? Why did she leave him alone with the white shapes?

Somewhere in the same place, not far away, someone is groaning, and just a little farther away there is a piercing noise, maybe a screaming.

We are at the kitchen table, making phone calls. We are drinking Diet Coke, asking each other why deVere White seemed so sweaty, so irritated.

15:05. BP: 72/48. Problem/Focus: Hct Sent.

He is rising and falling on the bed. Or is the bed rising and falling, tossing like a ship? Seasick. Dizzy. Trying to breathe underwater. Two white shapes again. Hands with needles. "Hold still, it won't hurt, it'll only take a minute."

I'm lying on our bed in the condo, darling. It's cool and comfortable, and I'm so tired. The blue blinds rattle in the wind leaking through the screen. They let in little bursts of light, but the room is really sweetly dark.

16:00. BP: 112/61. Pulse: 123. Problem/Focus: Pain. Observations/Treatments: R: Quiet w/ int. periods of wakefulness.

Pain. It presses up and out from inside, coils in the belly like another one of those tubes. But it's necessary, he tells himself, waking up, trying to lie still and quiet, trying to rest. The pain is part of the treatment, the pain is what he is here for. He lies very still, waiting for the pain to be over, resolving to be calm. And the bed, too, is silent and motionless, as if encouraging him to bear what he has to bear.

The pain *is*, darling, *is* part of the treatment. You just have to get through it. You know you can. Think of all the times you've had cavities filled without novocaine! You're the most stoic person I know.

16:30. BP: 99/62. Pulse: 117. Problem/Focus: CXR done. Observations/Treatments: awake and coop. Denies pain. Restraints off.

"No," he tells the nurse—for that is what the white shape is, a nurse—"I'm okay, okay, feeling no pain." He is sinking into the bed but trying to smile. Maybe he's going to tell a joke right now. A Rabinowitz joke. "See, Rabinowitz went to the hospital, he had to have a prostatectomy, but he was feeling no pain, except suddenly Mrs. Rabinowitz appeared and Rabinowitz said . . ."

That's what he's doing. He's telling a Rabinowitz joke in a very low voice, a very muffled voice so they can hardly hear him and don't understand the joke the way I would. That's what he did the time I took him to the emergency room with an asthma attack ten years ago.

He told jokes. He laughed and quoted Keats as they drew arterial blood for an oxygen count. "I know the color of that blood, that is arterial blood. John Keats," he said, though he was practically on the verge of death from status asthmaticus. *"Who's that Keats fellow he kept quoting downstairs?" the technician asked me later, when he was recuperating in a regular bed upstairs.*

We're all about to wake up. We're drifting toward consciousness, up out of the underwater daze of our naps. Now we're going to rush back to the hospital. And we're sure you're going to be angry at us because we're coming back later than we were supposed to.

17:30. BP: 114/70. Pulse: 126. Observations/Treatments: Feeling "Awful." Loc Pale. Rare PVC noted. A: Dr. Storer apprised of condition.

The cross face again. Leaning over him, snapping at him. "How do you feel, how do you feel?" And where—here!—is Dr. deVere White. The Irish brogue. "How are you feelin' now?" "Awful." The word comes out like a groan, a grunt. "I feel awful." What does it mean? Awful all over. Sinking into the bed, though the bed has begun pitching again. Pitching and tossing. He can't control its motion anymore. He's gasping for enough breath to get through the pain.

We're driving toward the hospital, late and panicky. The girls are squabbling.

18:00. BP: 54/0. Pulse: 113. Observations/Treatments: Dr. Jones & Storer At Bedside. Loc—Arouse—Shaking.

Tipping backward. Backward into the dizziness, the nausea. The white clicking.

The white.

6:15 P.M. Sacramento. Outside the hospital. Lights going on in the windows. The doctor in his official starch. "I just saw him. He was woozy, woozy from the anesthetic. Said something like 'I feel lousy.' You might as well go to dinner."

"Perhaps the most dangerous consequence of injury is the loss of blood," says Jonathan Miller, the author of one of the medical books I've been reading. "The efficiency of the heart and of the circulation depend on the maintenance of an adequate blood pressure, or fluid volume, and, if more than a pint or two is lost in a short space of time, the system goes into a state of almost irreversible hydraulic shock. . . . The most delicate organ, the brain, fails first—which is why people feel faint and lose consciousness when they lose blood rapidly."

Tipping backward. Dizzy. Breathless. "I feel awful."

"The body is unable to stop a major haemorrhage," writes Miller, "but up to the last moment it strenuously adjusts itself to the continuing loss by a process of reallocation. As the blood pressure starts to fall, organs which have a less urgent need for oxygen and nourishment are put on short rations: the arteries which let blood into the skin, for instance, shut down and limit the blood flow, shunting it to the more vital parts of the circulation. This is why patients with haemorrhage go white and feel cold to the touch."

The girls kept on squabbling in the Chinese restaurant, darling. Everyone was weirdly mean.

19:20. BP: 65/0. Pulse: 36. Observations/Treatments; Dr. Jones to bedside. Unresponsive, BP. Attempting to intubate. BP non palp—code blue started—

Won tons. Thick and soggy. Pale. *Loc: pale.*

The brain fails first. Which is why people feel faint and lose consciousness, go white and feel cold to the touch.

And fortune cookies that we barely read. And the three ice cubes have long since melted in my glass, though I'm drinking my scotch and water anyway.

It tastes pretty good.

Donatello looks good too. He's colored in very neatly.

I get up and go into the kitchen to see what time it is.

3:15 A.M. according to the clock on the microwave.

As I watch, a new number slides into the little window. 3:16 A.M.

Why patients go white, lose consciousness.

3:16 A.M., April 10, 1991. Exactly two months ago, on February 10, 1991, we were asleep, side by side, in the Davis condo. His body in the bed with mine. Warmth and warmth. His gray and white pajamas, my blue and white nightgown.

Five hours from now, we would get up and start packing for the trip down the road to the UCDMC.

"What if this is the last time I'm driving down this road?"

We inadvertently left Raggedy Andy and Orlando Furrioso behind in Berkeley, but Kathy and Liz brought them along later, so "the boys" could sit on the windowsill and gaze with mild approval at me and Elliot and the doctors.

Go white, lose consciousness.

Tipping backward.

Backward.

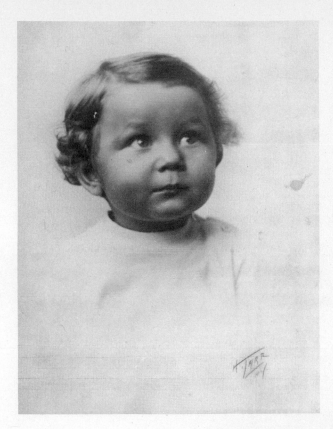

This is one of
the "baby Elliot"
pictures that still
lives on my desk.

Elliot with his little
brother, Richard. Elliot
must have been four
when this was taken.

Elliot was probably fourteen or so here, just starting out at the Bronx High School of Science.

Here's Elliot as a senior at New York University, age twenty-one or twenty-two.

Elliot around the time we got engaged, in 1956. He's standing in my dorm room at Cornell, in front of the guitar I never could play very well.

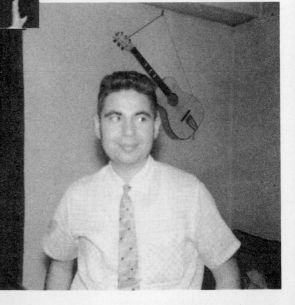

Elliot as a private first class in the army in 1957, just before we were married.

On field exercises in Germany, winter of 1958: Elliot was a radio operator in an "armored personnel" unit.

The official portrait of the
groom, December 1, 1957,
our wedding day.

Still in his getting-
married clothes,
listening to wise
advice from his
grandfather (left)
and his father.

Here we are, driving away from the church where we were married in a happy, ecumenical ceremony.

Elliot on the beach in California in the late 1970s with our youngest daughter, Susanna, then around twelve.

Elliot on the same beach, probably the same vacation. He's in his middle forties here.

This picture of Elliot, one of my favorites, was taken by a young friend in the early 1980s. It still sits on my desk, along with "baby Elliot."

In a motorboat on Lake Como, 1988, one of our last European trips together. We were both working at a faculty retreat owned by Princeton.

The same next-to-last trip: we're visiting a ruined castle in the west of Ireland, not far from the Yeats Summer School, where I was teaching that week.

14

The truth is that by and large, no matter how calm and con-trolled and accepting a face she may present to the world, a new widow is miserable and can be a very difficult creature.

What else could she be? The most important person in her life is no longer there. She has lost the love and companion-ship of the person with whom she has shared much of her life. She has lost status, both social and economic. She has lost her future.

—DR. JOYCE BROTHERS, *Widowed*

TUESDAY, APRIL 16, 1991, 4 P.M.

With its flowery curtains, Chippendale end tables, striped wing chairs, and soft blue carpet, the little office where Roger, Kathy and I are sitting looks like nothing so much as the writing room in an English country house. Actually, though, this is just one of a series of such offices—or perhaps the phrase "consulting rooms" would be more accurate—in the rambling main build-ing of the Sunset View Cemetery. We're finally forcing ourselves to order a headstone for Elliot's grave because we're beginning to feel guilty at the thought that *our* loved one, unlike most of his neighbors, still occupies an anonymous patch of ground.

We've learned a lot, lately, about what I now call "cemetery culture." We know, for instance, that the grass is always greener on the other side of the "plot," and that if you want to keep up with the Joneses you have to constantly put bouquets in the flower holder.

The assistant funeral director who's helping us pick the marker is a youngish, almost parodically lugubrious man. He has on a dark suit and tie (of course), an expression of frozen concern, and an unlikely smile that merely intensifies the look of concern.

If Elliot were in the room beside us instead of out there under the hillside, I know what he'd say. He'd laugh and tell us that any minute the assistant director will turn into Digby O'Dell, the friendly undertaker on "The Life of Riley," an old radio show, and say, "Cheerio; I'd better be shoveling off."

They dig the marker into the ground, don't they? Shovel a new hole and set the stone into the earth just about where the dead person's head must be?

". . . which is why a number of families decide on the bronze. On the other hand—" the assistant director turns the page of a glossy brochure positioned on the desk in front of us—"many feel that granite offers even greater resistance to the elements and is equally attractive so that—"

"Mom? What do you *think*, Mom?" Kathy nudges me gently.

"Simple," I say. "I want to keep it simple. Daddy never—"

"Daddy wouldn't like the bronze," she interrupts in an undertone.

"Sort of vulgar," I agree.

"He really wouldn't like those fancy letters." Roger points to a sample epitaph eulogizing someone's "adored husband, father, and grandfather" in pseudo-Gothic script.

"Simple, Daddy would want us to keep it simple," I reiterate, pointing to black-and-gray color "chips" embedded on the page at which the assistant director has now arrived. "That sort of thing. Or maybe a gray between that light gray and the black?"

"A kind of charcoal?" the assistant director wonders.

"Charcoal, yes, Elliot would like a kind of charcoal gray." I have an irrational vision of Elliot when he was twenty-six years old, wearing a charcoal suit from Brooks Brothers at our engagement party. Charcoal gray was all the rage in the fifties. "Your father used to have a suit in that shade," I tell the kids, then turn politely back to the assistant director. "Do you have any samples of the charcoal-gray stone?"

He hesitates. "Actually, in the back I may have a few stones that—" He motions ambiguously toward us and then toward the door. "You can see them if you like."

"The back?"

"A storage area," he explains, leading the way down the hall into a great, bare, cavernous space that looks surprisingly like the backstage of a small opera house.

Along one wall, there is a rack of women's dresses—rather formal ones in discreet pastels—and somber men's suits. Neatly displayed in the foreground there is a selection of coffins. At the *back* of "the back," there are a few headstones leaning casually against another wall.

And here's the charcoal gray. Just what I'm looking for.

We choose polished granite, with simple white letters that cross the top half of the stone in a terse inscription:

Elliot Lewis Gilbert
1930——————1991

It does seem unfair to me that just because Elliot was born in December and died a month and a half into 1991, everyone who looks at his grave will think he died at the age of sixty-one when he was really only sixty.

Anyway, deceptive as its dates are, the marker will bear no sentimental flowers or sappy angels. No corny epithets.

The whole effect, I decide, is one of restrained elegance. Rather Ivy League, actually, like a Brooks Brothers suit.

Elliot would surely approve.

And there's still space on the lower half of the stone for *my* name.

Some spouses save money, we understand, by having both names engraved at the same time. In fact, the whole stone can be completed for quite a good price, with just a blank where the living person's date of death has to be filled in at the appropriate moment.

But though I do feel as if my life is over, I think that contemplating such a stone would be somewhat unnerving. Every time I went to see Elliot, I might feel as if I were "seeing" myself too, mightn't I? Bringing flowers to my own grave, as it were, which seems like a rather selfish and tasteless thing to do.

Anyway, even if I believe my life is over, I've started teaching again, if only because my children and my close friends keep urging me to try to get out of the house, try to tear myself away from 2/11/91, and manage at least a toehold on the outside world.

I'm teaching a graduate seminar in modern poetry, a subject I ordinarily love to think about, but I can't handle Davis very well, actually. Whenever I'm on campus, I'm terrified that I'll bump into one of the doctors from the UCDMC. Then what would I say or do?

And worse, my office is in the UCD Humanities Institute, which, unfortunately, overlooks the Davis Funeral Home—the last place we saw Elliot. In his golden oak coffin. In his blue-and-white striped shirt, dark blue tweed jacket, Liberty tie. Looking rueful.

Still, my class is going pretty well. The only thing is, I hadn't realized how much modern poetry is about death and dying. Or anyway, how much of the poetry *I've* always taught is on these subjects.

And another problem I hadn't anticipated was posed by the name of one of the major authors we're examining: T. S. *Eliot.* Of course my husband spelled his first name differently from the way T. S. Eliot spelled his last name. Nevertheless, to my horror, I find it increasingly difficult to identify T. S. Eliot as "Eliot" during the course of seminar discussions. I can't seem to pronounce the name out loud in front of my students.

Which reminds me that spelling is crucial. The assistant director has been assiduously filling out a number of different forms for the marker. He assures us that it will be "installed" within six weeks or so.

"What happens if the stone arrives and my husband's name isn't spelled correctly?" I ask severely. "It should be E-L-L-I-O-T, with two l's and one t," I admonish.

"The marker can of course be returned and redone." His long, pale, funereal fingers, clasped around a black pen, keep on writing.

"How about *this,* Mom?" Roger has been pacing the room, frowning. Now he comes over, his mouth set in a small strained smile, and hands me a postcard that boasts a glamorous aerial shot of the cemetery, its main office, and its crematorium.

"The beautiful eighty-year-old Sunset View Cemetery is located in the tranquil hills of El Cerrito, overlooking San Francisco Bay," says a caption on the other side.

Kathy grabs the card and begins to laugh, although her voice, like Roger's, has a bitter edge. "This is what we should send those guys at the UCDMC!"

"Dear Folks," Roger expands. "Having wonderful time. Wish you were here."

"Sign it Love, Elliot," she says.

"Two l's, one t," he adds.

The assistant director, still writing, looks bewildered but faintly censorious.

Tuesday, May 14, 1991, 2 p.m.

Sun glaring through the skylight, flooding the dining room table, flashing across the condolence letters we're trying to answer.

Every few days, Roger, Kathy, and I set ourselves up at the table like a sort of cottage industry: mostly I scribble a phrase or two on the thank-you cards, and the kids address envelopes, unless we're responding to something from one of their friends, in which case we reverse the procedure.

We usually spend an hour or two at a time on this dreary task, although it doesn't seem to me that we've even begun to make a dent in the stacks and stacks of letters that Susan and Leah think I ought to answer.

But at least one good thing happened today. This morning the trapper came by to tell us that he's finally caught the opossum, which means that maybe we'll at last be rid of the skunk too.

Roger wanted to be sure that the trapper had really set the animal free, the way he'd promised he would.

"We leave it in the trap, put it in the back of a pickup, and drive it outside the city," the man said. "Sometimes we take it over the Contra Costa line, in Tilden park, sometimes into the hills outside Hayward. Then we let it go."

"Doesn't it ever try to come back? Back to where it was before?" we'd wondered.

"Usually they like the new place. Usually they settle right in," the trapper said reassuringly.

I've never seen an opossum, or even a picture of one, but anyway I imagine a small undaunted creature, looking something like one of the characters in *The Wind in the Willows*, carrying a knapsack and setting out through tall dry grasses toward a new life. A new life far from the midnight snarls and brawls under the oak trees in my backyard.

Fresh fields and pastures new.

Unlike Elliot, who "left"—"he's been *gone* three months now, hasn't he?" someone said the other day—but didn't go anywhere, nowhere special, as far as we can tell.

"With love and thanks, Sandra." I sign a note to one of my cousins and push it toward Kathy, to be addressed.

But what if that's what he wanted? I ask myself again. And I say it out loud again to the kids. "What if he *wanted to die?*"

"Mom." Roger looks sick. "Mom, we've been *through* it over and over again. We just can't know, can we? But there's no reason to suppose—"

"Mom," Kathy says at the same time. "That's *enough* Mom, just stop it."

I've been reading books about the psychopathology of illness, of mortality even. Six months ago I had bought Elliot a self-help treatise by Bernie Siegel, M.D., a surgeon-turned-therapist who's famous for believing that people's attitudes can influence the course of their diseases, and the other day I started rereading it.

Bernie Siegel, M.D., says that you're more likely to die of cancer if you're despairing and pessimistic than if you have a lot of confidence in yourself and your good luck. More important for us, he claims that patients can influence the effectiveness of their *surgery*, depending on how they feel about the procedure. If you're hopeful and trusting, Bernie Siegel observes, you're in less danger from complications. In fact, he declares, he knows of cases where patients died *on the table* or *in the recovery room* because, even though they were anesthetized, they "heard" the doctors and nurses say bad things about their prognoses for recovery.

Suppose that's what happened to Elliot? Suppose while he was ostensibly "under" he heard deVere White make some negative comment about his chances?

"We got it all out. We made the right decision." That's what deVere White said to *me*. But what if he said something very different in the OR? What if he turned, sweating, to Poonamallee and said something like, "It's stuck, stuck, we'll *never* get it all out!"

"Bernie Siegel is very reputable, actually," I tell the kids. I automatically sign another note and hand it, this time, to Roger. "He teaches at *Yale*, Roger," I add pointedly.

Roger got his B.A. and his Ph.D. at Yale, so I hope Bernie Siegel, M.D.'s affiliation with his alma mater will impress him.

But he just grimaces. "There are lots of weirdos in New Haven, Mom."

I glance up at Elliot's picture, which is virtually glowing in the afternoon light. Elliot merely looks enigmatically wistful.

He was so frightened of the surgery, so frightened of what it might do to his body—impotence, incontinence—that I finally said I wasn't experienced enough to help him with his terrors, he should really see a shrink.

"Then I won't tell you how I feel anymore," he'd answered angrily. "Won't tell you what I'm thinking."

Was he thinking that he'd rather die from the surgery than live to be impotent, incontinent? Did he *make* himself die?

"That's right, blame the victim," Susan said ironically, when I confided this latest fear to her last week.

"It isn't likely, Sandy," Dick said on the phone a few days ago. His tone, too, was dry, sardonic. It isn't likely, I guess he meant, that somebody could *make* himself bleed to death.

Go white, lose consciousness.

But maybe you could deliberately "go white"—go white and *let go*, let go of everything that scared you and try to escape to, escape to, where? someplace else.

"Anyway," I say out loud to both kids, "it's nice about the opossum, isn't it?"

FRIDAY, MAY 31, 1991, 4 P.M.

Memorial Day weekend. Sunset View is festive with flags and flowers. The whole green hillside dotted with springy colors, swarming with families patting and clipping the graves, or even picnicking—that's what they seem to me to be doing!—under the stands of evergreens. And way off in the distance, suspended lightly, lightly on the thin glitter of San Francisco Bay, there are dozens of tiny sails this afternoon.

Charcoal gray. It's shiny and charcoal gray.

We're seeing it for the first time. The kids are putting flowers in the flower holder.

You have to part the grass and dig the flower holder out of the ground, wriggle it hard to get it loose, then go fill it with water at one of the faucets scattered among the graves, then put the flowers in—today's are deep red roses, blood-red roses—then shove the flower holder back into the ground, then fluff up the flowers, make sure they're arranged properly—

Charcoal gray, and the letters shockingly white. "Too white," I tell Roger and Kathy and Gina. "Too white, it's scary."

"They'll weather, Mom, the whole thing'll weather," Roger says.

Shiny charcoal gray and shiny, glaring, deeply carved white letters. His name.

His name on the ground at my feet.

Elliot Lewis Gilbert
1930————1991

Now he's really here. Here in the new place. Now we know.

If he weren't really here, if he weren't really settled in just *here*, his name wouldn't be written on this stone, would it? This stone tangled in this particular plot of grass.

FRIDAY, JUNE 28, 1991, 1:30 P.M.

"My God, I saw him in the bank, saw him just now in the bank!"
I'm standing in the parking lot outside the Albany branch of the
Bank of America, leaning against Elliot's brown Toyota and
shouting at Susanna, who's looking puzzled and worried.

"Saw *who*, Mom?"

"DeVere White! What the *devil* was he doing in *my* bank? He
doesn't even live in the Bay area—he actually lives in Sacramento—what was he doing here?"

Susanna just came back from Santa Barbara for the summer,
and we're on our way to the Sea Ranch; Roger, Gina, and Val
and Kathy and Liz are coming too, but in different cars. We
stopped at the bank so I could get some money. While I went in,
Susanna went across the street to mail a few letters.

We're both kind of nervous: this is our first trip up to the Sea
Ranch since Elliot died. The place has been rented a lot to weekend visitors—and, after sadly clearing out all the important personal stuff my husband and I left there and bringing it back to
Berkeley, we've rented the condo in Davis for a year. But I finally
decided that it would be best for the seven of us to go *en famille*,
as it were, and check up on the Sea Ranch house.

Dr. deVere White—or a person who must surely be his
clone—was standing chatting amiably with the teller nearest
the door of the bank. If I had stayed in my place at the end of the
line, I'd have been just behind him.

He looked exactly like himself. The bald spot, the grayish
curls. Getting money from the teller, probably. "Nice day,
how're ye doin' today?" No doubt that's what he was saying in
his brogue. Bland and affable.

"Mom, you're making it up, Mom, what would deVere White
be doing in this bank? He lives in Sacramento!" Susanna gives

me a pitying look and a small bag of potato chips. "C'mon, Mom, forget it."

"I had to run right out of the bank." My heart is pounding fast. "I didn't know what I'd do," I tell her. "Suppose I started screaming right there in front of everybody!"

"Oh Mom, c'mon, you just probably saw somebody who *looked* like him."

"His twin, then." I take a deep breath and push hard against my stomach with the flat of my right hand. This procedure is supposed to nip a not-so-bad attack of tachycardia in the bud. "Or suppose, Susanna, just suppose I met him and I didn't say anything or I just said 'Hi, how are *you*' and hugged him or something the way I did that night outside the hospital after Daddy died?"

"I couldn't feel worse if it were me own father," he'd said. And I'd ceremoniously hugged him goodbye.

———

THURSDAY, JULY 18, 1991, 5:30 P.M.

I'm sitting on the back deck at Sea Ranch, staring out at the meadow, which is ripe and golden at this hour, lapped in what Elliot and I used to call "the kindly light" of summer late afternoon. And there's a path of light across the sea that shines gray-blue beyond the cypresses in the windbreak at the edge of the cliff. And the meadow larks are whistling the tune that Elliot always said sounded just like the opening bars of Richard Strauss's the *Bourgeois Gentilhomme*.

July 23 is less than a week away.

"July 23, if you can make it. I want to see you all in my office," Dan Kelly said on the phone this morning.

"Does this mean you're taking the case?" I could barely get the words out.

His tone was noncommittal even while he seemed to be committing himself. "I'll need to see all of you—you need to know the awful truth about lawsuits for medical malpractice." The deep, brisk, authoritative voice was wry. "I'm going to show you and your whole family the dark side of the moon." With a laugh.

"Does this mean the consultants were—?" My own voice was high and thin; it floated around my head like a dry leaf.

"Positive. The consultants were positive."

"Positive?"

A moment's hesitation. "Neither feels that the treatment of your husband was professionally up to par."

"I see."

"I'll have to have you all sign some papers, too. Okay? Tuesday, July 23, at 3 P.M. Call my secretary to confirm the day before."

Susanna is standing on the deck behind me. "Want to go swimming, Mom? Some of us are going to walk to the pool. You could meet us there."

All my kids and several friends are staying at the Sea Ranch right now—our friends at a house down the road because Susanna, Roger, Gina, Val, and Kathy have taken up just about every bed at *my* house. But all together, especially when we meet for picnics or barbeques, we seem to constitute one big holiday party. At least that's what an outsider would think. Someone who didn't know why Raggedy Andy and Orlando Furrioso, arms around each other's waists, are still mournfully guarding my bed.

"I don't think so, dear, I don't feel like swimming," I tell Susanna, and turn back to stare out at the meadow again.

It's the same meadow it always was, not a bit different at all. The kindly light, the opening bars of the *Bourgeois Gentilhomme*, the yellow lupine, the tall dry grass, the wall of cypresses along the cliff, their roots dipping toward the sea.

Maybe if I sit very still, very quiet, Elliot will decide to show up here just one last time. Maybe he'll remember the way up from the beach, the way to hang on to the roots of the cypresses and scramble to the top of the cliff, the way to get onto the path that winds among the lupine bushes toward the deck where I'm sitting, waiting.

Maybe this once, just for me, he'll come walking through the high grass, the grass that must be almost as tall as he is. He'll be wearing his old blue parka, and the kindly light will be behind him, so I won't see his face clearly, but I'll know it's him anyway, no matter how blurry he looks.

Yes I will. I'll know it's him.

PART THREE

CLAIM

Plaintiffs complain of defendants, and each of them, and for a cause of action allege:

. . . On or about January of 1991 and prior thereto, Elliot Gilbert came under the care of defendants and their agents, servants and employees, and each of them, for purposes of obtaining medical care and treatment. Defendants, and each of them, undertook to and did treat Elliot Gilbert and agreed to do all things necessary and proper in connection with his care and treatment.

. . . Defendants and each of them, so negligently and carelessly diagnosed, failed to diagnose, treated and failed to treat Elliot Gilbert so as to proximately cause his death on or about February 11, 1991.

. . . As a further proximate result of the carelessness and negligence of defendants, and each of them, plaintiffs were deprived of the love, care. comfort, society, services, support and earnings of decedent, Elliot Gilbert, all to their general and special damages in an amount according to proof.

. . . WHEREFORE, plaintiffs pray for judgment against defendants, and each of them . . . as the Court may deem proper.

—**Complaint for Damages (Wrongful Death),**
August 13, 1991, *Sandra Gilbert,*
Roger Gilbert, Katherine Gilbert and Susanna Gilbert,
Plaintiffs, **v.** *Regents of the University of California*
and Does One through Fifty, Defendants

15

Given the nature of Athenian attitudes toward homicide, if the death of a patient appeared to the relatives of the deceased to have resulted from . . . incompetence or negligence . . . they might have felt bound to charge the physician [in order to] ensure that they fulfilled their duty to the spirit of the dead.

—DARREL W. AMUNDSEN, "The Liability
of the Physician in Classical Greek
Legal Theory and Practice," *Journal of the
American Medical Association* (April 1977)

TUESDAY, AUGUST 4, 1992, 9:30 A.M.

It is almost two weeks since Dan Kelly deposed Ralph W. deVere White, and we're still waiting for the court reporter's transcript of the doctor's testimony. Clinging to Raggedy Andy as if he were a life raft, I wake weeping and sweating in my bedroom at the Sea Ranch. I have had The Dream—the dream I never had before, the dream of closure and farewell that all my grief books talk about.

Susan and Susanna and I came up here last night to get some work done. Susanna is finishing a graduate school paper, and Susan and I are trying to complete the last chapter of a book of criticism we've been writing for several years. As I huddle under the covers, I can hear them chatting in the kitchen, unloading the dishwasher, putting coffee mugs on the table, doing all the things that I should be doing too.

Yellow light glazes the drapes that cover the tall window near me; its brilliance hurts my eyes. Evidently we're going to have a nice day today, no fog, good beach weather.

Although I don't usually record my dreams, I get up, find a notebook, and crawl back into bed to write this one down.

I've been visiting my mother and a strange man she lives with. They're trying to get me medical help. They take me to a lot of doctors. After a while, there's some problem, they've brought me to the wrong doctors in the wrong series. I've done something illegal—or they have.

I'm sick; I'm living in a YWCA and have trouble sleeping. I take a Halcion but then someone comes in and gives me two injections of a strong sedative. But now, just as I'm going to be knocked out, I have to flee.

It's raining hard and I get into an open horse-drawn chaise with another strange man who is supposed to help me but is very ineffectual. First we set out for one place but then we are intercepted by someone who tells us to go to a different address, on 23d street, a small nameless hotel.

We rush through the rainy streets. I am carrying a black umbrella. Get to the hotel. Someone slips me a bunch of badges, all with my name on them, as at a convention. Someone else says you have to enter a lottery to stay at this hotel, only one out of three will get in. Then I pull out a nametag and say I AM THE SANDRA GILBERT YOU ARE LOOKING FOR. *All kinds of action now. Everyone very excited.*

Then I am in an elevator going to my room. The elevator is huge, the size of a small living room, and decorated in green and white French provincial. It has a big picture window at the back through which I can see a beautiful grassy hillside and gardens.

I am told this is a magical hotel. Every city has one on 23d street but few know about them.

Some people come into the elevator with a large luggage cart or golf cart in which they are carrying an enormous bundle wrapped in mattress pads, blankets, and bandages. They follow me to my room with this cart. When we get to the room, which is spacious and pleasant and overlooks the hillside, they unwrap the package—and there is Elliot, in his gray-and-white-striped pajamas. He looks handsome and says he's well.

I hug him and he feels the same as always. He tells me again that he's perfectly fine and he still loves me. He is absolutely real and solid: I can touch him when I hug him, I can feel the warmth of his body, the prickliness of his beard.

I say I'm glad he's fine, that's great, and now let's get out of here. He says I'm sorry, darling, but I can't come with you.

Does he or doesn't he add that I have to go by myself? I can't remember. What he does say, he says sadly but firmly, pointing me, pushing me, toward the door.

Although I know all about this kind of dream—I've read about it in at least three different grief books—and although I knew I'd probably have to have it sooner or later, I'm still crying, and surprised to be crying, as I write. My tears splotch the pages of my notebook, blur the ink.

It is the dream in which the lost one says goodbye. One woman watched her husband swim away toward the island of Mont St. Michel, waving calmly. Another was told that he couldn't accompany her on a camping trip. A third had to move out of her house and leave him behind in a trunk because he refused to get into the car with her.

It's standard. It's a classic. Why do my tears surprise me?

Of course, I go out to the kitchen, pour myself lots of coffee, and read my transcription of The Dream to my daughter and my collaborator, who are dutifully sympathetic and supportively analytic. Rightly or wrongly, we all agree that the elevator (going up and *down*) has to do with burial, and that the green and white hotel, situated on/in the hillside, stands for the cemetery. We speculate that the recurrent "strange man" might be some sort of lawyer or *ombudsman*—especially considering that we're waiting to hear what deVere White had to say to Dan Kelly—and we decide that the lottery (obviously) has to do with the randomness of life and death.

After we've pondered the story for a while, though, we do begin to wonder about one weirdly important detail. *23d Street.* Why is *23d Street* so crucial here?

Just as my shrink would, Susan and Susanna urge me to "associate" with the number 23. But I can't seem to think of any particular reasons why it should be so significant to me.

(It will be weeks before I remember that we first met Dan Kelly, first arranged to file our claim for medical malpractice against the UCDMC, more than a year ago, on July 23, 1991.

Do I still believe that the lawsuit will, if only temporarily, resurrect my husband?)

———

Monday, July 23, 1991, 3 p.m.

"Close that notebook. This minute." Dan Kelly's voice is frighteningly sharp. He glares at me like a fifth-grade teacher who's caught me playing tic-tac-toe during a spelling lesson. "That *is* a notebook, isn't it?" he adds, ironically. "And just what do you think you're doing with it?"

"Well—" My nervousness surprises me. "I was just going to write down a few, take a few, you know, notes on what we're talking about here. I *always* do that."

"*Always* do that?" He's still unnervingly elementary-school-teacherly. "Not here, you don't. Not if *I'm* going to represent you in this case."

Ranged around the conference-room table on either side of me, my children look shocked. They're used to their professorial mother getting at least relatively deferential treatment. Rudeness might be okay in stressful family situations, coming from *them* anyway, but such language from a stranger strikes them as intolerable.

I'm feeling especially proud of my children, who are all three gotten up for this occasion like the adults I know they really are. Kathy and Susanna are wearing with-it blazers and skirts (as am I)—the kind of clothes we hardly ever put on these days—and Roger, too, is sporting a classy tweed jacket, striped shirt, rep tie. I tell myself that we must surely appear "respectable," Ivy League. Why would anyone want to insult such a suavely bourgeois family?

Susanna leans forward frowning, as if to rebuke him, the sleeve of her beige linen blazer grazing the edge of the table.

"Mr. Kelly, my mother is a *writer,*" Kathy interjects. "She's a scholar and a *researcher,* she always writes things down—"

Roger looks gloomily out the window. The Walkup law firm's majestic view of San Francisco Bay, the Golden Gate Bridge, and the Marin headlands puts all this nonsense in perspective, his expression seems to me to suggest.

Dan Kelly is unphased. A trim, graying, compact man in a dapper charcoal suit, he has an elfin Irish face quite different (or so I believe) from De Vere White's, and he had greeted us with smiling amiability in the modest but comfortable Walkup reception room. Now, though, he keeps on scowling. "First rule," he says, banging alarmingly on the sleekly polished walnut. "If *I'm* to be your attorney, you do what *I* tell you to do."

Like Roger, I gaze at the view—an enormous sky filtered through vast expensive sheets of glass along with green-gold hills and a blue puddle of bay. "Okay," I concede with an elaborate nod. "It's up to you. *You're* the professional."

Actually, I want my daughters to back off. We don't even know for sure whether Kelly's really accepted the case, and at this point I'm afraid even to ask his opinion of its merits. What if he's only looking us over, trying to decide whether we have a strong argument or are just a bunch of crazies?

Focusing on the turquoise blur of the bay, I realize I'm slightly breathless with anxiety. Because I *am* certain that, no matter how irascible Dan Kelly may seem, we need him: he was highly recommended, and we have to have a lawyer, for ourselves, for our own emotional and spiritual survival, and most of all for Elliot, for the dead one who suffered and was lost.

To my relief, Kelly softens. "The thing is," he explains more quietly, "you can't take any notes or the other side could subpoena them." Toughening again, he gives me another ironic look. "I'll have to teach you a lesson in the law, even if you *are* a professor. Any notes you've made, any writing you do about the case while it's still in discovery—if the other side finds out about it, they can get hold of it. Unless you've written something specifically for *me*. Anything you write for *me* would be covered by attorney-client privilege."

Again I nod deferentially.

"And another thing." He jabs at the air with a pencil. "You mustn't discuss the case with anybody. *Nobody.* You'd be surprised at what gets around. And we don't want anything getting back to the other side."

The "other side." I find the phrase chillingly definitive. Now "they"—deVere White, Reitan, Poonamallee, the entire U. C. Board of Regents, even perhaps my own chancellor—all are the "other side."

Or maybe The Other Side, in caps. I've hardly ever seen a courtroom, except in the movies, but now I imagine the doctors, the chancellor, maybe even one or two regents, lined up in a kind of pew on The Other Side of the room and transfixing me with angry stares. Worse, I envision deVere White in a witness box, Kelly quizzing him. Two Irishmen, one from the Old Country, one from the New World, *mano a mano.*

"And so, doctor," Kelly begins, "how do you account for the blood? Half the blood in the body!"

DeVere White is unperturbed. "I told ye," he says directly to me, "warned ye it was stock, stock."

Stock! I smile at Kelly, stiffly I suppose. "Can I at least doodle?" I wonder, biting my ballpoint pen. Like all San Francisco office buildings, this is a No Smoking location, and I seriously want a cigarette.

Kelly grins back. "Doodling is allowed," he agrees. "And now"—briskly—"I have to find out just who everybody is."

And as at the first meeting of a peculiar graduate seminar, we go around the table, introducing ourselves. *Sandra:* poet/critic/professor of English at U. C. Davis/*bereft widow of the deceased. Roger:* Yale graduate and postgraduate; assistant professor of English at Cornell/husband of Gina, father of Val/*bereft son of the deceased. Kathy:* aspiring soprano, Indiana M.A. in Voice Performance/graduate student of business at Cal. State, Hayward/*bereft daughter of the deceased. Susanna:* Yale graduate/graduate student in English at U. C. Santa Barbara/*bereft daughter of the deceased.*

Kelly whistles. "English literature. Quite a family business." He turns to Kathy. "What kept *you* out of it?"

"I don't know," she says in a tight voice. "I guess I just wasn't interested." Plainly she still hasn't forgiven him for his behavior toward her mother.

"Well, I'm sure you all have questions." Kelly resumes his teacherly tone. "But first let me fill you in on some of the details of malpractice litigation."

I fix my eyes on my notebook and begin drawing black squares, black x's, black crosses, as he launches into a practiced lecture on the ins and outs of a case like ours. If we go forward with our suit, he tells us, by the end of August our claim will be filed in Sacramento. Not a bad jurisdiction, he observes in an aside, though not as sympathetic to plaintiffs as some. Four to six weeks later, we'll be required to respond to "written interrogatories" from "the other side." Then, a few months after that, we'll be deposed—that is, interviewed under oath by lawyers for the regents (really the UCDMC). Still later, our attorneys will depose relevant parties on "the other side." In addition, medical experts will probably testify for both sides.

Experts. I take a deep breath, still longing for a cigarette. Sokolosky's southern drawl: "Ah expect they'll say he shouldn't have bled to death followin' this procedure."

Now as to damages. The formula for calculating economic damages is an unfair one, Kelly remarks rather bitterly, but it's fixed, there's no getting around it. Roughly speaking, economic damages are based on the decedent's salary at the time of his death, multiplied by the number of years that he might have been expected to live and work. But there are no allowances for raises he might have received, had he continued on the job (as we are persuaded Elliot would have) for, say, another ten years. In addition, the projected cost of the dead person's annual "consumption" must be subtracted from these damages.

"So if your husband liked to gamble," the lawyer comments jovially, "and he gambled away his whole salary, you obviously wouldn't be entitled to any financial compensation at all!"

We assured him that Elliot never gambled, nor did he have any other expensive habits. Didn't drink or smoke, hated to buy clothes. His only extravagances, and they were minor, were books, classical CDs, and videotapes of movies, most of which he bought on sale.

All to the good, Kelly replies, adding that he hopes our marriage was a good one too. If there were marital problems, he notes, the widow's compensation can also be reduced, since she might have been planning to leave her husband in any case—or anyway he might not have been "worth very much to her."

We must all look vaguely shocked, because he illustrates this point with a weird story about a client of his whose deceased husband turned out to have been a wife-batterer—the "other side" found out that he'd once broken her jaw!—and that revelation practically destroyed the whole case.

Well, Elliot wasn't a batterer or abusive, I assure him, and while we're on the subject of pain and abuse, I ask, what about my *husband's* "pain and suffering"—to use one of the few official legal phrases I already know. Aren't victims of medical negligence routinely awarded significant sums of money in token of what they have suffered? I read about such awards in the papers often. Editorial writers complain about them all the time. According to many columnists and politicians, huge sums for "pain and suffering," gratuitously awarded to greedy plaintiffs, account for the escalating cost of medical malpractice insurance and drive all our doctors' bills up.

"Not compensible in California," Kelly answers curtly. "In wrongful death, pain and suffering aren't compensible. He's dead, so he can't recover. His pain and suffering are irrelevant."

I bend closer, closer to the page on which I'm doodling, leaning hard on my ballpoint, carving black boxes and x's into a big circle. The recovery room. *The white clicking. Tipping backward.*

Cases of wrongful death, Kelly explains, typically result in lower awards than cases of severe injury precisely for this reason. A survivor can sue for pain and suffering; a decedent can't, nor can his relatives. Besides, juries are much more sympathetic to miserable people in wheelchairs or on crutches than they are to dead people whom they'll never have to see.

I begin counting the x's in my notebook. *Half the blood in the body.* Not compensible.

"Not compensible either," Kelly is saying, in answer to a question from one of the kids. *"Your* pain and suffering aren't compensible either, unless you were witnesses to the event. And you weren't. Precedent for that was set by—"

"But we *were* witnesses," Kathy interrupts rather truculently. "We spoke to the doctor several times, he kept sending us away, we're sure he lied to us, we *suffered*—"

"You weren't witnesses to the *actual* event," Kelly answers firmly, "and you couldn't have been unless you'd been in the OR and *understood* what you were seeing. Seen the scalpel slip, for instance, if that's what happened."

Seen it slip. *Seen the blood spurt.* Known what we were seeing!

"But that's not right, is it?" Susanna begins. "I mean we *have* suffered, my *mother* has suffered—"

"A flat sum." Kelly looks severe. "In cases of wrongful death the state of California allows the surviving spouse a flat sum of up to $250,000—and absolutely no more—for loss of care, comfort, and consortium."

Care, comfort, and consortium: the alliterative phrase seems to me to have a kind of grim charm. "Consortium" is when you go to bed with someone, isn't it? I will never again "consort" with Elliot between the sheets, so the state of California might require the UCDMC to compensate me for this loss.

My breath comes faster. "And *punitive* damages?" I ask, staring at Kelly's dark lapels.

He looks back at me blandly. "No punitive damages for medical negligence in the state of California, no matter how egregious the negligence may have been."

"No punitive damages!" Kathy and Susanna both gasp; Roger frowns.

"Why not? I thought that in *all* these cases—at least from what I've read—" I start another line of black x's and gaze at the lawyer plaintively.

"Not in the state of California," Kelly says sardonically. "Not for medical negligence. In almost every other case of personal injury you can sue for pain and suffering, for punitive damages, for the works—for example, if you walk out of this building and you're crossing California street and you're minding your own business and a Standard Oil truck hits you, you can sue the company for your pain and suffering and if you can show they were careless, negligent, sent out a truck with no brakes or something, well then you can recover punitive damages, too. But not a hospital, not a doctor. No way."

"Why not? It seems very strange." Roger is frowning more deeply.

Kelly produces a bark of a laugh. "The doctors' lobby. They got to the legislature." He shrugs and turns to me. "But hey, I told you I'd show you the dark side of the moon, didn't I?"

"Well, of course money isn't the issue," I tell him, forcing myself to adopt my own lecturing tone. "But accountability *is*. How do you ensure accountability without punitive damages? How do you keep irresponsible doctors from killing people if they don't have to pay for their mistakes? I mean, no sum of money can replace my husband, but—"

I hear my voice skid to a halt. No sum of money. I stare at my hands, Kelly's hands, the hands of my children. All alive, pinkish, in motion, clasped around pens or touching the table, sensitive, *sentient*, nervous, blood flowing through them. Unlike Elliot's hands in his coffin, grayish-white, rigidly clasped.

How would one calculate a sum to replace the dead person? Would some jury decide on, say, $100,000 for his hands, $50,000 for his beard and his thick dark eyebrows, $75,000 for his hazel eyes?

"Tough," Kelly is saying. "These cases are tough. And don't get me wrong, they're hard to win, the doctors stonewall, experts are often reluctant to testify, you're going to be put *through* it, and I hope, I hope—" He glances at me keenly. "Are you ready for it? I hope you are."

I bite my lip. "I'm ready and my kids are."

"Okay, okay, well I hope so." He relaxes a bit. Have we passed some kind of test? "We've got a few papers to sign and then—" He goes to the door of the conference room for a minute, summoning his secretary I guess, then comes back to the table. "I'll tell you," he says, shaking his head. "A lot of these doctors can be really *something*. If only they'd level with people, half the time they wouldn't get to this kind of point, things like this wouldn't come to *my* office."

"They didn't tell us anything," I say slowly. "They *still* haven't told us anything."

Nothing, the kids reiterate bleakly. They've told us nothing. Stonewalling. Just as Kelly says they do.

"I'll tell you a story about that." The lawyer leans back in his chair, toying with a pencil. "A guy from down the Peninsula came to me. Wealthy man, good Catholic. A big contributor to a Catholic hospital down there. A *patron*, a benefactor. And his wife went in there for routine surgery. Never mind what. Woman in her fifties. Came out of the OR in a coma. Lived for a month or two in a nursing home, then passed away."

"Terrible." I frown sympathetically. So do the kids.

"Happens all the time. These things happen all the time," Kelly responds. "But the doctor could have leveled, could have made it better. This man and the doctor, they belong to the same club in San Francisco. The guy takes the doctor out to lunch at the club, once, twice. Each time, he looks at the doctor and says, 'What happened, Doc? What happened to my Mary?' 'I don't know,' says the doctor. 'It was God's will, Frank. These things are mysterious. Who knows what happened. It was God's will.' "

Kelly snorts. "God's will! Well, the man came to *me*, had to find out what happened to his wife. And we deposed the people who were in the OR, found out what everyone knew all along. The perfusion machine—that's a machine that keeps the patient breathing during the surgery—the perfusion machine ran out of oxygen. Someone just forgot to fill it. And you only have two minutes in a situation like that, then she's brain dead. Comes out of there comatose."

"Oh my God." We're horrified, who wouldn't be horrified. (Although is there anything much that can horrify us after what we've heard, after, "Ah imagine they'll say he shouldn't have bled to death?")

Kelly grins. What Elliot would call, remember, a "rictus of a grin." "Happens all the time. But this guy was a good Catholic, a patron of the hospital. If the doctor had leveled with him, he wouldn't have sued."

And why *don't* physicians "level" more, I wonder. Pride? Self-deception? Or, in fact, the fear of precisely the kind of lawsuit that Kelly says this doctor could have avoided by telling the truth?

"Well, anyway, did he win?" I turn inquiringly to the lawyer. That's what I really want to know.

"Won a settlement." Kelly gives me another keen look. "I hope you understand that a settlement is what you want. Most of these cases, if they go to trial, the plaintiff loses. Sixty to seventy percent of the malpractice cases that go to trial are lost by the plaintiff."

Sixty to seventy percent! The kids and I glance at each other nervously. What are our odds? Elliot, we want the best odds for you, we want "the other side" to *pay.*

"*Our* case?" I've finally gained the courage to ask the real question. "Do you think *our* case has any chance?"

"Who knows?" Kelly raises an eyebrow impishly. "Especially if we have to go to trial. But I wouldn't take it on if I didn't think it had merit. He certainly shouldn't have bled out like that, that's what Wes and the experts say."

"Bled out." The phrase is new and terrifying. *Baby, you shouldn't have bled out; darling, you shouldn't have bled out, out, out.*

"The coding summary," I murmur to Kelly. "Acute post-hemorrhagic anemia. What are they going to say about that?"

"Who knows what they'll say? *I* don't, not right now. And as I told you, they stonewall, they lie, they cover-up." He leans forward and taps the glossy walnut with his pencil. "But let me tell you, I wrote the book on personal injury law—anyway, I wrote *a* book, I'll show you a copy—and I'll do my best to scare the shit out of them. Everyone who knows me knows I'm a shark. A baby-faced shark."

16

*When a loved one dies from a physician's malpractice . . .
grief is often put on hold until the legal proceedings are
completed. For some, this contributes to a delayed grief reaction. For others, these proceedings themselves are thera-
peutic, since they afford a way to channel the rage and give
it a focus.*

—Rando, *How to Go On Living*

WEDNESDAY, SEPTEMBER 25, 1991, 2:15 P.M.

"I believe I wrote you about it. The claim was filed in Sacramento on August 15." Dan Kelly is crisp and perfunctory on
the phone.

I tell him I realize that. I found his letter in a stack of mail on
Monday, when Susanna and I got back to Berkeley. In fact, I
have it in front of me right now, with my list of questions to ask.

Re: *Gilbert v. Regents of UC*

Dear Mrs. Gilbert:

Please be advised that the complaint in your case has today
been sent to the court in Sacramento for filing. I will keep you
posted as to pertinent developments during the pendency of
the case.

Best personal regards.

Very truly yours,

DANIEL J. KELLY

Kelly's signature has a special dark flourish, I notice, and I'm charmed by the capital letters in which his name appears. DANIEL J. KELLY. Baby-faced shark.

"You should have the written interrogatories by now too," he adds.

"I do," I tell him. I know I do. I just haven't been able to force myself to focus on them yet. It's too scary to read the legal language, the chilly queries.

My fist is clenched around the receiver, my palm is sweaty. After a month in Italy and a week on the East Coast, re-entry is difficult.

More than difficult. Unendurable. The empty house is unendurable.

Susanna left yesterday to go back to school in Santa Barbara. Kathy and Liz moved to Boston weeks ago: Liz will be attending law school there, and Kathy wanted to experiment with a different way of life, in New England. And Roger, Gina, and Val returned to Ithaca at the end of July. For the first time since last February, I'll be staying here alone, without my husband or my kids. I try to console myself with the thought that, since I'm on sabbatical, in a few weeks I'll be away again, this time to Yaddo, a writer's colony outside Saratoga Springs, in upstate New York. But even so, I can hardly bear to drag myself through the hollowness of the rooms, though I understand I have to be strong about it.

"Anything new from the outside consultants?" I ask Kelly, trying to keep the eagerness out of my tone. This is of course my major question, this and *what is our deadline for answering the interrogatories*, since all of us feel sick when we read the legal forms. We're going to need a little extra time, if it's at all possible.

"Yes, something pretty interesting, actually." Kelly's voice livens up; he suddenly sounds cheery, gossipy. "We've been in touch with an emergency room specialist, a woman over in the

East Bay, who had a few sharp comments. She pointed out that after a patient has been transfused, his blood doesn't equilibrate right away so the first hematocrits that are taken can be misleading." He chuckles. *"Equilibrate. I like that word. It's new to me. Pretty fancy. I guess 'doesn't equilibrate' means the red blood cells don't get distributed evenly throughout the whole body. So the first hematocrit they got from your husband in the recovery room—hematocrit of 32, I believe—might not have been a valid indication of his true red blood count."*

"Equilibrate." I write the word down in the flyleaf of one of the grief books that's lying on the telephone table next to the bed. "Equilibrate. God. You'd think they'd have known that."

"You'd think so, wouldn't you?" Kelly chuckles again, with what I've come to realize is his customary bitter wit.

I guess you can't spend week in and week out being a personal injury lawyer and dealing with stupid or irresponsible doctors, drunken hit-and-run drivers, and manufacturers of defective machinery without getting kind of bitter.

"So she thinks—thinks his treatment was unacceptable? Negligent?"

"Well, yes." He hesitates a minute. "To be frank, I sent her over two cases, significant similarities between them. Both hemorrhages. One your husband. The other, a woman who was in labor, delivered the baby, and then she bled out and died, the way your husband did. Only it should have been more obvious. This emergency room person thought the woman's case was clearer, maybe stronger."

"Stronger? Does that mean this specialist doesn't—?" Doesn't think we have a good case, I want to say, doesn't think Elliot was *maltreated*?

As always, I wonder why I hope the experts will say Elliot *was* maltreated? Wouldn't I prefer to have someone come up with a plausible reason for his death? It would be better, wouldn't it, to be told that everything possible had been done for him?

Increasingly, though, I know why I feel as I do. Because every day I'm surer that Elliot didn't have to die, surer that it wasn't the "fault" of his own mind or body, and more fearful that "experts" and "consultants" will cover-up: afraid the right hand will wash the left hand, the doctors—all the doctors—will band together and keep on stonewalling.

"The woman's case was only *marginally stronger*," Kelly comments reassuringly just before we say goodbye.

I get up and go into my study to unpack some more books and papers. The sofa is piled high with manuscripts and letters that have to be filed as well as postcards and photographs of Lake Como, St. Moritz, the other guests at the Villa Serbelloni in Bellagio, the gardens of Lugano, and who knows what else.

Susanna and I spent five weeks at the villa, a *grand luxe* study center for scholars from around the world that is run by the Rockefeller Foundation, reading, writing, and meeting interesting people. I should be happy about that, shouldn't I?

Of course, Elliot was supposed to come with me. The Villa Serbelloni welcomes the spouses of its guests. Elliot loves—I mean, loved—the Italian lakes, and would have adored the villa. But then so did Susanna. The director and his wife discovered that she has a terrific voice, so almost every evening she sang in the *sala* along with some of our new friends.

Elliot would have loved to hear her singing, too. Whenever I thought about that, I'd go back to my room, open the shutters, look out at the lake, and cry. Sometimes cry for hours, sometimes stop crying and try to write poems.

Then, when Susanna came in later on, the two of us would often sit up half the night, trying to figure out which person it was in the recovery room at the UCDMC—a nurse? a resident?— who forgot to get the 3 o'clock hematocrit back.

There was another widow at the villa besides me: the wife of the former director. Her husband—a few years younger even than Elliot—died last fall in a Milan hospital, under what she thought were suspicious circumstances. We talked about our shock and grief sometimes, but only in the most desultory way, staring out at the lake as if its flat, green sheen might offer an answer, an explanation—something neither of us could provide for the other.

But the worst day was September 11, the seven-month anniversary of Elliot's death, when Susanna and I went to St. Moritz and took a cable car up to the Diavolezza, the cloud-shrouded glacier that caps one of the highest ranges in Switzerland.

There are pictures of the Diavolezza in the stack of stuff on the sofa, but I don't want to look at them, don't really want to remember how we were borne up and up into a gray-blue heart of ice that made us want to cling together as if we were both first-graders on some demonic field trip. White fangs of other Alps below the glacier. Dead rubble on the slope beneath the cable car. Ceaseless wind, crashing against the observation platform at the summit.

Did Elliot fall into that emptiness the way I feel I've fallen into the emptiness of the house—only fall much farther, far more terribly?

Dr. Joyce Brothers, I tell myself, talks about *my* problem, anyway. In her book about her own experience of widowhood, she says the loneliest time is coming home from a trip, when you're greeted by this kind of emptiness. No one to hug you. No one talking on the phone. No music playing.

Maybe I should write her a letter and ask her how she handles hollowness. Or maybe I should just walk around the house a little bit, instead of sitting here obsessing about the Diavolezza and equilibration and Elliot's clothes.

Maybe I should sit down at my computer and begin on the interrogatories, then go into the dining room and say hello again to Elliot's picture, which still broods over the table, looking apologetic. Probably I ought to tell him our lawyer said the dead woman's case was only "marginally stronger" than his.

———

SATURDAY, SEPTEMBER 28, 1991, 4:40 P.M.

Attorney or Party Without Attorney (Name and Address)
Thomas A. Minder (054146)
Lillick & Charles
300 Capital Mall, Suite 1590
Sacramento, CA 95814-4339

Attorney for (Name)
Defendants: Regents of University of California

Name of Court and Judicial District and Branch Court, if Any
Sacramento County Superior Court

Short Title of Case:
Gilbert v. Regents

FORM INTERROGATORIES

Asking Party: Defendant REGENTS OF UNIVERSITY OF CALIFORNIA

Answering Party: SANDRA GILBERT

Set no.: One

Sec. 1. Instructions to All Parties

(a) These are general instructions. For time limitations, requirements for service on other parties, and other details, see Code of Civil Procedure section 2030 and the cases construing it.

The humming of my computer, usually reassuring, sounds sinister right now. The hum ordinarily means the mechanism is healthy and ready to help me with my work, instead of flashing, blinking, beeping, and turning into a technological obstructionist. But at the moment this completely impersonal electronic murmur seems to me to echo the unnerving abstraction of the legal system into which we're slowly being drawn.

Again and again I strain to reread, to *analyze*, the judicial instructions. The scholar-critic in me evidently feels it's essential to master their secret meaning.

(c) Each answer must be as complete and straightforward as the information reasonably available to you permits.

I decided to start on these interrogatories in the late afternoon so that, after working on them for a few hours, I could pour myself a good stiff before-dinner drink, then go out to a restaurant with some friends. But I know I have to be clear-headed about what I write, even though Dan Kelly and his assistants will "clean up" our responses—so they told me—before putting all the information together in the correct form for the court.

The lawyers for the other side have only marked certain questions for me to answer on the "form interrogatory." The kids will have to answer the same queries too. But I have an additional document to deal with—a "special interrogatory," which asks a series of specific questions about *Elliot*.

A few of the early questions in the "form interrogatory" have a weird glamour. For instance,

2.0 General Background Information—Individual

2.1 State.
(a) Your name;

(b) every name you have used in the past:
(c) the dates you used each name.

This demand for names makes me wish I were an interesting enough person to have had a series of aliases. Instead, my maiden and married names are all I can offer.

A number of the other questions on the form strike me as almost theatrically peremptory, although after studying them for a while I figure out that most are addressed to the victims of automobile accidents rather than to the survivors of medical malpractice.

Do you attribute any physical, mental, or emotional injuries to the INCIDENT?
 Will you lose income in the future as a result of the INCIDENT?
 Was a report made by any PERSON concerning the INCIDENT?
 Have YOU OR ANYONE ACTING ON YOUR BEHALF inspected the scene of the INCIDENT?

At first, actually, the bullying tone established by the capitalizations makes me want to laugh; reminds me, indeed, of some of Elliot's funniest "one-page novels," where apoplectic bosses hector paranoid subordinates or absurd melodramas issue in italicized moralizings.

But after a while, I am not amused. Not amused, Mr. Kelly. Not amused, Mr. Minder. Not amused, Dr. deVere White.

Was a report made by any PERSON concerning the INCIDENT?

No, actually, unless you count "Dad's had a heart attack," or "I don't know, luv, his pressure just dropped," or "Probable liver failure," or "The results of the autopsy are inconclusive," or "We made the right decision, the surgery was a complete success, we got it all out."

Have you or ANYONE ACTING ON YOUR BEHALF inspected the scene of the INCIDENT?

No, Your Honor. No, I can't even identify the scene of the INCIDENT. Did the INCIDENT occur in the OR (a slip of a scalpel, a rush of blood) or did the INCIDENT occur in the recovery room (a tossing of the PATIENT on the BED, a turning away of the NURSE or the RESIDENT or some other PERSON in attendance)?

And Your Honor, how did the scene *look?* Was the OR painted green, was there a great white ring of fluorescent light overhead, aimed at my husband's body, at the scalpel as it entered, sliced, and maybe slipped? And the recovery room—was it white, did its MACHINERY click and hiss as I believe? What color was the wall, the bedspread, the IV bag, and which of them was the last earthly object my HUSBAND saw as his eyes closed, as the *feeling awful* swelled in him, as *irreversible hydraulic shock* took over and shaped the absolute finality of the INCIDENT?

————

SUNDAY, SEPTEMBER 29, 1991, 2:20 P.M.

Although it, too, opens rather comically with a request for names and pseudonyms, the special interrogatory, propounded to me alone, is even grimmer in its insistence on detailed information about the dead PERSON.

As the computer hums its indifference, I struggle to reconstruct my husband's *curriculum vitae*—his education, his career, his life and death. The Bronx High School of Science, where he wrote the senior play with his friend Irwin, a farce about a genius named Aristotle Goldfarb, who built an atomic bomb for his sophomore physics project and fell in love with Ecstasy Geffner, the Grade Guide's Daughter. New York University, where he developed a passion for Mahler and Strauss as well as for Gilbert and Sullivan, immersed himself in Dickens, and resolved to go on studying the Victorian novel in graduate school. Cornell, where he met me, or rather where I met *him,* where I had such a deep crush on him (especially on his beautiful thick eyebrows, now I come to think of it, and on his wavy hair, and the way he could sing Mozart arias better than anyone else) that I used to wait for him for hours outside the English department library, making up phony questions about philosophers and poets in the hope that he'd notice me—I was merely an undergraduate and he was not just a graduate student but a Teaching Assistant!— and I thought if I could engage him in some sort of serious conversation he'd invite me to dinner, take me to the movies, maybe even seduce me.

If you contend that the negligence (includes failure to comply with the applicable standard of care) of defendants was the proximate cause of the decedent's death, state in detail all facts (not conclusions) which support this contention?

I was married to him, Your Honor, for thirty-four years, so I can state in detail many facts that support my contentions about his childhood, his education, his wedding, his teaching, his children, but none, Your Honor, none about his DEATH, none because I didn't witness the INCIDENT, because all I know is that there are a number of us who believe this DECEDENT should still be alive, this INCIDENT shouldn't have happened.

Nonetheless, I dutifully clatter at the keyboard, inserting questions for Dan Kelly where I'm not sure what I ought to say. I'm determined to finish this task by tonight, so I can ask my friend

Bob to proofread my responses and comment on them when he comes over for dinner.

I've also resolved actually to cook for Bob this evening, because he's been bringing me so many meals. The day before yesterday, for instance, he and Moneera proffered Mexican chicken soup, osso bucco, and Chinese long beans.

It was depressing for the three of us to be alone in the house, without the kids rushing in and out, taking Val to the playground, hurrying off to work or to the library. But Bob observed that at least we'd all be able to smoke as much as we please.

Bob and Moneera are the only other Berkeley people I know who smoke, and my children, reasonably enough, hate our cigarettes. Now, with the house so empty, Bob said comfortingly, each of us could even light two at once if we wanted to.

In fact, that's what I did Friday night. As Bob and I sat at the kitchen table, looking over the interrogatories and having a drink while we waited for Moneera to get here, I noticed that I was somehow smoking two cigarettes at the same time.

———

FRIDAY, NOVEMBER 1, 1991, 5 P.M.

It's hot and stuffy in the Yaddo phone booth. One thing I've learned here is that all artists' colonies—not just Yaddo—have uncomfortable telephone facilities. This is because the administrators of these places quite rightly don't want the writers, painters, and composers in residence to be tempted by the phone during working hours. So here in West House, where I have a bedroom and studio, there are only two tiny cubicles that you can use for calling people, if you absolutely have to talk.

As I wait for Dan Kelly's secretary to get him on the line, I glance down at the copies of the official Responses to Form Interrogatories that arrived this morning and rehearse the question that Liz helped me formulate when she and Kathy visited me a few days ago. The question about "Dillon," about the "pain and suffering" of the so-called "bystander."

"COMES NOW Plaintiff SANDRA GILBERT and responds to Defendant's first set of FORM INTERROGATORIES as follows.

For some reason, I love the curious legal formula "COMES NOW." I imagine myself COMING FORWARD with due solemnity before a packed courtroom, before the hostile glances of the other side, before a black-garbed judge, with my responses to the FORM INTERROGATORIES. Here, NOW, I come forward to state my claim.

When he gets to the phone, Kelly says he's glad I've got the copies, hopes I'm having a good time on the East Coast—it must be great to have gotten away from the devastation of the awful East Bay firestorm—and he doesn't have any news; there's nothing more from the experts right now and nothing more from the other side. Although, he adds, they'll soon be scheduling *our* depositions.

When do we interrogate *them* in writing, I wonder.

Never, he tells me curtly. Never, because we don't know who "they" are. The regents of U. C. are the defendants, he points out, but they can hardly be expected to answer questions about my husband's death at the UCDMC.

Haven't I noticed, Kelly remarks, that we are suing the "Regents of the University of California and Does One Through Fifty"—"Does" as in "John Does," arbitrarily named but unknown persons?

Yes, I've noticed. I confide that I was bemused by "Does One Through Fifty." I worried—I *worry*—that the mystery phrase means we don't know whom to target. DeVere White is a Doe. Poonamallee is a Doe. Reitan is a Doe. Several OR technicians and a few recovery room nurses are also Does. Which Doe is the *guilty* Doe?

Therefore, I reiterate, when do we hear *their* story, *their* explanation of what happened? I tend to repeat this question to Kelly again and again, since it often keeps me awake at night. *What will they say, how can they explain, what's their story . . . ?*

Once in a while I get up at around three in the morning, toss on my raincoat (I forgot to bring a robe) and wander out into the cluttered fin de siècle public rooms of West House—the library, the vast parlor weighted down with treasures from the Gilded Age.

Grand as it is, West House was originally a kind of guest cottage adjoining the Mansion, the main building of Yaddo. Katrina Trask, the founder of the colony, moved in here during the First World War, I'm told, after she was widowed and when it got too costly to heat the Mansion.

A number of artists at Yaddo—"colonists" we're called, actually—are reputed to have encountered Katrina's ghost, especially in the Pink Room, a big upstairs studio/bedroom that was once her private parlor. Everyone says she appears as a friendly, well-intentioned, Wilkie-Collinsesque Woman in White.

One composer said Katrina occasionally hovered at the foot of her bed in a kind of inspirational, maternal capacity, to help her finish a chamber piece she was having trouble with.

Sometimes, as I roam around the half-lit downstairs rooms in the middle of the night, I wish Elliot would manifest himself to me—as ghost, demon, shadow, apparition in white or in pajamas or in a raincoat just like mine, I don't care what. It would be even better if he'd show up in my bedroom, the way Katrina appeared at the foot of that woman's bed.

Maybe *he* would tell me the story that so far no one from the UCDMC has divulged. At any rate, he'd keep me company in the lonely hours: even disembodied, he'd be my closest friend.

As it is, I only have Raggedy Andy to hang on to here in the East. I left Orlando Furrioso back in Berkeley, in charge of the home front.

Patiently, reasonably, as he has so many times before, Kelly is reminding me that we will hear the UCDMC's story when he deposes the other side in a few months. Then and no sooner.

Okay. Okay. I know I have to accept that. And now, about "Dillon." I clear my throat and tentatively mention that "a law student I know" says "the Dillon v. Legg case" implies a possibility that we as bystanders *can* recover for our "pain and suffering." The Dillon case is evidently even a California case, I add. It is the case of a mother who was awarded damages for her own pain and suffering because, as I understand it, she was nearby when something horrible happened to her child.

There's a silence at the other end of the line, then an explosion of sarcasm from Kelly. "Would you like this little *law student* to represent you instead of me?" he asks irascibly. "I mean, would you rather work with this *law student* or with *me?*"

"Well obviously I, I mean obviously *you're* our attorney, I didn't intend to suggest that you—"

"Well, when this *law student* represents you, then you can take *his* advice. In the meantime, you'd better take mine." He still isn't placated.

His advice. I guess Kelly is an old-fashioned sort who can't even imagine that the anonymous law student might be a *she*. Feminist though I am, I keep on trying to calm him down. Here we are in medias res, and we need him badly. "Of course I realize you—but I just wondered—" I'm annoyed with myself and Liz for even getting us into this.

But Kelly has relented now and is explaining himself more calmly. "I just wrote an update on this for the *California Practice Guide* on *Personal Injury,*" he says. "It's here on my desk. 'No bystander recovery if injury-producing event cannot be perceived: Per *Thing v. La Chusa* . . . plaintiffs suing on a 'bystander' (*Dillon v. Legg*) emotional distress theory must have *personally observed* the injury-producing event and resulting injury to the victim; and must have had an *'understanding perception'* of the event at the time it occurred. Where the event is of a type that simply *cannot be perceived, no* bystander negligent infliction recovery is allowed.' "

I am properly chastened, should have all along known better than to challenge his judgment. After all, the <u>Responses to Form Interrogatories</u> that I have in front of me are dazzlingly professional, full of impressive evasions and objections. For example,

<u>Question:</u> Was a report made by any PERSON concerning the INCIDENT?

<u>Answer:</u> Objection. This interrogatory seeks the premature disclosure of information and other data which a consultant expert has provided plaintiff in the preparation of this case as such violating the attorney work-product and/or attorney client privilege. Without waiving said objection and in the spirit of good faith in the discovery process plaintiff has knowledge of the following reports having been prepared: An Autopsy Report dated 3/8/91 prepared by Dr. Boris Ruebner and Dr. William Ellis; Death Certificate; and the decedent's medical records from UC Davis Medical Center, 2/10/91–2/11/91, contain various reports.

To reiterate, plaintiff's investigation and discovery are continuing at this time and plaintiff therefore reserves the right . . .

I hadn't just been haunted by the PERSONS who had made the reports—all the suspects who populate the "other side" in my mind—I had also sweated over that question when I was drafting my own answers to the form interrogatory.

As always, I thank Kelly profusely for his time and his kindness.

It's already dark now in upstate New York, and I go back to my room for a few minutes, to put on lipstick and brush my hair for dinner. There's Raggedy Andy, affably holding down the fort on the colonial maple single bed where I sleep this month. There's my September 1991 picture of Elliot, me, and our Iraqi friend, Husain—me in the middle, one arm around each of the others, the three of us small and blurry on the desk in my studio.

Katrina Trask hung huge oil paintings of her four children in all the public rooms at Yaddo. She founded the colony in memory of these four dead children—the only kids she ever had. Her husband didn't die until many years after all the children had long since succumbed to the usual turn-of-the-century maladies: tuberculosis, scarlet fever, and so forth.

Which would be worse: if all your kids died suddenly and unexpectedly or if your husband did? Obviously you couldn't choose, though just as obviously sheer quantity would have to play some part in your decision-making, should you be *given* a choice.

Objection, I say to myself as I brush my hair too hard, too fast. Either way more than half of you dies too.

Although at least poor Katrina Trask knew just what killed her kids.

———

SUNDAY, NOVEMBER 24, 1991, 10 P.M.

"The guys I spoke to at NCI had nothing but the highest regard for him," Dick says sadly, gazing into the fire.

"I know," I nod. "You told me." After Elliot was diagnosed with prostate cancer, Dick had asked around at the National Cancer Institute about several of the urologists we saw, including deVere White.

"The highest regard," he repeats. "They said he was a superb clinician, and he had a great bedside manner."

"Well, he does," I concede. "Does have a great bedside manner. And after all, we don't know he was responsible, don't know *who* was—"

Dick leans forward and looks at me earnestly. "Remember that, Sandy," he says. "You don't know and maybe you never will."

I too study the flames, my eyes stinging. *You don't know and maybe you never will.* Never to know, never: can I bear such blankness? Maybe Kelly was really right. If doctors would only "level," patients probably wouldn't sue.

"Or maybe you'll find out it was simply procedural," Dick continues. "Bad recovery room procedures. Smug. Taking things for granted. Slow as molasses."

We're both silent, listening to the crackling on the hearth, the sudden soft fall of a log, the swish of the dishwasher in the kitchen, where Leah insisted on cleaning up after dinner by herself so Dick and I could have a chance to talk alone about the case for a few minutes.

Although I feel almost overwhelmingly obligated to Dick for all the help he's given us, I haven't seen him since Elliot died, so after I left Yaddo two days ago, I flew here to Bethesda to see him and Leah before going to New York to spend Thanksgiving with my mother and my daughters.

Kathy is driving down from Boston this coming Wednesday, and Susanna is flying in from California on a frequent flyer freebee the same day. The girls and I have made elaborate plans because we're all hyperconscious of what my grief books define as the danger of holidays for the bereaved.

Even under the best of circumstances, lots of people fall into depressions during the holiday season, my books point out, but for people who are still coping with a severe loss, such a time is especially perilous. *Plan ahead*, the grief counselors warn. *Don't stay home alone. Try to do something a little different from what you'd usually do.*

Kathy, Susanna, and I are going to splurge and have dinner at the Plaza Hotel with my mother and one of Susanna's college roommates. Short of getting on a plane to Acapulco, that's about as different from what we'd usually do as it can be.

Under ordinary circumstances—in an "ordinary" world we'll never inhabit again—we'd be in Berkeley, and Elliot would roast a twenty-pound turkey with Grandpa's spinach-and-sausage stuffing. We'd invite lots of friends, and everyone would laugh too much, eat too much, and later complain about feeling full.

"The point is, Sandy," Dick reiterates, "these things can be fairly complicated to untangle, you may never be sure who—"

"I'm writing about it, Dick," I interrupt, somewhat to my own surprise. "I wasn't going to tell anyone, but I seem to have to write about it. I can't think about anything else. So I started a book at Yaddo."

Actually, I didn't begin the book at Yaddo. I began it in Berkeley on July 23, the day of our first meeting with Dan Kelly, though I didn't realize then that it would have to be a book. That evening I had dinner with some friends who were nearly as distressed as I was, not only by the circumstances of my husband's death but by what I had just learned from Kelly: the constraints with which malpractice litigation in California is hedged round.

"Look in the *Times* for the last few months," remarked one of them, a journalist. "Bush and Quayle have been giving speeches about this lately. They want to make the California system a model for federalized procedures. Cap awards, do away with punitive damages, reduce accountability."

"You should write an article about it," somebody else suggested. "Tell your own true story."

"I probably wouldn't be able to publish it," I worried. "The other side would probably try to gag me."

Later that night, though—or more accurately, at three in the morning, when as usual I couldn't sleep—I went into the kitchen with a notebook, and began, weeping as I wrote, to try to write. Began to try to remember what happened to Elliot and me and the kids so people who get angry at supposedly greedy plaintiffs, and so maybe even doctors who self-righteously deplore the escalating costs of malpractice insurance, might understand the impact of medical negligence on one "real-life" family.

Sunday, February 10, 1991, 7 P.M.: First thing tomorrow morning my husband, Elliot, is scheduled for major surgery.

I wrote no more than a few hundred words that night, but in my time at Yaddo the pages multiplied.

Now Dick is saying that he thinks a book is a good idea; he'll be glad to help in any way he can because he too finds this case upsetting.

"I spoke to a colleague about it after I finished going through the records for the third time," he confesses. "And he said it's the kind of thing that keeps him awake all too often. The kind of medical horror story that gives him nightmares as a physician."

He'll be happy to suggest some relevant journals I might read, Dick adds. There are often useful pieces on medical malpractice in the *Journal of Public Health* and the *Journal of Law and Medicine.* There's been a series recently in the *New England Journal of Medicine.*

"I know about that one," I tell him, and Liz, whom I've signed on as a sort of legal research assistant, has been sending me copies of articles from the *Journal of Law and Medicine.* That's how she happened to find out about *Dillon v. Legg.* But I'll be grateful for any references he can produce.

When Leah comes in with coffee and liqueur for all of us, he's promising that he'll do a computer search at the NIH library.

"I heard what you were saying, Sandy, and I think it's great," Leah interjects. "It'll probably be cathartic for you."

No, I tell her rather sullenly, it's awful reliving the whole thing over and over again. What's more, I add ironically, it's hard to write a book when you don't know the whole story.

For example—I turn back to Dick—what about the conversation with deVere White outside the hospital that haunts me so, the one in the early evening when he remarked, "I just saw him. He was woozy, woozy from the anesthetic. He said something like 'I feel lousy.' " According to Dick's time line, Elliot was already dying then. His blood pressure had plummeted, his heart rate had shot up, he was pale, he was—must I go on?

"No, you don't have to go on," Dick says. "What's the question?"

"You know what the question is as well as I do," I answer, cross even though it's absurd to be cross with Dick and Leah, of all people. "Why was deVere White leaving the hospital at that point, why was he walking away from a patient who was in mortal danger?"

Dick shakes his head. Leah looks at the floor.

I've asked myself about this repeatedly, I tell them, and I think there are only two alternatives. "DeVere White either didn't understand what was happening or he did and he didn't care. One, he saw the patient, looked at the chart (or *didn't* look at the chart), and couldn't even interpret the signs of complication, so he left. Or two, he saw the patient, knew there was something terribly wrong, and didn't care or didn't want to be responsible, so he left."

Dick shakes his head again and gets up to poke the fire. "There might be another alternative, Sandy," he comments with his back to me. "He might have seen the signs and understood them but not wanted to acknowledge them." He sits down again and starts pouring cognac for all of us. "He might have been so panicky that he—"

"You mean he might have been scared?" I ask sharply. "Might not have wanted to face up to what was happening?"

Dick is silent while Leah passes around the cognacs. "Even if you don't know all the answers yet, Sandy," she says, handing me my glass, "you have to write about it. Write about it the best you can."

17

BE IT REMEMBERED that on Friday, the 27th day of December, 1991, at the hour of 1:23 p.m., of said day, at the Law Offices of Walkup, Shelby, Bastian, Melodia, Kelly, Echevarria & Link, 650 California Street, 30th Floor, San Francisco, California, before me, Julie A. Carroll, a Notary Public, personally appeared Sandra Gilbert, who was examined as a witness in said cause.

> —Deposition of Sandra Gilbert,
> Sandra Gilbert, et al., Plaintiffs, v. Regents
> of the University of California, et al.,
> Defendants

THURSDAY, DECEMBER 26, 1991, 1:30 P.M.

The dreary debris of the day after Christmas litters the living room. Warming our hands on mugs of fresh coffee, the kids and I perch wherever we can, pushing aside new books and records, shiny stick-on bows, puzzles, windup toys. From the dining room, where Val is watching a video, we can hear the violently cheery crescendoes of *Loony Tunes.*

We cleaned up pretty well after the first round of unwrapping, the family round, but there's still a lot of stuff strewn about from the second round, the exchanging of gifts with the friends who came to dinner in the evening.

It's damp and chilly, grayish, looks like rain. The dense thick Christmas tree in front of the sliding door to the deck, laden with all the old ornaments, offers color, yes, but it darkens the room too.

We took precautions, the way we're supposed to, made sure we were all together and surrounded by close friends. But I still don't remember much about yesterday. In my mind it's curiously muddled with last Christmas, a *normal* Christmas, when Elliot was here.

Well, I remember one thing: people gave me extra gifts yesterday because my husband wasn't alive to give me anything. I tried to get special stuff for the kids, too, but I don't think I was very good at it myself. I ordered a lot from catalogs, which was probably impersonal of me, but I couldn't face the crowds of regular-looking people in the stores.

Roger and Kathy made Grandpa's stuffing for the turkey, arguing over the proportions of spinach, sausage, mushrooms, parmesan, and breadcrumbs. I tried, half-heartedly, to nag them about the consistency as I always nagged their father— "Grandpa's was smoother, finer, he put it through a meat grinder," I'd fret—but in the end I didn't really notice whether the stuffing was too coarse or not.

We set the table with the snowman candles I inherited from my favorite aunt, and everybody pretended to be quite jolly.

I can't seem to recall who carved the turkey. Bob? Roger? No, I think it was Kathy.

Having Val here helped, though. He got a fancy racing-car set, and it took all afternoon for Roger to put it together, while the rest of us kibbitzed.

After we finished eating the turkey and stuffing and mashed potatoes, I showed everybody the Christmas card that came for Elliot from the UCDMC. "Exhibit A," I said, as I handed it around. It arrived just a few days ago, in a thick cream-colored envelope addressed to Mr. Elliot L. Gilbert—a fancy card with a beautiful wreath on the cover and, inside, a message engraved in blue, the school color: *SEASON'S GREETINGS and BEST WISHES FOR A HAPPY NEW YEAR, from ALL OF US AT THE UNIVERSITY OF CALIFORNIA, DAVIS, MEDICAL CENTER.*

We decided to bring it to Dan Kelly tomorrow, in case it might help support our claim about the carelessness of the procedures at the UCDMC.

"Why do we have to be deposed? Why do *we* have to be deposed?" Kathy says now, setting her mug down on the coffee table with an angry bang.

"I don't know, I'm not sure, but—" I get up and turn on the Christmas tree lights. "It's dark in here, isn't it?"

Susanna assumes a look of forbearance. Before she started graduate school, she spent a couple of years as a paralegal, so in Liz's absence she tries to explain the law to us. "I told you already," she says. "They want to be sure we're not—"

"Crazy," I finish.

"Or irresponsible," she adds.

"*And* they probably want to know what we *know*," Roger puts in.

"*And* they'll probably try to impugn our motives," I suggest. "I mean, they'll probably try to imply we're greedy or—"

"Let's do some role-playing again," Susanna interrupts. "You be me," she tells me, "and I'll be the attorney for the other side."

We've been having this conversation, and doing role-playing too, for several days now, but nothing seems to make us feel much better about what we anticipate will be tomorrow's ordeal.

Kelly's office has sent us a pamphlet with background information—*ABOUT YOUR DEPOSITION: 95 QUESTIONS AND ANSWERS*—which has been fairly useful, even reassuring. For example,

<u>Question:</u> Will the opposing lawyer try to trick or confuse me with his questions?

<u>Answer:</u> **This is a general misconception brought about by what you may have seen on television or at the movies. If the opposing lawyer's questions are of this nature, your attorney will be quick to recognize it. He will take the proper measures to prevent the continuation of this method of questioning.**

Still, the only one of us who's ever been anywhere near a deposition is Susanna, and her reaction, when she learned last summer that she'd have to be deposed, was hardly reassuring. "Deposed! My God, I don't *want* to be deposed! You have no idea how unpleasant it can be!" She made a deposition sound worse than root canal.

As for me, I'm not just anxious about the deposition, which is to take place in Dan Kelly's San Francisco office tomorrow, but about the problem of getting there. Kelly wants us to arrive early, no later than 8:30 in the morning, to rehearse for the actual event, which won't begin until ten. When I nervously explained to his secretary that I'm the very opposite of a morning person and tried to arrange a late-afternoon rehearsal time earlier in the week, she was recalcitrant.

"Mr. Kelly likes to work with clients right before the other side comes in," she told me.

We'll have to leave by 7:15 or 7:30 as if we were catching a plane to the East Coast, the kids have admonished me, because the traffic going to San Francisco is so bad.

I turn to Kathy. *"You* be the attorney for the other side, I just don't feel like it right now."

My friends think it makes matters worse that tomorrow is my birthday, but I'm not so sure. As I've told almost everybody, the only birthday present I want is the assurance that we really are suing the UCDMC for what I believe to be my husband's wrong-ful death.

"What are your feelings about doctors? Have you personally ever had any negative medical experiences?" Kathy is asking Susanna.

"Well, I—" Susanna hesitates, obviously realizing that this is a mock-question designed to Impugn Motives.

"Remember, you're under oath," Kathy adds in her best Perry Mason voice.

I turn toward the tree and fix my eyes on one of my favorite decorations, a chubby gilded cherub swinging inside a crescent moon. Thirty-four years ago, when we were first married and Elliot was in the army, stationed just outside Nurnberg, we bought that along with a bunch of other brightly painted wooden ornaments.

Although he was Jewish—energetic teller of Rabinowitz jokes, enthusiastic eater of corned beef sandwiches—Elliot loved to cel-ebrate Christmas.

Every year he put a homemade, hand-drawn, wittily versified card in my stocking. After we had kids, the cards usually elabo-rated some conceit based on the two of us as Mr. and Mrs. Santa Claus.

Last Christmas, when he was thinking ahead to surgery, the outside of his card featured a picture of a stoically smiling Santa Claus lying on an operating table. Inside, there was a surprised looking doctor holding up a tiny beaming lady in a red dress, over the words, "The Doc who cut old Claus apart/Found Mrs. Santa in his heart."

I still have it in the top drawer of my bureau, where I keep all my good jewelry. Maybe that's where I should keep the card from the UCDMC too, when Dan Kelly is through with it.

———

FRIDAY, DECEMBER 27, 1991, 1:23 P.M.

Q. Good afternoon, Mrs. Gilbert.

As you know, my name is Mark Muro, and I represent the University of California Davis Medical Center in this lawsuit brought against them by your family.

A. Uh-huh.

Q. Have you ever had your deposition taken before?

A. No.

Q. I'm going to go over briefly what we're going to do here this afternoon. I don't expect it will take a long time.

The atmosphere in the Walkup conference room is as severe as I'd feared it would be: not one but two court reporters wearing neat pastel separates and stooped over a peculiar-looking transcription machine; a gray-suited lawyer across the table from me, and two gray-suited lawyers next to me, one on either side; the long walnut table littered with papers, water glasses, and coffee cups; rain pelting the giant glass windows behind me, obscuring the view; a box of Kleenex thoughtfully placed in front of me, in case I should break down I suppose. I breathe deep, swallow hard, try to pull myself together.

After all, everything's gone okay so far. For instance, getting up at six in the morning wasn't as hard as I'd feared it would be, even though it was of course still pitch dark at that hour. There was a curious air of emergency in the house, or anyway an air of the *unusual,* as if we were all indeed preparing to take off for some distant clime.

The kids let me sleep later than anyone else. When I went to get myself some coffee, they'd already put breakfast on the table, along with a Happy Birthday note, and Susanna was on her way into the shower. Roger and Kathy were dressed, reading the newspaper in the brightly lit kitchen.

Their father was like that. Efficient and cheerful in the morning, the very opposite of me. It seemed appropriate that we were doing this for *him*.

He would be proud of me for getting up with such alacrity, I thought as we climbed into the car at 7:25, and pleased, too, by how spiffy we all look, Roger in the tweed jacket and tie that he saves for special occasions (mainly visits to Kelly's office, so far as I can tell), Kathy and Susanna once more in their professional blazer and skirt outfits, me in the black silk jacket, the black scarf, and the black dress with tiny white dots that I wore for his memorial service—my widow's weeds, as I call these garments.

Kelly's rehearsal was somewhat unnerving, though. We'd jotted down a list of questions for him—for example, what if the other side asks us if Kathy's brain surgery has made us suspicious of doctors? What if they imply that my decision to commute between Princeton and California for four years meant that Elliot and I had a troubled marriage?—but his admonitions were rather more daunting than the potential problems we ourselves had thought up. Most of our difficulties were manageable ones, as he pointed out. Kathy's brain surgery? None of their business. The Princeton commute? A professional decision. But he himself knew his principal advice wouldn't be easy to follow.

"It's going to be tough for this family, I know," he kept reiterating sardonically, "because you're all talkers, you all love to speak up. But you're going to have to do as I tell you. *Just say as little as possible. Keep your answers short. Don't volunteer any information they don't ask for.*"

I gave him what I hoped was a meaningful look. "How do you think I got to be a professor, Dan?" I asked. "By being a good student. So you can stop worrying about me. I'll do just what you tell me to do, and so will the kids. They're good students too."

He wasn't convinced, however, and neither was I. "Just keep the answers short," he repeated, surveying us all skeptically, or so I thought. "Don't start telling them how you think doctor so and so did such and such, don't start giving them all your opinions about everything. That's not what you're here for. That's what we'll do in court, okay?"

Q. What year did you meet Mr. Gilbert?
A. I met him in 1954.
Q. One thing that I neglected to tell you is that if you wish to take a break at any time, you have the right to do that. You just need to let me know.

  And you also have the right to speak privately with your attorney.
A. I understand.
Q. You were married to Mr. Gilbert in December of 1957?
A. That's right.
Q. Where did you meet him?
A. I met him at Cornell.

I guess my voice is shaking. I guess that's why the lawyer for the other side keeps telling me we can take a break if I want to, and keeps assuring me that I can speak privately with my attorney.

But I have nothing to hide, after all. Yes, I met my husband at Cornell. I already told them so in my answers to the written interrogatories.

Kelly thinks the day is going remarkably well. The kids have already been deposed: each one came out of the conference room looking exhausted but relieved. The questions have apparently been very easy.

"They sent a baby out today," Kelly says, grinning like the cat that swallowed the canary.

It's true that the lawyer for the other side is quite young, but he seems smart. He's here because Thomas Minder, the man in charge of the case, went to Hawaii for Christmas.

"What kinds of questions do you think he'll ask *me?*" I murmured to Kelly in his office, just before I went in for my own deposition.

He was telling me that he had to leave early in order to make a court date in Benicia and introducing me to one of his partners, John Link, who would take over for him halfway through my deposition. "I was filling John in on a little more about the case," he said. "Told him how they're denying everything but it doesn't seem as though they have a leg to stand on." He turned to Link, a tall, affable-looking man in what I now recognize as a regulation dark gray lawyer suit. "At the last minute, they're pouring blood into this guy, his pressure has dropped and they're pouring blood into him, and they claim they didn't do anything wrong!"

"What if they ask me about *Dick?*" I wondered.

At lunch, the kids told me the kinds of questions they had to deal with. Simple ones, so far as I can see, about family life, about their schooling and their careers, and in particular about their relationships with their father.

We went to a Japanese restaurant down the street from the law office—the first time I've agreed to set foot in a Japanese restaurant since Elliot's "last meal" on February 8, 1991, when he had the Bento box and we argued about the Gulf War with two old friends.

"He wanted to know the kinds of things I did with my father," Kathy said, picking at her sushi.

"That's right," Susanna said. "I told him we listened to music and watched videos together, we went to Sea Ranch, he read my papers, he—"

"I said I learned all my jokes from him, and opera, and I went into the family business, and he played with Val." Roger looked down at his plate.

"I said I had so much fun with my father that I used to go along with him when he had errands to do, like going to the Price Club or something, just because it was so neat to be with him," Kathy told me.

All three seem somewhat abashed to find that they've been uncharacteristically sentimental.

Back in Kelly's office, I confessed how nervous I was. Especially because, as he had just pointed out to John Link, they blandly refuse to admit they did "anything wrong." "What if they ask me about *Dick?*" I reiterated.

"No, you don't mention him," he said for the third or fourth time. "Your friend at NIH counts as an expert consultant. You have no obligation whatsoever to disclose his identity. And as I've told you, if you do, the next thing you know they'll be subpoenaing him and bringing him in here and—"

"I know, I realize, I understand," I admitted, "except that"—I must have looked at him plaintively—"I'm under *oath* and it seems so—"

"Not to worry," Kelly said, as he and Link walked me down the hall for my deposition. "Just keep the answers short."

Q. When did you first find out that he had prostate cancer?

A. In August—actually, I think it might have been July 31st, 1990, but it was certainly that week or the first week of August.

Q. Is there something in particular about that week that you recall that it was during that week?

A. I just can't forget.

Q. Who told you?

A. He was diagnosed by Dr. Humphreys, his regular urologist in Berkeley.

Q. Were you there for the discussion with Dr. Humphreys, the initial one?

A. Yes.

Q. What did Dr. Humphreys say?

A. Dr. Humphreys said that he—I'm trying to remember what he said the Gleason grade was. He told us what it was. He wasn't sure about the size.

He strongly recommended surgery but said that radiation would be an alternative. And he told Elliot to begin donating blood, autologous blood, in preparation for the surgery if he wanted to have surgery.

The more questions Mark Muro asks about Elliot's illness, the more I find myself tensing up. What kinds of admissions is he trying to elicit from me? I'm pleased to see that for the most part I've kept my answers short, as Kelly advised, but I keep trying to psych out the other side.

Do they want me to confess that *no one* recommended surgery, that Elliot (and I!) stubbornly insisted upon an inappropriate treatment, and that's why he died?

But deVere White *did* urge Elliot to have a radical prostatectomy, so where is this line of questioning going to go?

Now the young lawyer is snapping out the names of Elliot's various doctors as I reported them in my responses to the written interrogatories, and now he's asking about pulmonary difficulties and heart problems.

Well, I can see where *this* is going: Muro wants me to admit that my husband was sick already, that he had bad lungs and maybe a bad heart too. But Elliot didn't have any problems, unluckily for the other side. Unluckily for them, he was basically a healthy man.

Q. Have you had any conversations at all with anybody affiliated with the medical center since the time of your husband's death?
A. I spoke to—I think the only person I personally have spoken
to is Dr. deVere White.
Q. Initially you spoke with him at the hospital on the day of his
death, correct?

I think I've got it. I think this is so Muro can lure me into admitting that they leveled with me from the start. But they didn't. So he can't.

Behind me, a great gust of rain sweeps over the window, al-most like a wave cresting over the side of a ship. It's pouring now, with singleminded gravity.

Q. And he's the only one you've ever spoken with at the Med
Center regarding your husband's death?
A. Yeah.
Q. Have you talked to any physicians other than those affiliated
with the medical center about your husband's death?
A. No.

The question about *other health care professionals*. The ques-tion about Dick. But Kelly is right. Dick is an expert consultant. His advice is "privileged," as the lawyers would put it. Still, I feel as though Muro is looking right through me, analyzing my every stammer and fidget.

I have to try to remember how pleased Dan Kelly was with the kids' depositions. "The other guys are hitting their heads against a stone wall," he said smugly. "They're not going to get anything out of *this* family." And he looked at my children with what almost seemed like fondness. "Anyway," he added, "they shouldn't have sent a boy out to do a *man's* job!"

Q. Why don't you tell me what types of things you and your husband used to do together other than the obvious, eating together.

A. Well, of course we did a lot together. We were colleagues; we were in the same field. So I suppose you would have to say number one was talk.

   We listened to music, we went to the opera, we watched movies, we traveled, we went to restaurants, just the whole range of activities.

Q. What type of traveling did the two of you do?

A. Well, we—we went to Europe a lot, usually to do research, each of us with different projects. We went to London a great deal. We—a couple of times we traveled to give talks together.

   We went to Florida to see his mother. We did obvious vacation travel. We went to the Sea Ranch. We went to see our kids.

Our "consumption"—or, rather, Elliot's consumption? Is he trying to force me to concede that Elliot spent so much money that I'm not owed any damages? He traveled too much?

But surely all I'm telling him is how much we loved each other and wanted to be together.

Q. Have you, yourself, incurred any medical bills as a result of your husband's death?

A. What kind of medical bills?

Q. Either counseling or even for any physical problems that you—

A. I have had some counseling, yes.

Here's where he's going to imply that I'm crazy, going to impugn both my sanity and my motives.

Q. Did your treatment . . . have anything to do with your marriage with Mr. Gilbert?

No, now it's about the marriage. He wants to show that I was seeing a shrink because my marriage was in trouble so, like the wife-batterer who broke that woman's jaw, Elliot was of no use to me and therefore I'm not owed any damages and the case might as well be dismissed. Is he trying to confuse me or trick me? Should Link "take the proper measures to prevent the continuation of this method of questioning?"

Q. Is anybody living with you right now?
A. Well, there's the person in the apartment.
Right now, my daughter Susanna is at home for vacation. My son—the three kids were obviously here for Christmas.
Q. What I really mean is: Is anyone permanently residing at your house right now?
A. No, no.

What's he getting at this time? I bend low over the notepad on which I've been doodling and struggle to figure out the point of all this. Either he wants to show that I'm crazy but always *was* so my grief isn't worth compensation, or he wants to show that I'm just fine, not crazy at all, and therefore my grief isn't worth compensation.

But why does he want to know who's living in my house? As I puzzle over this, another gust of rain dashes against the window, so hard that the two court reporters gasp, then smile sheepishly.

Q. I don't think I have much more. I'm going to look over my notes for a second, and I think we'll be done.

A. Okay.

    (Pause in proceedings.)

Q. Were you present for the consultation with Dr. deVere White about the options that your husband had prior to the surgery?

A. Yes.

Q. I think we covered this a little bit. I just want to know specifically what he said to you and your husband about treatment options.

A. The first time we saw him in August of 1990. . . . He was very strongly in favor of surgery because he said that for men at my husband's age . . . surgery could give him a complete cure and give him 20 to 30 more years, whereas radiation would only, in effect, hold the cancer for eight or nine years, and then the cancer might recur.

I know what this is about. He's pressing me to tell him what the doctor said to us because he wants to find a way of suggesting that deVere White never really recommended surgery, that the surgery was dangerous from the start and it was all *our* idea! And even though I know he's wrong, even though I know deVere White really did urge Elliot to have the operation, I'm tired, tired of being so tense and watchful.

. . . I mean, he never told anybody what to do, but he said that I—you know, surgery is the best option.

    Mr. Muro: Those are all the questions I have. Thank you.

        (Conclusion of proceedings.)

As Kelly had warned he'd have to, he left halfway through the deposition, but John Link was a patient presence by my side throughout the whole tense business. Now he accompanies us to the door of the Walkup offices, smiling approvingly.

"A really good deposition," he says. "Dan will be pleased."

I thank him, but he interrupts: "Of course, that guy was a pushover."

"Was he—?" I wonder. "I thought some of his questions were tough. But you know best. Only, why would they—?"

"That's what Dan was saying earlier," he observes.

We all hover a moment in the lushly carpeted hall, halfway to the elevator.

"Well, maybe this case will get them to change some of their recovery room procedures," Roger remarks, and his sisters echo his sentiment. Surely the point of cases like this, they agree, is at least in part to encourage doctors and hospitals to change their ways.

Link shakes his head rather benignly. "They almost never do," he says with a bitterness considerably more amiable than Kelly's. "We see it over and over again. Even when they lose their cases or have to settle, they just keep on in the same old groove. Nothing changes. You probably can't even imagine the kinds of guys who keep right on practicing even after three, four, *ten, twelve,* malpractice suits."

We murmur our astonishment. Politely, though, because I guess we all secretly agree that nothing much can astonish us anymore.

"Guy up north," Link says. "An alcoholic in OB/GYN. Lost at least *five* suits—wrongful deaths of mothers and babies, severe harm to mothers and babies inflicted through negligent behavior, and so on and so forth—and not only does he keep on practicing, the patients keep right on coming."

We don't want to hear this now, we really don't, even though Link is obviously a kind, decent man. When the elevator dings just down the hall, we rush for it, shouting back our thanks and best wishes for a Merry Christmas and a Happy New Year.

We're off, the deposition's over, we're hoping we can forget about it for an hour or two. Rain or no rain we're going to go out to celebrate my birthday, the first birthday I've had without Elliot since I was seventeen or eighteen, I can't remember which.

And as we hurry into the elevator, relieved to be leaving the scene of inquisition, I suddenly realize why Muro asked that weird question about whether anyone is "permanently residing at your house right now." He's hoping that I may have already replaced my husband with another man—a lover or something, taking up space not just in my house but in my heart and bed!

I should have told him that the only man waiting for me at home now is Raggedy Andy.

18

*What proportion of the aggrieved, though they may not like
it, 'lump it' . . . either because they are too poor, too timid,
or too resigned to initiate litigation; or because they believe
that they can never win in litigation, or because litigation
is not part of their problem-solving set?*

> —ALLAN R. MEYERS, PH.D., " 'Lumping It':
> The Hidden Denominator of
> the Medical Malpractice Crisis,"
> *American Journal of Public Health 77,*
> no. 12 (December 1987)

TUESDAY, JANUARY 14, 1992, 1 P.M.

"Please review the deposition, writing any corrections on the
errata sheet enclosed, noting the page and line number, and
return it to us in the self-addressed, stamped envelope."

I toss the letter from Kelly's secretary aside, tuck the copy of
my deposition—beautifully bound and covered in clear plastic—
under the "People" section of today's paper, and collapse back
onto the pillows. My temperature is still up, nearly 101 though
it's comparatively early in the day, and I can't stop coughing.

I've had this awful flu for weeks, ever since we were deposed. I
guess the stress made me sick, that and running around San
Francisco in the rain after we left Kelly's office. We had to park a

block away from the restaurant where we celebrated my birthday, we'd forgotten to bring an umbrella, and we all got soaked.

New Year's Eve was especially terrible. I had prudently arranged to go to a close friend's party and to have dinner beforehand with a couple of other friends. But then I was too sick to do anything except lie under three or four quilts and shiver. My temperature soared to more than 103, and my kids, though bound for parties of their own, took turns piling on more blankets and bringing me mugs of broth. As Elliot would have done.

It hadn't yet occurred to me how unpleasant it would be to have to be *ill* without him.

One good thing, though: I was so knocked out by the fever that I didn't even notice the end of 1991, the most horrible year I've ever lived through, and the beginning of 1992 and of maybe all the other years in which, so it seems, nothing will ever get very much better.

———

THURSDAY, JANUARY 30, 1992, 12 NOON

Damp sand weighs down the hem of my skirt as I walk away from the flat white seething of the surf toward the parking lot. It's gray and mild, kind of gloomy, kind of desultory, on this Santa Barbara beach, where I've been sitting half the morning, staring at the trawlers, the freighters, the offshore oil platforms, and trying to write a poem for my husband—in his honor, in his memory.

I had to give a talk in Los Angeles this week, so I came up here yesterday to spend a little time with Susanna. She's in class at the moment but maybe later this afternoon we'll go shopping to cheer ourselves up.

It's especially important for at least two of us to be together right now because a year ago today they started the whole thing. "They" started it—that's how I put it to myself—when "they" couldn't manage to intubate him, couldn't do the surgery that had been scheduled for 11 A.M., Wednesday, January 30, 1991.

When Elliot woke up with his throat raw from all "their" futile efforts to poke, jam, *ram* a breathing tube into him, he was enraged. We'd actually *warned* them that his chart said he was "hard to intubate," he reminded me.

He didn't need to remind me, I told him.

His voice kept on cracking. He flushed with anger, clenched his fist against the coverlet. "I make my living with my voice," he said. "I make my living *talking.* If they've damaged my vocal cords, I'll sue them, by God I will."

I handed him one of the lozenges the anesthesiology resident had prescribed and urged him not to strain, not to speak.

Climbing over the low concrete wall that separates the beach from the parking lot, I wonder how I'm going to make my skirt respectable enough for Nordstrom's. I shake and brush, but the navy blue jersey is still streaked with sand.

Between my rental car and Cabrillo Boulevard, a line of palm trees bends in the sea wind, sword-shaped fronds rattling.

In the poem I'm struggling to write, I explain to Elliot that I can't stop talking to him as if he were here, even though I know he's dead. Now I tell him what I guess is the major fact of the day: *They damaged a lot more than your vocal cords, darling, and I am suing them, just the way you would have.*

———

TUESDAY, FEBRUARY 11, 1992, 5:30 P.M.

It's decades since I've gone to mass, but the *brrring, brrring* of the sacramental bell that signals the transubstantiation is still familiar, still, to my ears, exactly like the jangle of a telephone.

St. Peter's Church "in the Loop," Chicago, is impressively crowded. Susan and I are in town for a conference at the University of Chicago, but she told the people in charge that we'd have to stay away from the proceedings today.

We weren't sure what to do, but we both knew it had to be something ceremonial.

Finally we settled on a visit to the Art Institute, where I thought I might stand for a while in front of Seurat's *Sunday Afternoon on the Island of La Grande Jatte*, followed by a trip to the nearest Catholic church, so I could light a candle for Elliot.

But to our surprise, there are late afternoon masses at St. Peter's Church, downtown in the center of Chicago's business district. And Susan said she'd be glad to come with me if I wanted to go to one.

Sunday Afternoon on the Grande Jatte is about life, I decided, about the long luminous moment my husband and I shared for thirty-four swift years, while the church and the candle and the mass are about death, or anyway about what is not life as we know it.

Brring. The holy bell pierces the silence again, and the rows of overcoated office workers all around us bow their heads, clasp their hands. A few delicately tap their breasts with closed fists, in a manner I remember from my childhood.

Lord, have mercy. Christ, have mercy. Lord, have mercy.

Brring! This is my body and this is my blood. Take. Eat. Drink. Brrring!

The mystic telephone line is open, or so I used to think when I was a kid, studying my catechism, going to Sunday mass with my father or my aunt.

Nothing's all that different now, either, except that the priest faces the congregation instead of the altar and speaks English instead of Latin.

2/11/92. The lessons for today are from 1 *Kings* 8:22–30 and *Mark* 7:1–13. The archaic messages are still powerful, even put into modern English as they have been in the revisionary spirit of John XXIII.

Kings, not inappropriate: *"Solomon stood before the altar of the Lord in the presence of the whole community of Israel, and stretching forth his hands toward heaven, he said, ". . . Look kindly on the prayer and petition of your servant, O Lord, my God."*

Yes, I want the Lord, my God, whoever or whatever he or she or *that* is, to look kindly on my prayers and petitions for my husband.

And *Mark,* too, seems relevant: *"The Pharisees and some of the experts in the law who had come from Jerusalem gathered around Jesus . . . . He said to them: "How accurately Isaiah prophesied about you hypocrites when he wrote, 'This people pays me lip service but their heart is far from me.' "*

Well, *Mark*'s a little harder to take personally—but maybe the experts in the law and the hypocrites are important.

Anyway, I wish this church itself were rather more archaic. With its cantilevered ceiling and indirect lighting, it looks a bit too much like an airport terminal or a hospital lobby. And it's very high-tech. As we discovered just before mass, you don't light a candle by dipping a taper into the flame of another candle, you light one by pushing a button which turns on a little electric light in the glass-covered bank of "candles."

5:34 in Chicago, 3:34 in Sacramento, California. A year ago, we weren't in the hospital lobby where we'd really planned to be: we were napping in the Davis condo. In the recovery room, Elliot was beginning to wake up, woozy. Twenty-nine minutes earlier, his pressure had fallen. 3:05. They had sent a hematocrit to the lab, the one that never came back.

This is My Body. And this is My Blood. My Blood.

The white-and-green-robed priest is quaffing—*quaffing,* not drinking, is the only word for what he does—the sacred wine. His shiny chalice flashes. The man on my right genuflects, then rises and brushes past me into the aisle. A line of communion-takers is forming, people in boots and scarves, eyes cast down, hands clasped.

I wish I could join them but I can't. *I don't think I believe in it, Elliot, though I wish I did and though I crossed myself so obsessively as they led me down that hospital corridor.*

A choir—of course there's a choir, I should have realized there would be a choir—and an organ strike up somewhere above us, behind us. Something vaguely Schubertian but not as good as Schubert. More like the sappy, Hershey Bar hymns they used to sing at the little half-French church in Vermont where I was taken every Sunday when I was a kid at camp. *Jesus loves us, Jesus needs us/Jesus holds us, Jesus feeds us:* that sort of thing.

To my chagrin, my eyes are filling, my shoulders are shaking, Susan is pressing a handkerchief into my hand, and I'm murmuring the Hail Mary, I can't stop myself, over and over again. *Hail Mary, full of grace, blessed art thou amongst women and blessed is the fruit of thy womb, Jesus. Holy Mary, Mother of God, pray for us sinners now and at the hour of our death. Amen.*

Now and at the hour of our death. Amen.

What I said under my breath in the hospital, in the lobby, in the elevator, and in the white room, while crossing myself.

Susan leans toward me and whispers in my ear. "See that woman two rows up on the left? The one in the gray fur coat? She's crying too. See?"

Everybody's in mourning today, Elliot. Everybody.

———

THURSDAY, FEBRUARY 27, 1992, 4:25 P.M.

"By the way," Kelly adds casually just as I'm about to hang up, "I ran into a guy from Lillick and Charles the other day when I was out in Vallejo, not Tom Minder but one of his associates, and he passed along an interesting rumor."

"Oh?" I pick up my ballpoint and begin scribbling again on the piece of scratch paper where I've been taking perfunctory notes on our conversation.

Even though Dan Kelly was censorious about my notebook at

that first meeting, I often jot down crucial points he's made on the phone, just so I have something vaguely factual to hang on to.

Not that today's skeletal record offers anything in the least consoling. On the contrary. Everything it says is disheartening, one way or another. *Jog payroll re records. Jan will call benefits re pension but get name(s?) for her. No depos of DVW & P for a few mos.*

"The word is I may be hearing from a claims man one of these days—"

"A claims man? What's a—?"

"Somebody from the risk management office that handles these cases for U. C."

"Oh, there's a special office? I didn't know there was such a—"

"Yeah, and this guy, associate at Lillick and Charles, said he thinks they may have a claims man call, may want to discuss a settlement with us."

"A settlement!" I breathe in sharply but keep on scribbling. *DK says someone at L & C said a claims man may—* "But isn't it awfully early to talk about a settlement?"

"Early?" Kelly laughs. "It isn't early if they know they don't have a leg to stand on."

"Well, of course they don't, of course I'm sure they don't," I agree, beginning to doodle a border of x's and little black boxes around my notes. "But do you really think they might settle even before you depose the *doctors?* I mean, if they settle before you—if they settle *now*, we'll never find out what happened, will we?"

"Maybe they don't want us to depose the doctors," Kelly says coolly. "Maybe they don't want us to find out what happened."

"Oh my God, but I—" I can hear my voice rising, feel my throat tightening.

"Hey, look, don't get too excited, it's just a rumor," Kelly says quellingly. "And besides, these things have to go through lots of committees, so it'll take quite some time in any case."

Sure, I understand, I tell him. Naturally it'll take some time.

Furthermore, he points out, a settlement is what we're really hoping for, isn't it? If it isn't, it should be.

I know that, I concede. He knows I know that.

And I do, I remind myself, as I carefully replace the phone on the receiver, not slamming it down, not screaming. I agree with him about a settlement, and I agree with all the friends who constantly assure me that "it'll be better when the lawsuit is over."

Then why do I feel so sick as I fold my notes and slip them into the pocket of my jeans for filing under "Wrongful Death"? Why am I grinding out my cigarette in the ashtray as if it were some noxious insect? Why am I murmuring curses to myself, why am I muttering *damn them, damn those bastards?*

————

WEDNESDAY, MARCH 4, 1992, 2 P.M.

Ash Wednesday, and a few wild irises are hesitantly opening, nervously unfurling their dark blue streaky petals in the sunniest, mildest meadows at the Sea Ranch. It's rained a lot lately— too much, as far as I'm concerned, though not as much as it did last year at this time—so the grass is exuberantly, luminously green.

Ashes to ashes, dust to dust, is that what the priests used to say (I remember how I hated it) or was it *dust thou art and unto dust thou shalt return?* They crossed our foreheads with some kind of gray stuff, *real ash* maybe, though it was greasy and hard to get off, and they intoned these portentous words in Latin. I always felt dizzy as they spoke, then vaguely nauseated on the way home, stumbling along with clasped hands when I was trying to be "good," trying to meditate, as they had told me I should, on how I was ashes and dust and would have to become ashes and dust again very soon.

I'm sitting at Elliot's end of the long table in the Sea Ranch study, staring out at the joyful meadow, the assertive green, the tentative irises. My "Wrongful Death" notebook blurs in front of me: where is this passage going? I'm writing about Dick's time line, about what it was like to read it for the first time, but the writing (and the rereading of the time line itself, which is open, too, on my left) is painful and scary.

From the living room comes the sound of a late Artie Shaw recording, cool, complex, and syncopated. Comforting. "Artishaw," Bob calls him, or sometimes "Artichaud"—at least I think that's what he's saying.

Bob is "Yaddoing" here this week: he invented the verb ("to Yaddo, to be Yaddoed, to have Yaddoed, etc.") in order to define the kind of security I decided I got at the writer's colony last fall when I began my book about Elliot's death, a security so salutary that he and a few other friends resolved to replicate it for me by being "around" when I was working on hard parts of the manuscript.

When he "Yaddoes," Bob does his own thing in the living room or the kitchen or out on the deck, and often he plays music like "Artishaw," so I know he's there and I don't get too distressed by the worst sentences in, say, Dick's time line. Or, rather, if I do get too distressed, I can go out and chat with him for a while, have him distract me, console me, even now and then cheer me up and on.

Dorrie is coming this weekend to "Yaddo" too—and to check out the wild irises, the lush sweet miner's lettuce that's growing under the cypresses, the mushrooms burgeoning in the windbreak.

Neither knows, though, about the greeting on the answering machine. I just discovered it last night.

There's an old answering machine in the study here: Elliot and I turned it on occasionally, if we were going to be up at the Sea Ranch for more than a week or two. None of us used it or even noticed it last summer, so Elliot's greeting wasn't erased; as I learned last night in the middle of the night, it's emphatically still there.

I can't imagine how it got plugged in or why I pressed the PLAY button on the machine, which sits next to my old type-writer from graduate school, but anyway I did. Maybe I really unconsciously understood that I'd hear Elliot's message, the same sort of message we erased with such alacrity from the machine at home the day after he died.

Hi (clearing his throat selfconsciously, I can tell), *this is Elliot Gilbert. None of us can come to the phone right now, but if you want to leave a message for me or Sandra or Roger or Kathy or Susanna, please leave it after the sound of the beep.*

I played the greeting over and over again, a ritual nine times altogether, then cried half the night.

Hi, this is Elliot Gilbert. Dust thou art and unto dust thou shalt return.

———

THURSDAY, MARCH 19, 1992, 11 A.M.

"This is Sandra Gilbert, I'm returning your call."

"Yes," says Michelle, Dan Kelly's secretary, "Mr. Kelly has been out of town this week but he calls in regularly, and he wanted me to tell you that there was a trial-setting conference this week."

"A trial-setting conference?"

"Yes, a trial-setting conference, that's what they call it."

"Oh? Does that mean we're definitely going to trial?"

"No, not necessarily. It's just that they all go in there, and they decide about the dates for the trial and the settlement conference and so forth."

"Oh, I see."

"Mr. Kelly is out of town this week but one of the junior people here went and sat in for him, it was on Monday, Monday in Sacramento of course."

"Oh, okay. So—?"

"Well, I have the dates for you. The trial and the settlement conference."

"Uh huh? Yeah? So when—?"

"Right now, the settlement conference has been set for the twenty-eighth of May, May twenty-eighth, and the trial date has been set for the seventeenth of June, June the seventeenth, that's a Wednesday and the twenty-eighth is a Thursday a few weeks before, so Mr. Kelly wants you to know that you should keep those dates free—"

"Well, of course, of course I will."

"Good, that's great. I'll tell him I spoke to you."

"Yes, please do, tell him I said hi. Although, my God, the seventeenth of June is my son's birthday, it's weird, we were deposed on *my* birthday and now the trial date—"

"Well," says Michelle, "between you and me, don't get yourself too upset about it. I mean, they just set those dates arbitrarily; they're never firm. In other words, I wouldn't count on any of those dates if I were you."

———

MONDAY, APRIL 6, 1992, 3 P.M.

"No matter how strong the case is, I would anticipate discounting any settlement for medical malpractice by a substantial percentage," Kelly says dryly. His voice, crackling through the receiver, rises a little. "Hey, I'd expect a substantial discount on the demand even if they threw the guy out the window!"

As usual, I scribble in my notebook. *Even if they threw the guy out the window.*

Kelly has rather unexpectedly begun interrogating me about my notion of a proper settlement.

A minute ago, I nervously mentioned a sum that the kids and I had calculated last fall: we multiplied Elliot's annual salary by ten, added miscellaneous expenses mentioned in the official "Complaint" (medical bills, funeral and burial costs, etc.), subtracted a modest annual amount times ten for what we consider my husband's quite low "consumption," and then added the flat $250,000 that the state of California allows for "loss of care, comfort, and consortium."

Kelly laughed noisily into the phone. "You'd probably be lucky to get a third of that," he said, explaining that claims for medical malpractice have to be significantly discounted because, contrary to popular opinion—*very* contrary to popular opinion—judges and juries are for the most part recalcitrant not just about awarding substantial damages to plaintiffs but even about ruling in favor of plaintiffs. "And of course the other side always knows that. Their settlement offer is always predicated on that. Even if they also know they threw the guy out the window." He chuckles. Clearly he's fond of his bleakly comic little example.

For some reason, I am too, and I too chuckle. I imagine a *New Yorker* cartoon: a middle-aged man in a hospital gown struggling and protesting as he is wrestled out a window by two white-coated doctors.

The man in my cartoon isn't Elliot, of course. Although they might as well have thrown *him* out a window also, I guess.

Kelly is filling me in on the risks the plaintiff faces in going to trial. Strong cases settle *before* trial, he emphasizes for the umpteenth time. Sixty to seventy percent of the malpractice cases that go to trial are won by defendants, he reminds me. Why just the other day he was at a meeting with—and here, with un-characteristic reverence, he intones the names of what I suppose are a group of local legal luminaries—"and hey, we're not a bunch of stumblebums, we're not some Willy Lump Lump from out on the avenues trying his first case, but what we all had in common was we just lost medical malpractice actions!"

The lawyer sighs. On the one hand, he confides, he's still ex-pecting to hear from a claims man; on the other hand, the other side keeps sending special interrogatories. Too many special in-terrogatories.

Why are they doing that, I wonder.

"Too many lawyers," he says with surprising glumness. "Too many lawyers, too many special interrogatories. The firm's too big, like a lot of others. I keep telling people that, I keep pointing it out. I tell them, hey, Dr. Ruth has been preaching for years that size isn't everything."

At least he leaves me laughing, I reflect. "Thanks for making my day," I tell him.

"Think nothing of it," he replies, "anytime you want to see the dark side of the moon I'll show it to you."

"The dark side of the moon" is obviously his favorite meta-phor, and I have to agree that it's apt.

———

MONDAY, MAY 18, 1992, 11:15 A.M.

I'm staring down at the table, idly tracing the wood grain with one finger. This is a smaller table in a smaller room with a less spectacular view, but it's the same glossy walnut as the long conference table. "It doesn't seem fair, it seems awfully unfair," I protest, not looking up.

"Who said it was fair?" Even Kelly sounds vaguely regretful. "Of course it isn't fair. But it's the law. You and your husband had the foresight to purchase the insurance, you and he paid for the insurance, the money is yours by right regardless of any compensation they may owe you. Nevertheless, when calculating economic damages, they're entitled to subtract the amount of the life insurance you've received."

"It isn't even that I care about the money, really. It's just that I'm tired of everything seeming to be so *easy* for them. I mean, it looks as though they can just kill somebody and hardly pay for their negligence at all."

Kelly grimaces with comic helplessness. "They certainly have to pay less for wrongful death than for severe personal injury."

"It isn't fair, it's bizarre," I reiterate plaintively. "What about the man in Vacaville, or is it Vallejo, whose eye doctor gave him the wrong glasses and he got so sick and crazy that he couldn't have sex with his wife, and she just won two million dollars or something for loss of consortium. I saw it in the *Chronicle* the other day."

"That award is going to be overturned," Kelly assures me. "It won't stand in California. The appellate court will cut it in half, at least—"

He wanted me to come in this morning so we could discuss the specific details of my "demand," in case (as is still rumored) the other side is really inclined to offer a settlement.

By now it seems to me we've drunk at least a quart of coffee, or anyway *I* have, and my doodles have filled so many sheets of paper that out of sheer embarrassment I've been reduced to rubbing the tabletop instead of scribbling.

And anyway, I observe, still plaintive, how can they begin to talk about settling when Kelly hasn't even deposed deVere White yet?

The deposition has been scheduled for early next week, Kelly reminds me again, Monday the twenty-fifth, but then the settlement conference is slated for early in the morning on Thursday the twenty-eighth, so it's imperative that we—

My self-pity swells. I really do feel like crying. "How can we be sure what we ought to ask for when we aren't certain yet about what happened and we won't be until you depose the damn doctors!"

"You may have to face the fact that we'll never know more about what happened than we know right now," Kelly answers sternly. Just what Dick said a month ago.

"Another thing," Kelly adds. "What about a structured settlement? They may offer a structured settlement. They often do in these cases."

"A structured settlement? What's that?"

"A lump sum upfront, usually, then monthly payments over a certain period, maybe for your lifetime."

"I don't know." This is a completely new idea to me, and I'm confused by it.

"I just did a structured settlement in another wrongful death case," Kelly confides. "Woman in Marin county. She's getting a pretty good lifetime annuity, but I bet you might do better."

"What kind of case?" I'm sulky, not looking up.

"Open and shut. The husband was a man about your husband's age. Had a history of cardiac problems. Goes to his doctor with crushing chest pains. The doctor says he's strained his muscles. Three hours later he's dead of a heart attack."

That sounds ghastly, I concede, it sounds *open and shut.* Why in the world might my case be stronger?

Well, because this particular guy had a "history," he explains. Which on the one hand does suggest that the doctor should have been able to diagnose his problem, but on the other hand implies that the man might have died from the heart attack anyway. Whereas, of course, Elliot didn't have a history of hemorrhaging, so—

"But even if you do better than she did," he warns again, "you'll have to reconcile yourself to the fact that, since you can't sue for punitive damages in California, the award in a wrongful death action is going to be a lot smaller than you personally think it should be."

I attempt an ironic smile. "You've made that pretty clear," I admit. "And I've been reading a book that says the same thing. You'd probably like it. I'll lend it to you when I finish it."

Kathy sent me this novel last week. She found it in a second-hand bookstore in Boston. It's by a Wes Sokolosky type, a doctor-lawyer named John R. Feegel (M.D., J.D.).

I dogeared the relevant passage this morning. Maybe I'll copy it tomorrow and send it to Kelly, though of course he knows it all already. *"Some big negligence lawyer from Miami had once remarked in a seminar that the purpose of that big ax you always see hanging on the wall of the railroad car was to allow the conductor, after a wreck, to go through the train, killing the injured survivors, thereby keeping damages to a minimum."*

———

WEDNESDAY, JUNE 3, 1992, 4 P.M.

It's too hot and bright under the skylight this afternoon: the glare whitens the pile of old medical bills I'm shuffling through, makes them hard to read. But I don't want to move, I want to sit right here at the dining room table so I can look at Elliot's portrait and chat with him in my head while I rummage for the Coding Summary and the other documents Kelly still needs.

Jan, Kelly's paralegal, will be here in a few minutes to pick up some materials I forgot to send her. I guess I forgot about them because I really didn't want to do this job.

I've sent the Coding Summary to the Walkup offices several times already, but I want to be absolutely certain they have it. Besides recording the crucial diagnosis of "Acute Posthemorrhagic Anemia," it's also a bill for more than $100,000—

$102,113.07 to be specific—for Elliot's disastrous day in the hospital, including the services of the code team that spent fifty-five futile minutes trying to resuscitate him.

I gaze ruefully at my husband's rueful image. *It cost you $102,113.07 to die, darling.*

Of course, as Kelly has pointed out to me, the hospital won't be required to reimburse Blue Shield for these costs, even though some were incurred because of medical negligence. The law doesn't require the hospital to reimburse insurers in such a situation, just as it doesn't oblige doctors to pay punitive damages.

I'm glad, though, that Jan is coming over. Maybe I can ask her a few questions in confidence. I want to know why "they" (and who are "they?" Kelly? the other side?) cancelled the settlement conference scheduled for the twenty-eighth of May, and why Dr. deVere White still hasn't been deposed.

And I especially want to know why the other side has now asked for *my* medical records.

"Do you have a GP, family practice doctor, or something?" Kelly asked on the phone the other day. "I got a call from a guy at Lillick and Charles. They want to look at your records, at least for the last six months."

I was shocked. "Why in the world would they—?"

But he was unperturbed. "He's just doing his homework, just doing what he's supposed to do."

"But why *my* records?"

"Well, frankly, they need to know *you're* not terminal. I mean, if *you're* about to kick off they won't need to offer a settlement, will they?"

TUESDAY, JULY 7, 1992, 5 P.M.

"You sound awful," I tell Kelly, cradling the phone on my shoulder as I fumble for a pen.

"Upper respiratory infection," he says lugubriously. "Had it for a few days."

"Well, I'm just returning your call, I won't keep you long—although I *would* like to know what's been—"

"Happening?" I can hear him blowing his nose, clearing his throat. "We're in our trial mode now. I haven't heard boo from them about a settlement."

"Oh my God—I thought they were going to—"

"So did I. So did I. But there hasn't been any movement in that direction. No movement at all so far as I can tell. They've disclosed their expert witnesses, we've disclosed ours. I'm deposing deVere White on the twenty-first, then they're deposing one of our guys, then I'm deposing theirs. The new settlement conference is scheduled for July 29—be sure and keep that free—and trial is set for—"

"And what about Poonamallee? Reitan? Are you going to depose them?" I'm so energized by this news that I've pushed my chair back from my desk; I'm standing up and pacing back and forth in front of the bookcase in my study, flicking ashes on the carpet.

"Poonamallee?" Kelly coughs rather pathetically. "They're hunting him down. Seems he's not at the medical center any more, he's gone on to bigger and better things. But don't worry, don't worry. We'll catch up to him if we need him."

"And the experts? Who *are* they? What do they *say?*"

Kelly produces a rasping chuckle. "Funny. Both San Francisco men. Ours is Dr. Weber, theirs is Dr. Weiss. I can't imagine what theirs is going to say. Ours is prepared to testify that your husband's treatment was below the standard of care, ready to testify that it all happened more or less the way we know it did. And we've taken some advice from several other consultants, too."

"So what exactly do they think did happen, when did—"

"Well, as you realize, that's not clear yet. But maybe we'll find out something more from this deVere White of yours when I depose him. Of course we'll focus on the hematocrit, the one that came back at 6:30, probably sent at 3:05—"

"The hematocrit that came back at 6:30 was probably sent at 3:05?"

For some reason, Kelly and I have never talked at much length about the crucial hematocrit, perhaps because its relevance to the case seemed so obvious.

"Do you really think that the hematocrit sent at 3:05 came back at 6:30?" I ask him. *"The hematocrit of seventeen?"*

"It's certainly possible," he replies.

"But if that's what happened . . ."

Until now, I didn't think (and didn't think Dick thought) that the hematocrit sent at 3:05 might be the very same hematocrit whose results were returned at 6:30, although from a logical point of view—"by Ockham's razor," as my husband used to say, the principle of reasoning that suggests one should always look for the least complicated explanation of a problem—it would make perfect sense.

Maybe Dick hasn't told me about this possibility, I speculate, because it seems too awful to consider. In fact, my reading of Dick's story has perhaps self-protectively evaded such a conclusion. "The notes," Dick wrote, "indicate that a hematocrit was sent to the laboratory at 3:05; *there is no report of this hematocrit in the record. Note that a 'Critical Lab Report' dated 2/11/91 lists no hematocrits between 2:45 and 6:30 P.M."*

And later Dick wrote: "A hematocrit of 17 was recorded at

6:30. *It is not clear when this sample was obtained since there was no order for one and no notation of 'hematocrit sent' as there was at 3:05."* And later still, as if he too sought to evade the chilling possibility that the 6:30 hematocrit reported on blood that had been drawn at 3:05: *"I presume the sample was obtained at 6:00,"* he wrote, *"since the drop in blood pressure would essentially have required it."*

I sit down heavily in my chair and stare at the Baby Elliot photos on my desk. With his golden curls and his cherubic Campbell kid cheeks, eighteen-month-old Baby Elliot gazes back quizzically, his raised eyebrows seeming to say *World, what are you all about anyway?*.

Baby, I tell him silently, conspiratorially, *baby, if they let you lie there for three-and-a-half hours with a hematocrit of seventeen, they killed you, baby. They killed you, sweetheart, just as surely as if they threw you out the window.*

19

Q. Were you involved at all with the resuscitative efforts of this patient?

A. I arrived when he was just terminating.

—Deposition of RALPH W. DEVERE WHITE, M.D.,
Tuesday, July 21, 1992

SATURDAY, OCTOBER 24, 1992, 2:20 P.M./ TUESDAY, JULY 21, 1992, 10:37 A.M.

"Some of these questions and answers may look pretty innocuous to you, Sandy," Dick says slowly, putting his Diet Pepsi down in the only bare spot he can find on the coffee table, "but they're all important." He gazes mildly at me over the top of the plastic-bound deposition. "Your guy was brilliant—jumping around, crazy like a fox, building his case one brick at a time."

Dan Kelly. He means Dan Kelly was brilliant in his deposition of R. W. deVere White. Well, that should be no surprise. Although I've had this transcript for several months and so far haven't been able to see the point of half the exchanges between the lawyer and the doctor. "We'll go over it together, page by page," Dick had said reassuringly when he and Leah picked me up at Dulles a few nights ago. "Half the time they're talking in technicalities that a layperson wouldn't get, but I'd say the whole case is basically outlined right there."

I've been in the Washington, D.C., area since Tuesday: I did a poetry reading downtown on Wednesday and gave a talk at a conference there the next day, but of course I'm staying in Bethesda, near Leah and Dick. The tiny living room of my hotel suite, overlooking the Ramada Inn parking lot and a long wide street beyond, is already littered with books and papers I needed for the reading or the talk. Now the general clutter has been swelled by copies of the deposition, along with more books and papers on malpractice that Dick has brought me. *Expert Witness*—a collection of rather sickeningly gripping "true stories" by a doctor in Chicago who *has* been willing to testify against other doctors from time to time. A fat file on the Andy Warhol case; an even fatter file on the Libby Zion case—both notorious dramas of wrongful death arising from what was alleged to be medical negligence at New York Hospital. Plus a stack of other articles Dick has been gradually accumulating in his office at NIH.

"I don't *get* a lot of what's going on," I admit to Dick. "I mean, for example, what's all this stuff about "volume" and "low fluid" and "high output" on pages 42 and 43? And the stuff about the change in urine output? And the—?"

"Hang on, Sandy, hang on," he says soothingly. "It'll be best if we begin at the beginning and go through the whole thing one step at a time so you can get a sense of how your lawyer develops his argument. That is—" he casts a worried frown in my direction— "if you think you can take it."

"Okay, sure. Sure I can take it," I tell him as I get up to pour myself some more coffee.

I can take it, Elliot, if I have to, for your sake. I know you'd do the same for me.

Dick is sitting on the sofa, calmly turning pages. Ballpoint in hand, I settle myself in a tub chair opposite him. "Okay, sure. Okay, let's begin."

BE IT REMEMBERED THAT, pursuant to Notice of Taking Deposition, and on the 21st day of July 1992, commencing at the hour of 10:37 a.m., at the University of California, Davis, School of Medicine, 4301 X Street, Suite 2210, Sacramento, California, . . . personally appeared RALPH W. DEVERE WHITE, M.D., produced as a witness in said action. . . . DANIEL J. KELLY, ATTORNEY AT LAW . . . appeared as counsel on behalf of the Plaintiffs. THOMAS G. MINDER, ATTORNEY AT LAW . . . appeared as counsel on behalf of the Defendants.

At the UCDMC. Sacramento. Searing summer air, hot and dry: desert air. Dusty palm trees outside the windows. A not-quite-properly-air-conditioned conference room, no doubt.

BE IT REMEMBERED and so forth. The familiar formula. Dick and I turn pages in silence. The usual exposition. *Who are you? What do you do? How long have you been doing it?* DeVere White doesn't have to be told to answer *yes* or *no* and/or as fully as he can. Perhaps this means he's been deposed before. Perhaps all doctors are deposed with numbing regularity, even this doctor we had thought so trustworthy, so incapable of negligence.

"Take a look at page 5," Dick says. "Start with line 12."

I turn dutifully to the passage, but It seems fairly routine to me, just more exposition.

Q. What condition did Mr. Gilbert have that you were treating him for surgically?

A. Prostate cancer.

Q. He had had some prior hormonal therapy for the tumors; is that correct?

A. That's correct.

Q. Is it the purpose of that type of therapy to reduce the size of the prostate?

A. Yes.

Q. Is one of the purposes of such therapy to—by reducing the size of the prostate to make surgery a bit easier?

A. You can say that, yes.

"So? So what? It's all true." I'm puzzled and frown at Dick.

"Notice he doesn't say anything about having *warned* you about possible consequences of this treatment, although later on he claimed that the gland was 'stuck' because of the hormones."

"Oh." I stare down at the page.

Q. Have you yourself used that type of therapy with patients with this condition?

A. Yes.

MR. MINDER: That he intended on operating on?

MR. KELLY: Yes.

THE WITNESS: Yes.

MR. KELLY: Q. Where did he receive that hormonal therapy?

A. Here.

Q. Under your direction or somebody else's?

A. Mine.

"You see," Dick observes, "now they can't claim that the hormone therapy was problematic. And keep on reading this page, page 6."

Q. He had had other consults regarding his condition, correct?

A. Correct.

Q. Do you recall—again, this is not a memory quiz—one was at Stanford?

A. Yes. I mean, he came to me in August having had the diagnosis and he saw, as well, Peter Carroll in San Francisco. He saw Dr. Stamey in Stanford, and he saw Dr. Bagshaw in Stanford.

Q. And had he received, as far as you know, from those consults differing opinions regarding whether to operate or not operate?

A. Yes.

"And this," Dick says, "this is to establish that surgery was *not* the only option. But keep on going."

Q. Did you tell him you were of the opinion that surgery was warranted for treatment of this condition?

A. Yes. I mean, we had long discussions about various forms of treatment over those ensuing four months, and, yes, I told him I thought the best way to treat it was surgery.

Right, darling, he said that to you over and over. Though you were so scared. "I mean," he said, "I can't tell you what to do. But ye're a young man. Ye could have thirty more years."

"And *now*," Dick notes, "they can't say that *you* somehow insisted on surgery despite their best advice. And the next discussion they have—where he asks deVere White about the surgery having been postponed because of the anesthesiologists' inability to intubate Elliot—*that's* there because he wants to put that issue on the record."

Put it on the record, Elliot. He wanted to put it on the record that you lost your voice, and you might have sued them yourself, you told me so.

"Page 9," says Dick. "Go to page 9. Here Kelly is trying to establish that the surgery took longer than usual."

Q. . . . generally, what's the ballpark time frame for the surgery?

A. . . . I expect the actual surgery to take me three to three-and-a-half hours.

Q. In this particular case, do you recall what the surgical time was?

A. No, but I know I was down in the office by 1:00 o'clock. So it wasn't excessively long.

Q. When did you start the surgery?

A. He would have gotten in the room around 7:30.

Q. Is it your testimony that some of the time was spent awaiting results of the frozen sections?

A. Yes.

"Well, he certainly wasn't in his office at *1:00*," I tell Dick bitterly. "It was around 1:45 when he came to see us in the lobby, still wearing his greens. He *said* he'd just come from the OR."

"Of course, neither of you can be absolutely certain of the timing, can you?" Dick is in a benefit-of-the-doubt mood on this one.

"*I* can," I reply sullenly. "I'll never forget any of it."

"Do you think you can keep on reading?" he asks.

"Yeah, sure. Okay, sure."

Q. Were there any complications with the surgery that you re-call, the actual surgical procedures?

A. There were no complications. He had a fairly large gland . . . and it was a stock gland. It didn't just sort of peel away, so it was a little trickier. He oozed a little more because there was a little more stock. But at the end of the case I was extremely satisfied with the result.

"Stock!" I can't help laughing. "Remember, I *told* you, he kept saying it was 'stock, stock,' and I didn't know what it meant until the kids said he meant 'stuck'! The poor court reporter must have made the same mistake."

Dick smiles blandly, humoring me.

Stock, Elliot! As if you were a pot of soup, a side of beef boiling down!

Q. The—you might consult the operative report, Doctor.

That report notes that at some point in time two sutures slipped off the dorsal vein plexus causing brisk bleeding. Do you find that?

A. Well, what I'm finding—when we—we normally put two types around it [ties?] rather than sutures and then you have to cut across. And sometimes they do slip and that's why you put them there, to bunch it up, and then we just take a 20 chromic suture—

THE REPORTER: Excuse me, what kind of suture?

MR. MINDER: 20.

THE WITNESS: Our 20 chromic suture. So, I mean, we like to not have them, but we prepare that as a regular possibility.

"This is to establish the source of the bleeding in the OR," Dick says, "and to show how much blood loss there was. Quite a lot, in fact. Estimated as 2,500 cc's. But they argue that it's within the standard deviation, so-called. That is, it's a little higher than normal, but not out of sight."

Q. And in closing up the patient, Jackson Pratt drains were used?

A. Yes. . . .

Q. How do you—I hate to use the word ensure, but ensure the patency of such drains? Is there a way to do so?

"Patency means openness," Dick explains. "Kelly wants to know how they can be sure the drains are open and actually *draining?* As you realize, this is going to be important later on. He's laying a lot of groundwork here."

Q. Is there any way that you know to ensure the patency of such Jackson Pratt drains once they're placed in the patient and the patient's closed?

285

A. No, I suppose there's no way of assuring it except that if the drains are draining, you presume they're patent.

"This of course begs the question," Dick comments, "because drains may drain *some* but not *all*—as was evidently the case with Elliot. And now, you'll notice on the next few pages the other *dramatis personae* in the case are introduced: Poonamallee is introduced as chief resident (important because *he's* the one who wrote 'liver failure' on the death certificate), and another urology resident named Fishman is introduced, along with Reitan, the anesthesiologist. But on page 16 we begin to get to real meat, stuff about the hematocrits and so on."

Q. The anesthesia record has, as I look at it, a notation for hematocrit of 32.
A. Yes.
Q. There appear to be some other hematocrits that are recorded. This one I really can't make out. It could be a 23 or a 28 and then another one of 25.
A. Okay. Yes. These are intraoperative, are they?
Q. After the fluid replacement—do you know what his hematocrit was when he was back to the floor post-surgery?
A. 32.
Q. Do you know when that hematocrit was done with reference to the conclusion of surgery?
A. Approximately two hours.
Q. There's a word in medicine, equilibrate. you're familiar with that in terms of hematocrit in a surgical patient who's received fluids?

"He's raising this issue in an anticipatory way, Sandy," Dick interjects. "But obviously, it's going to get crucial."

A. Yes.

Q. And is it not true that the initial hematocrit may be a bit deceptive because the patient is not equilibrated?

A. That's true.

Q. The hematocrits in this case, how often were they ordered post-op?

A. They—I don't understand an order for that. Another one would have been done that evening and one the next morning.

"He's already admitting they weren't following the hematocrits closely, despite the blood loss in the OR."

Q. Let me again show you the chart.

Tom, I apologize for doing this, but I've got these by numbers and we'll be here all day trying to figure this out.

MR. MINDER: That's all right.

MR. KELLY: Q. There's an order 2/11/91 for medication given this patient for tachycardia; is that correct?

A. That's what it says.

"He's moving fast. Now he's laying the groundwork for cause of death, hinting at what his argument will be. Tachycardia—a racing heartbeat, with some irregularity—can be a sign of shock."

Q. What is that medication?

A. I'm not sure. It was ordered by one of the anesthesiologists. I mean, it looks like propranolol, but I'm not sure. . . .

Q. That medication does not treat what's causing the tachycardia in the patient, does it?

A. Again, probably the most appropriate person to answer it is the anesthesiologist. I would presume that they thought it was.

Q. Well, tachycardia can be some indication that the patient's in shock, correct?

A. Correct.

Q. And what I'm saying is, as far as you know, that medication would treat the symptom but not the underlying cause of the tachycardia, if you know?

A banging in the chest, a nausea, a dizziness, a trembling. Make it stop.

They did make it stop, Elliot. But the wrong way. Like treating a brain tumor with bufferin, Kelly told me.

A. Could I rephrase it?

Q. Sure.

A. I think if you thought the patient was in shock, that's not the drug you would use. If you thought the patient had tachycardia for a different reason, I presume that's why the drug was given. . . .

Q. Would you agree with the statement that assuming the tachycardia was not life threatening that treating tachycardia before determining its cause is poor practice?

MR. MINDER: Well, by poor practice, you mean practice not within the standard of care?

MR. KELLY: I mean in terms of the patient.

MR. MINDER: Well—

MR. KELLY: I'm not asking a standard of care question.

"He's jumping around, very cannily jumping around," says Dick. "Very crafty."

THE WITNESS: I think you really have to ask the anesthesiologists because it's a very—it's become a very specialized field and patients receive lots of medication. So I presume, again, they thought that it was being given for a specific reason.

"He's on the ropes here," Dick murmurs.

MR. KELLY: Q. As far as you know, though, was the tachycardia that was being addressed, was that life threatening at that particular point in time?

A. No, I don't think so.

"The point is," Dick reiterates, "if the tachycardia had been a life-threatening arrhythmia of cardiac origin—the kind of thing associated with a heart attack—it might have been okay to give the propranolol, but here he makes the key admission that it *wasn't* life threatening, so it wasn't okay to give the propranolol. Instead, they should have tried harder to figure out what was wrong. To consider the drops in pressure, to trace the hematocrits."

Q. If you have a patient that has a high pulse and a low blood pressure, that can be indicative, can it not, of a low fluid status?

A. Correct.

"Low fluid status, Sandy, means not enough volume in circulation—that is, not enough *blood;* the high pulse and the low pressure should have made them consider the possibility that he might be bleeding."

Q. Were you involved at all with the resuscitative efforts of this patient?

A. I arrived when he was just terminating. I arrived before he terminated, but he had not responded at that time.

Trying to control myself, I turn to Dick with one eyebrow ironically raised, impersonating a tough-cool-cookie-Lauren-Bacall detective lady. "Terminating," I say viciously (though why I should be vicious to Dick I can't imagine). "I suppose that's the sort of language you as a physician are used to."

He looks back at me sadly. "Not at all," he says. "Not at all. I find it just as offensive as *you* do. But maybe that's the way these guys think they have to talk for the record. Maybe they talk differently among themselves."

Terminated, Elliot. How strange that you, who were so curiously fond of flicks like Terminator 1, 2, 3, ad nauseam, should have terminated—or been terminated?—instead of just plain dying. The trembling, the tremors, the tipping backward, darling—that was all termination!

Q. Are you aware that the Jackson Pratt drains were suctioned as part of that resuscitation?

A. Yes.

Q. And do you recall what the blood volume was that was suctioned from the patient?

A. There was a large serous—it was serous sanguineous fluid that I saw. I mean, it was a large quantity. I don't know the exact number. It looked like blood-tinged fluid.

Dick sighs and shakes his head wearily. Plainly he doesn't believe the testimony.

MR. KELLY: Off the record.

(Discussion off the record.)

MR. KELLY: Q. Let me show you the—I think it's the code sheet on the patient, and the notation is, "drains JP." That would be the Jackson Pratt drains?

A. Yes.

Q. "Total output 2,450 red blood." Do you see that?

A. Yes.

Says Dick, "A minute ago he probably made what the lawyers call an impeachable statement. He probably impeached himself here, because, you have to get this, 'red blood' is ward shorthand. The phrase 'red blood' *means* 'this looks like real blood,' not 'serous sanguinous fluid.' In other words, some doctor in the recovery room wrote those words, 'red blood,' because that's what he thought he was describing."

Q. Is it your testimony that that's not what you saw being retrieved from those drains?

MR. MINDER: In other words, red blood?

"His attorney doesn't want him to answer too fast here," Dick comments. "He wants him to pull himself together and notice what's happening."

"Wake up and smell the coffee?" I ask sardonically.

THE WITNESS: Well, see, I wasn't there when that was hooked up. So it wasn't a matter of seeing it. When I came in, the code was just ending. So I just looked on the wall because someone said they suctioned a lot.

In my recollection of looking, it didn't look like bright red blood. It looked like serous stained fluid. I didn't go examine it. I was obviously more worried about the patient. I didn't see that, per se.

"He's trying to recover himself," notes Dick, "since he knows he may well have impeached himself, which would be disastrous. Red blood in the record, 'serous sanguinous fluid in his testimony.' Not good."

MR. KELLY: Q. Assuming that was red blood that was retrieved, that's a large amount, correct?

A. Agreed.

More than half the blood in the body, sweetheart. More than half the blood in the body. Kicking the door, smashing my toe, screaming, no voice left.

Q. At some point in time post-op this patient had a hematocrit of 17?

A. Correct.

Q. When was that with reference to the patient's ultimate death, if you recall?

A. It was approximately 1730. I would have to check that to be exact.

Outside the hospital. Blue and windy. "Can we see him now, Doctor? Is he all right?" "Fine, just fine. I just saw him. He was woozy, woozy from the anesthesia. Said somethin' like 'I feel lousy.' You'd better go to dinner. No use waitin' around here."

Q. Well, let me see. I might be able to—1800 hours, it says, hematocrit 17.

A. Okay.

Q. And the patient's cardiac arrest is noted at 1920. Is that your recollection?

A. Yes.

"It's as if they were moving through molasses," Dick said when he first read the records. "Every doctor's nightmare," he reported his friend who headed a major pediatric service had said.

Q. So that would be about an hour and 20 minutes?
A. Yes.
Q. Generally speaking, would you agree that a hematocrit [drop?] of about 3 percentage points for the hematocrit corresponds to 500 cc's of blood loss?

MR. MINDER: You're asking that in the abstract?
MR. KELLY: Yes.
THE WITNESS: In the abstract, I think where you've given lots of fluid, that may be a little—a little different.

"He's waffling, Sandy."

MR. KELLY: Q. But have you yourself ever used that type of calculation to try to figure out blood loss via what the hematocrit shows?
A. Yes, yes. No, I agree.

"Now he's getting nervous, Sandy."

Q. Do you know how it was that that hematocrit that we've referenced, the one for 17, was done?
A. When the team made rounds, which I think was around 5:00, 5:15, in that time, and he was making a lot of urine and because he was making a lot of urine, someone asked what it was and I think it was a while before it was 32, so a new crit was ordered.

I'm frowning at Dick, bewildered. "What does the urine have to do with it?"

"Too much urine might indicate that too much fluid had been given," he answers with professorial neutrality, "resulting in a dilution of red blood cells. Still, you could never get a drop from 32 to 17 that way. You could never get the kind of dilution, the kind of *acute anemia* that eventually occurred, just from giving too much fluid. Unless there are hemolytic causes (which would result in jaundice, and there was evidently no jaundice), that kind of dilution is a sign of bleeding."

Standing in the white room next to your body. The girls weeping. "What happened, Doctor? What happened to my father?" "I don't know, luv," he said. "I don't know. He was makin' good water." We thought the good water was being offered to us as a consolation.

Q. Do you know who ordered it?

A. I asked for it to be done. I don't know who actually wrote the order.

"Remember, Sandy, no order appears on the record."

Q. Who gave you information of what was going on with the patient?

A. The team did. I mean, I went up there.

Q. Did you see the patient?

A. Yes.

Q. And you say he was putting out a lot of urine?

A. Yes.

Q. Eventually that was not the case, correct?

"Here he's preparing for later, Sandy. An important step."

A. Eventually, no. At that time he was making lots of urine.

Q. What did that indicate to you as the operating surgeon that he was putting out a lot of urine?

294

A. I thought that he was receiving a lot of fluid, very good refusion (phon.), was probably a little more—too much and his kidneys were putting it out again.

"The word is 'perfusion' and that's a problem here, Sandy, because the kidneys are a principal organ of equilibration. But in this case it was misleading simply to focus on the kidneys."

Q. And why, then, did you order the hematocrit or agree to it?
A. Because they said he had had a drop in blood pressure and they gave him fluids, the blood pressure come [sic] back up. He was putting out a lot of fluid, slightly tachycardiac. His Jackson Pratts were draining. He was making an awful lot of urine.
 So his last crit was I think then about two hours, roughly, beforehand and so they said his oxygenation was fine.

"Not true about the last crit, Sandy. According to the record, it had been at least four hours since they actually *had* a hematocrit in hand because the one sent at 3:05 never came back."

I produce a bleak laugh. "Unless it was the one that came back at six or sixthirty!"

Q. Were you made aware of the hematocrit reading of 17?
A. No.
Q. Where were you, then, when they had that reading?
A. I had gone to a meeting at that time. It was around, I think, 7 o'clock.

"Didn't he say earlier that they got that reading at six?" I ask Dick.

He shrugs cynically, as if to say, what difference does it make what they say, at this point?

Q. Dr. Poonamalle [sic], I believe, ordered further hematocrits after that, correct?

A. He—I didn't write the order, so, yes, it would be—one of the residents would have—the whole team was there, so I don't know which one wrote the order.

"He's waffling again, Sandy."

The team. Doesn't the concept of the team have a sort of grim charm, Elliot? One imagines them—or imagines them imagining themselves—as a kind of star football team, gladiators (as one medical sociologist said of surgeons) holding the line in a rousing game against death. Except, evidently, nobody knew what position he or she was supposed to play.

Q. Well, is it—let me ask it somewhat hypothetical, but if you were there and had been advised or not there and advised of that reading, would that be of concern to you as a physician?

A. Yes.

Q. And why is that?

Dick sighs. "Here he's getting to the heart of the case."

A. Because his last crit was 32. He had a crit at 17 and I would want to correct that.

Q. And how would you go about doing that?

A. You start by giving him blood, recheck his crit, recheck his signs and then make a decision what was happening.

Q. Was that done here?

A. As I read the notes, he got two units of blood.

"Just for the record," Dick puts in. "He didn't. Or at least he didn't when he *should* have."

Q. When?

A. It's not—it's not exactly clear to me reading the note when.

"More waffling, Sandy."

Q. It appears that after 6 o'clock the patient's urine output went down in volume. Is that your recollection?

A. Yes.

Q. What would that be indicative of?

A. Change—it could be change in volume status, giving the patient less fluid.

MR. MINDER: You're asking him in retrospect what it was or—

"His lawyer is worried," Dick comments. "He's trying to slow the pace of the questioning."

MR. KELLY: Q. As I interpret these entries, and I'm sorry, I may be misinterpreting, but it shows a urine output of 140 cc's between 1700 and 1810 and 35 cc's between 1810 and 1900. Is that—

A. Correct.

Q. Would you agree that's a rather dramatic decrease in urine output?

A. Yes.

Once more I scowl at Dick. "I just don't *get* it, why is this urine business so important to everybody?"

"The decrease in urine output can be a manifestation of shock, Sandy," he says quietly. He looks at me compassionately, almost tenderly. "A sign that the kidneys aren't being perfused, the whole system of the body is closing down."

Q. Was it your testimony, Doctor, that had—and I don't mean to misstate it, but had you been aware of this hematocrit of 17 you would have ordered blood replacement?

A. Correct.

Q. And then rechecked the hematocrit?

A. Correct.

Q. Was there a recheck of the patient's hematocrit prior to his demise?

MR. MINDER: After the 17?

MR. KELLY: Right.

THE WITNESS: Not that I am aware of. There was one part of a blood gas when they were resuscitating him.

MR. KELLY: Q. I showed you the order of Dr. Poonamalle [sic] which was repeat the hematocrits every six hours for 24 hours. Again, the hypothetical question, had you been aware of the 17, ordered replacement fluids, when would you want to know the hematocrit level in that patient?

"Stat," Dick mutters. "Stat."

"Meaning right away?" I ask.

"Stat. At once. Right away. Immediately."

A. I think I'd have put in the first unit, rechecked his crit, depending on his vital signs, put in the second unit and rechecked the crit.

Q. By rechecking the crit, you mean doing it immediately after the—

A. Yes.

Q. —the units are—

A. Yes.

Q. —replaced?

MR. MINDER: You've got to wait until he gets the words out.

MR. KELLY: I tend to stutter and stammer.

THE WITNESS: Sorry.

MR. MINDER: He tends to jump in.

MR. KELLY: Q. Assuming that the JP drains were suctioned and it was red blood that was returned and the amount indicated, the 2,450 cc's, would that— that would be an explanation of the patient's low fluid status, correct?

A. Yes.

I turn to Dick inquiringly. "Obviously, yes?"
He grimaces. "Obviously."

Q. In other words, the patient was bleeding, assuming those things—

A. Yes.

Q. —to be true?

A. Yes.

"You'll notice here, Sandy, that Kelly is forcing deVere White to contradict himself. He said earlier that the patient *wasn't* bleeding—said it in the face of a notation on the chart that indicated *red blood* had been suctioned from the drains."

Q. It's my understanding that you attended the autopsy on this patient?

A. Correct.

Q. Was an area of bleed or source of the bleed found?

A. No.

MR. MINDER: Okay. You jumped in too fast. Source of the bleed assumes that there was one and it's his opinion that there wasn't one. So you got to back up one step from that.

MR. KELLY: Well, okay.

MR. MINDER: You'd asked him a hypothetical about the red
blood. It's his opinion it's serous sanguineous
fluid and that there wasn't 2400 cc's of red
blood like you would get from a bleed.

*A bleed, my sweet. A rush of blood? A pool of blood? Or a sort of
flower, a bleeding heart? That's what it should have been. Remember
the line from Shakespeare that you always loved—"Out of this nettle,
danger, we pluck this flower, safety." But I guess there was no safety
in that desultory chaos.*

"Notice, Sandy," says Dick, "that Minder is reminding his
client here of what his opinion is supposed to be. Not blood, just
colored fluid."

MR. KELLY: Q. Okay, then I guess we get down to the ultimate—

MR. MINDER: Yes.

MR. KELLY: Q. —question which is, do you have an opinion as
to why Mr. Gilbert died post-op?

A. I don't know why he died.

*"Just wanted to let ye know we made the right decision, luv. We
got it all out." The quiet kitchen behind me. "But if it was the right
decision, why did he die?" "Ah, that I don't know, luv, that I don't
know."*

Q. Let me ask you this specifically. Did you make any mention
to the pathologist about the drainage found upon suctioning
the drains?

A. I can't recall that specifically.

"Pretty incredible that he can't recall *that*," Dick says wryly.

Q. Let me ask you, there's a death certificate in this case that Dr. Poonamalle signed that said that the patient died of cardiopulmonary arrest due to probable liver failure. The best you recall, were there any indications to you that this patient had liver failure?

A. No.

Q. Do you know where Dr. Poonamalle got that information?

A. I would imagine it had something to do with the autopsy report, but I—

Q. Have you looked at the autopsy yourself?

A. Yes.

Q. Did you see anything in there that indicated liver failure?

A. No.

"Here's another point," Dick remarks rather insouciantly, "where he's probably admitting something that's impeachable."

"The death certificate? Do you mean he's impeaching himself or Poonamallee?"

"Maybe both," he answers with a sly smile. I can see that he does, indeed, admire Kelly's conduct of the deposition.

Q. After the patient's dead, did you have any conversations with Mrs. Gilbert or any members of her family?

A. Yes.

Q. How many such conversations?

A. I talked to them extensively that evening. I talked to Mrs. Gilbert on a couple of occasions afterwards. I can't tell you how many.

"I certainly can," I protest to Dick, as if he had suddenly turned into a personal representative of deVere White. "I had exactly four conversations with him: one the night Elliot died; another the next day; another the day after that; and the last one a few weeks later when he called to say that we made the right decision because they 'got it all out.'

Q. Did she or any family member ask how this happened or—
A. Yes.
Q. What did you respond?
A. "I don't know."
Q. That's what you told her?
A. Yes.
Q. In other words, "I don't know" was your response to her?
A. Yes.

"This is to establish," Dick tells me gravely, "that they might have been covering up. He's supposed to tell you everything he knows, and he clearly didn't. His withholding of information— about the hematocrits, the transfusions, the apparent failure of the kidneys—together with the bizarre notation of liver failure on the death certificate might well turn into a serious problem for the medical center."

"Could this mean that they're guilty of what some of the books I've been reading call 'fraudulent concealment'?" I wonder.

"About that I can't say," Dick answers, still unusually somber. "That would be very serious, and if you wanted to establish such a charge, you'd have to prove something about their intentions, wouldn't you?"

Q. Did you yourself attempt to find out how this happened, that is, by going back and looking at the chart and what was going on?
A. We discussed it extensively.
Q. Who is we?
A. The department, the department of anesthesia, surgery, together.

Q. Was this part of a—

MR. MINDER: Any conversation that's M and M conference or quality assurance, then you can't testify about. If they're conversations outside of M and M and outside of quality assurance, you can testify about.

MR. KELLY: Q. Do you understand that, Doctor?

A. Yes. The meaningful conversations were all in M and M's.

"M and M? Sounds like a bag of candy!" I essay a smile.

Dick ignores my effort at comedy. "M and M means 'Mortality and Morbidity,' Sandy. It's a conference physicians regularly have in hospitals about cases that have gone wrong, and it's legally privileged—they can't be questioned about it—because otherwise they might not be completely frank with each other about their mistakes."

MR. KELLY: Okay, so—

MR. MINDER: I assert the privilege under Evidence Code Section 1156 and 1157.

MR. KELLY: Q. And that would include conversations had with your team?

A. Yes, the meaningful ones.

"But Dick, when he called me the next day, Dick, he said everybody at the hospital was talking about it. And my kids talked to the daughter of an old girlfriend of Elliot's from New York—they went to school with her and she's a medical student there—and she said everybody was talking about it too!"

"He'd say those discussions weren't meaningful. But of course he's stonewalling, Sandy, stonewalling. What do you expect?" Another weary sigh.

Q. Using my hypothetical, and I know you disagree with it, that is, that the 2,450 cc's was red blood that was retrieved via suctioning the JP drains, that amount of blood could account for the patient's demise, correct?

A. I don't think that a patient of that age should die because of a crit of 17.

"An evasive answer, Sandy. Seventeen three hours after 32 is very different from a steady 17. Such a radical drop is far more significant, severe—and dangerous."

Q. Would that be true of a patient who was in a high output cardiac state?

A. Yes.

"Not true in this case," says Dick. "Someone who's suffering from tachycardia—whose heart is laboring rapidly—needs more oxygen than someone not in such a state."

Q. Your answer would be the same, that a crit of 17 shouldn't be an explanation for the patient's death?

A. Correct.

Q. Just so I'm clear, when the patient does have a low fluid status, the patient does go into a high output cardiac state trying to catch up or compensate for that low volume, correct?

What does Jonathan Miller say, Elliot, in the book I found on your shelf and began to read, avidly, assiduously, after you died? "Surgical shock is what happens when the . . . heart can no longer maintain the pressure needed to irrigate the vital organs, and the circulation begins to collapse. The patient is deathly cold to the touch, his pulse becomes rapid and thready, and his blood pressure drops to the point where it becomes unrecordable . . . unless the blood loss is replaced artificially by a transfusion the shock becomes irreversible: either the patient dies or his kidneys and brain suffer irreparable damage."

A. That's one—one explanation.

Q. Are there others?

A. Yes. Cardiac manifestations and that can give you high output states. I'm not an expert in high output states, but all high output states are not low volume states.

"See,"—Dick leans forward looking earnest—"here he's offering an opinion but confessing that he's not an expert. This certainly isn't an answer you'd want read in court. I mean, of course people can suffer from tachycardia for all kinds of reasons, but people who have lost a lot of blood from a hemorrhage suffer from tachycardia *because* of the hemorrhage and not, under ordinary circumstances, for any other reason."

Q. No, I understand. But I'm saying that an explanation for a high output cardiac state can be that the patient is trying to compensate for low fluid volume.

A. Yes.

Q. And to complete where we were going with that question, even assuming, hypothetically, my—whether it's red blood, the 2,450 cc's that's retrieved via the JP drains, your opinion is that still wouldn't be an explanation for this patient's death. Is that your opinion?

A. Yes.

"Okay, he's putting it together here," Dick says cheerily. "It's great, he's really putting it together."

Q. There was a drop in the patient's blood pressure, correct?

A. Yes. We talked about it earlier.

Q. And a drop in the patient's hematocrit?

A. Yes.

Q. What, in your opinion, would explain those two drops?

MR. MINDER: In conjunction with each other?
MR. KELLY: (Nods.)

He can't explain it, darling. or won't. This man you trusted so much.

Q. Is there a coding summary that you have in your charts here?
MR. MINDER: You mean—
THE WITNESS: For?
MR. MINDER: —in the whole hospital for putting complications and things like that?
MR. KELLY: Yes.
THE WITNESS: This.
MR. KELLY: Q. That's the one.
A. Yes. . . .
Q. There's an entry of acute posthemorrhagic anemia, correct?
A. Yes.
Q. And we have a last name for Reitan. Is that the anesthesiologist?
A. Yes.
Q. Does that mean he may have been the source of that information?
A. I seriously doubt that he was. I don't know. I mean, I seriously doubt it. They take the chart and they extract it. I don't know.
Q. I take it you would disagree with that summary for this patient, acute posthemorrhagic anemia?
A. Well, he had anemia.
MR. MINDER: But he didn't have posthemorrhagic anemia?

"Note that the lawyer is prompting him, Sandy."

THE WITNESS: Not that I know that that's the sole cause of it.

306

"Interesting," says Dick, sitting back in his chair—after all, we've almost reached the end of this ghastly text—"that he doesn't say that he *didn't* have posthemorrhagic anemia!"

"Oh, I'm so tired of them, Dick, so tired of them never really explaining anything. What's the point? Why won't they tell us what happened?"

"Just a little more, Sandy. Can you go on?" He sips his Diet Pepsi. "More coffee? Or a Pepsi? Some cheese and crackers?"

"No, nothing, thanks. I can go on. Or as Samuel Beckett puts it, 'I can't go on, I must go on, I'll go on.' "

"Well, here's the funny part, Sandy. Or at least moderately funny. Black humor. Go to page 46."

Q. Let me show you the—I think two notes regarding—from the anesthesia department. Do you know who signed off the one for 2/11?

A. No.

Q. And the same with the one—the next?

A. Yes, I'm afraid I don't.

Q. This is obviously, I mean, in error, as I read this. There's an entry dated 2/12/91 which is the day after the patient died that describes him as being hemodynamic, stable, comfortable and oriented.

A. I agree.

Q. You don't know who signed that or how it got in this particular chart?

A. No.

Q. It appears to be 6:15 A.M. on the 12th.

A. Do not know.

Q. But we can both agree on one thing and that is that the patient had died on the 11th so—

A. I agree. I agree.

Q. Okay. The notation is "extended stay, secondary to awaiting ICU bed." Do you see that?

A. If I can—

Q. Go ahead.

A. My speculation would be that it's meant to be 2/11 and that's meant to be 6:15 P.M. That would be my only—and that's just—the date was wrong, that could be my only explanation, that he was waiting to leave the recovery room to go to an ICU bed. That could be my only explanation. I don't know. I didn't write it, so I don't know.

Q. But we've gone over some chart entries that would say at about 6:15 everything was not hunky-dory with this patient, correct?

A. I agree.

"My God, Dick." I'm not smiling, even though I do realize it's funny—funny like something in MASH or in *Catch 22.*

Funny, Elliot, like the card you got last Christmas from the UCDMC, wishing you all the joys of the season.

"Just another sign of their incompetence," Dick says, "and it sort of clinches that point, doesn't it? Anyway, he's made it pretty clear here that if they go to trial, their goose will be cooked. He's shown them what his argument will be, the outlines of the case he has, and they're running scared."

Oh yes, now I remember, darling. Kelly called me after the deposition and he told me a little about that last exchange. "Your Doctor deVere White was very charming," Kelly said, "But he hung his head when I asked him about the last note on the chart. 'We can both agree on one thing and that is that the patient had died on the 11th so—' 'I agree. I agree.' "

"But of course I suppose these things happen," I say to Dick with an effort at a smile. "These little mixups in crowded busy hospitals."

"They shouldn't. They're not supposed to," he answers grimly.

"Yes, well—"

I gaze out the picture window at the October trees that circle the parking lot and the street beyond it. Here in northern Maryland they still haven't lost their leaves, though the leaves have mostly turned by now. Some are gold and orange, like burning paper—as if angels (whatever *they* are) were incinerating truckloads of old notes and letters.

Some are red, like blood—or maybe like "serous sanguinous fluid."

Whatever *that* is.

20

Significant numbers of respondents [in one study] believe
that they have been neither vindicated nor compensated for
their own or their relatives' illness, injury, or death; and
that they have not had the opportunity to protect others
from harm.

—Allan R. Meyers, Ph.D., " 'Lumping It':
  The Hidden Denominator of the Medical
  Malpractice Crisis," *American Journal of Public Health* 77,
  no. 12 (December 1987)

TUESDAY, JULY 21, 1992, 2:30 P.M.

"Your Doctor deVere White was very charming," Kelly says. "Just as you told me he'd be."

"Oh dear." My palm is sticky on the receiver. "That's what I was afraid of."

"But he hung his head at the end, when I asked him about the last note on the chart." The lawyer sounds unusually elated. "The one where someone said your husband was okay on February 12, when he'd actually been dead for almost twelve hours."

"Oh my God, I didn't know about that. How could they—?" I take a furious gulp of my milkshake. A few days ago I developed some kind of weird dental abscess, partly (according to my shrink) because of tension and anxiety about the deposition at the UCDMC and the upcoming settlement conference, and now I'm on a liquid diet.

"Hey, there's no end to what they can do." Kelly lapses back for a minute into his usual dark-side-of-the-moon manner, but his exuberance is really irrepressible. "It would've been better if this deVere White of yours had two heads or something," he confides. "I mean I can see where a jury would find him charming too. But he didn't do his side a lot of good this morning. He was *very* disingenuous."

"Really? How?" I take a calmer sip of the milkshake.

"Waffling, waffling on everything. Claimed the 'surgery couldn't have gone better' and strangely enough insisted that the 2400 cc's of blood suctioned from the drains was 'tinged fluid.' Tinged fluid!" Kelly snorts triumphantly. *"That's* not going to go down with a jury."

"I hope not."

"And he had to admit the significance of the drop in the hematocrit *and* that there was no evidence of liver failure *and* he waffled on the medicine given for the heart-rate problem."

"But did he say anything about what *did* happen? Why did *he* think my husband died? What was *his* opinion?"

"Not a word," Kelly says curtly. "Stonewalling. Just the way I told you he would. I said you shouldn't expect anything else, didn't I?"

I sigh theatrically, to let him know I agree, I understand, and stare down at the creamy bubbles in my glass. Elliot loved milkshakes and knew how to make them just right, thick enough, sweet enough, not too foamy, but I myself have hardly ever made one before so I guess I'd glad this one came out okay. "But otherwise you think it went well? Really well?"

"I'd say so. I'd say his answers will be useful in court if we have to go to trial," Kelly answers. "But I hope we don't. I hear they're having a risk management meeting at the medical center today or tomorrow. Going to decide about a number of cases, I hear."

"A number of cases!" I exclaim bitterly. "I just bet they have a *number* of cases." I gaze out the window to the shady deck, where my friend Bob is pacing around, smoking a cigarette. He came over to help me look at cars (and help me make my milk-shake) this afternoon; we were just about to leave when Kelly called. *Well, Elliot,* I murmur in my head, *will a shiny new car compensate me—and you—for the wafflings of the charming doctor?*

"Remember," Kelly warns, "last week I told Minder we wouldn't turn a deaf ear to a structured settlement."

"Okay, I remember, I'll obviously think about it and so will the kids. But we'd need to know *all the terms.*"

I still haven't confessed to Kelly about the book I'm writing, but I'm getting more nervous about it every day. Maybe that's why I developed this obnoxious abscess. Last week I was at a dinner party with some journalist friends who scared me, yet again, about the possibility of a gag. One man, in particular—an experienced editor—said settlement agreements frequently include prohibitions against any discussion of the issues involved in the case that's being settled. Another man, whose wife used to work for a personal injury lawyer, promised to call her former employer, naming no names, and ask *his* opinion.

The time is drawing near when I really will have to tell Kelly about what I'm doing, but I still don't seem to be able to mention the book. *As though I were involved in some furtive, illicit activity, Elliot? As though it were somehow curiously criminal of me to want to tell the truth, the whole truth and nothing but the truth about what happened to you?*

"I'll keep in touch," Kelly promises. "But don't forget that the settlement conference has been scheduled for 8:30 A.M. on the 29th. Sacramento courthouse. Jan'll send you a map. You've got to be there on the button."

I know, and I know I'm not looking forward to it. Will deVere White be there, and Reitan, and Poonamallee, and maybe even the chancellor? What will I do if, let's say, deVere White shows up, charming as ever in his starched doctor coat and matter-of-fact chinos?

———

TUESDAY, JULY 21, 1992, 9 P.M.

"He said a restrictive order isn't likely." My friend Jerry is on the phone with good news about the views of his wife's ex-boss. "He's a civil liberties type, you know, so he has lots of ideas about this sort of thing. He said he thought such an order would be unconstitutional, even if it's written into the agreement. It's a First Amendment issue."

"Well, yes, free speech. We've thought about that."

In fact, my kids and I have long since decided that when and if the possibility of a gag arises I should take my stand on free speech, First Amendment, academic freedom, that sort of thing. And my friend the editor agreed that, without mentioning my secret project, I could say that I'm a poet after all and I can't accept any legal stipulations that would constrain my imagination, etcetera, etcetera.

All well and good. But what if they then say, okay, you don't have to accept our terms, and we don't have to settle?

But *then*—and this is what the kids and I have told each other over and over again too—then we'll go to trial.

"He also pointed out that people have a right to know about cases like this," Jerry continues. "Sometimes clients agree to gags for the wrong reasons, because they don't *want* other people to know what happened, but in this case—"

"Well, but did you ask him the other question we talked about last week? I mean, did you ask him whether if I tell *my* lawyer about what I'm writing he somehow then has to tell the other side?"

"I did indeed," Jerry says, "and he said no of course he doesn't. In fact"—he laughs hearteningly—"his exact words were, 'it's none of their fucking business.' Those were his exact words. 'None of their fucking business.' "

———

Friday, July 24, 1992, 10 a.m.

Bright and hot. Bright even through the dark shades, bright frames around the edges. Hot under the covers, too hot. And the windows wide open, so birds rustling and cheeping in the oaks, squirrels leaping among the leaves, are loud, too loud. As is the ringing. I want to stay asleep but the ringing is piercing through the rustling, cheeping, leaping noises, and for some reason I don't want to leave the whole problem to the answering machine the way I usually do.

I drag the phone toward me, over the hot and heavy comforter under which, as always, I'm irrationally huddled. Raggedy Andy slips under a pillow; Orlando Furrioso almost falls off the bed.

"Dan Kelly here. Do you have a minute?"

"Of course." I clear my throat experimentally, grab my bedside water glass, and gulp. He sounds more unnervingly businesslike and brisk than ever.

"Well, I just had a call from Tom Minder." He barks out a laugh. "We've got a real cliff-hanger here."

"A cliff-hanger?" I'm dazed with heat and sleep but wide awake at the same time.

"Yeah, a regular cliff-hanger. Wes Sokolosky and I are sitting in the conference room, preparing one of our experts for deposition, and Minder's on his way down Route 80 to depose the guy, and let me tell you, Wes and I are sweating blood—"

"Sweating blood?" I struggle groggily into a sitting position, prop myself against the pillows.

"Our guy," he says bitterly, "*our* guy is being very conservative. Doesn't want to say more than that in his view your husband would have had a better than 50 percent chance of survival if his care had been up to the standard."

"Better than 50 percent?" I'm wide awake now. "But that's absurd. He was a healthy man, he never had any heart trouble, didn't have anemia, Dick says that if they'd given the transfusions in time he'd absolutely be alive today, so how could this person—"

"Haven't I told you all along? These guys don't like to testify against each other, they're very *very* careful about what they say, what they're *willing* to say. So it's a cliff-hanger, okay? And Tom Minder's in his car, right this minute he's in his car, on his way down 80 from Sacramento to do the deposition in our office, and he just picked up his carphone to offer us a structured settlement. How do you like *that?*"

"Oh my God." (This is what we wanted, isn't it? Yet I feel my heart beginning to pound a little too hard, too fast, tachycardiac.) "Well, what are the— what are they—?"

His voice darkens, becomes grave, almost solemn. "Now these are the terms and I think they're good ones—" he notes, then begins outlining the offer. A relatively modest sum up front, including enough to cover the contingency fee for him, plus an equally modest monthly annuity for me. For life.

I gaze at the glitter of light around the shades, the glitter Elliot will never see again, the glitter that they now seem to be admitting he should have been able to see again, and surprise myself with my legal acumen. "And if I die? What happens to that money? Do my kids have any right to it?"

He hesitates. "Actually, no, not as the offer is presently formulated."

"Well, in that case—" I straighten up, move over to Elliot's side of the bed and lift Raggedy Andy onto my lap—"I don't see how I can agree to it. I mean, after all, I have all kinds of bad habits, I might kick off any day—and besides, look at what happened to my husband!"

I mean, look at what happened to him, right? In the midst of life we are in death, isn't that so Mr. Kelly, isn't that so Dr. deVere White, and shouldn't any respectable settlement take such metaphysical matters into account?

"Tell you what," Kelly says in a conciliatory tone. "I'll call him back. Maybe we can get a guarantee."

"Guarantee?"

"Certain number of years for which they have to pay the annuity to your heirs if *you* aren't around."

"Well, sure, if you can, although of course I need to know more about the other terms of the settlement, too." Now my mouth is getting dry. Now I'm going to have to confess to my covert literary activities. Now we're approaching the moment of truth about the *telling* of truth. "For example," I continue as smoothly as I can, "might the settlement include any restrictions on my freedom of speech?"

"Restrictions on your—," Kelly sounds puzzled.

"I mean, suppose I wanted to write something about what happened to my husband—I mean, I'm a writer you know, a poet and—well, just suppose I decided to *write* something about him? Would the terms of the settlement preclude—"

"I can't see why." He's plainly surprised, impatient. "Sometimes there's a clause about the *terms* but I don't usually encounter anything like—"

"A gag? I mean, frankly, might there be a gag?"

He laughs. A little scornful, maybe? "Why would they want to gag you, what would be the—"

I'm inexplicably irritated, squinting at the light that glints around the drawn shades. "Well, I guess I'd better level with you. I *am* writing something, a book, and I take it pretty seri-

ously, so I'd have to be absolutely certain that I don't sign anything restrictive, anything that would in any way silence me,
you understand?"

"I do understand, and I think it's quite unlikely." He still
seems perfunctory to me, so much so that I feel a little sick,
although *so what* I tell myself, *so what, we'll go to trial, and that'll
be better anyway, we'll really nail the bastards if we go to trial.*

I gather my courage, bite my lip, stare at the glitter around the
window. "If they *do* put in a gag," I warn, "we'll have to go to
trial."

"I doubt that they'll do it, I don't think they're sitting around
worrying about what you might say," he answers calmly. "And
if they come up with a decent guarantee, I'm going to advise you
to accept the settlement. I've told you time and again you'd be
making a mistake to go to trial. Hey, when you go to trial—," he
laughs sardonically, more like his usual self, "when you go to
trial you're subject to a jury, and you know what a jury is a lot of
the time? A bunch of guys who couldn't rub two nickels together
even if they had an instruction sheet in front of them."

I smile reluctantly. "I'd appreciate it if you'd find out as much
as you can about the terms of the settlement, beyond the guarantee and the up-front sum and that sort of thing."

"I'll get back to you in a few minutes," he says energetically.
"Don't leave the house. Stay near the phone."

"Sure, sure." *Sure, of course I will. Where am I going to go, and
what am I going to do, now?* I slide out of bed, carefully restoring
Raggedy Andy and Orlando Furrioso to their proper places
under the quilt, and pad into the kitchen for some coffee. Now
I've come out of the closet as a memoirist. And what if he *does*
tell them? Who knows what he might say, what *they* might say.

" 'None of their fucking business.' " That's what Jerry's personal injury guy insisted. But Kelly might not feel that way,
might not be a big civil liberties man, although whenever we've

discussed political issues, just in passing, he's always seemed to me to be on the right side, meaning *my* side.

Back to bed. Raise the shades. Concentrate on the leafy crowns of the oaks. Try to call the kids.

Amazingly, in all their different time zones, they're all at home, and they all agree. Of course a guarantee, of course not just because it's in their interest but because they don't want to let the UCDMC off the hook if their mom should be dumb enough to go and die the way their dad did.

"But Mom, does this mean we'll never *know*—never really find out what happened to Dad?" Susanna is the most plaintive, and I share her feeling.

But we have to concede the facts of the case. "Yes, I guess that's what it does mean. At least, that's what it means if we decide we have to accept this offer. Which, you know, we don't have to do. We don't *have* to do it."

Yet we do, don't we? A settlement in the hand and all that.

A ringing and another ringing, and a piercing ring. I pick it up, but it isn't Dan Kelly, it's a friend who can't possibly know what I'm in the middle of and wants to discuss the next meeting of our poetry group. We blather on for a while, until a wave of anxiety sweeps over me and I remember that Kelly wanted to call me back.

And a minute later the phone is jangling again. But this time it's Roger, calling from Ithaca and sounding mildly censorious. "Kelly's been trying to *reach* you, Mom, he said he told you to stay off the phone, and he actually called *me* to ask if I'd get in touch with your next-door neighbors and get them to bang on the door and pry you loose from the receiver dammit!"

"Oh dear, I'm sorry honey. Sorry if he yelled at *you*."

"It's okay. In fact, I had a good conversation with him about the gag problem." Roger's tone has softened, and he even sounds rather pleased with himself.

"What did you say?"

"I simply pointed out that my mother is a poet who might want to write her memoirs some day and after all she couldn't be expected to leave out one of the most crucial events in her life. I said that's a First Amendment issue, free speech, and so forth."

As soon as I hang up, the phone asserts itself yet again, and this time it's Kelly, growling. "Have you ever heard of something called 'Call Waiting'?"

"Well, yeah, my friend Bob always—"

"Anyway, we got the guarantee. Sounds to me like they're running scared. They're going to raise the up-front money and, plus, they're willing to offer you a guarantee. I just spoke to him again—," Kelly proffers a small, smug chuckle—"in his *car*. He's still in his car."

Running scared. I stroke Raggedy Andy's locks of yarn. *They're scared, baby. Scared of what they did to you.*

"And the guarantee?" I ask. "What does it mean, specifically?" Again, I'm almost alarmed by my own assertiveness.

"Even if you die, the kids keep on getting the annuity for a fixed number of years."

"And the gag? Might there be a gag?"

"A gag? Well—" Kelly hesitates. "They won't let you discuss the sum of the settlement. They usually don't, that's standard—"

"So everybody will probably think I got lots of money," I interject bitterly. "But are you sure they won't *really* try to gag me?"

"A *real* gag? They couldn't do it. It would be unconstitutional. As I just told your son." He sounds as pleased with himself as Roger did a few minutes ago. "We talked it over and agreed. After all, you're a poet, a literary type. You might want to write your memoirs someday and couldn't be expected to leave out such a crucial event in your life. It's a First Amendment issue. Freedom of speech."

I stare down at the carpet. So is this the happy ending we've waited for, this anticlimax?

"So that's it? That's all? What happens next?"

Brisk and businesslike again. "We should get the formal papers in about a week. As soon as you and the kids sign, they'll issue a check for the up-front money. In the meantime, I'll have an accountant go to work calculating the value of the annuity. You'll get a statement from us within a week too."

"And that's it? That's all?"

"That about wraps it up." He's obviously relieved. "Oh and—and your Dr. deVere White's deposition? I won't be needing it now, but I should get a transcript sometime in the next few weeks. Want me to send it to you? You might be interested in reading it."

Yes indeed, I tell him, yes, I'd be very interested in reading it.

Perhaps, I tell myself, as I replace the phone in its cradle, reading deVere White's testimony will give me some feeling of closure, some feeling that—as the doctor himself once put it (but in how different a context!)—we've Done the Right Thing.

Midday. The house is quiet now. Even the birds and squirrels have stopped their chattering, chirping, rustling outside. Is it time for a siesta, here and in the hills to the northeast, where the same stillness, perhaps, has descended on the Sunset View Cemetery? Or are we all observing a moment of silence?

"What ceremony else?" I ask myself, quoting a line from *Hamlet* that my husband loved to declaim with theatrical irony, whenever he was disappointed in an official event, whenever rituals seemed skimpy to him.

"What ceremony else?" demands Laertes, as Ophelia is laid in her grave.

The doctor of divinity who's in charge of burying Ophelia has an answer that's pretty relevant here, too. "Her obsequys have been as far enlarged/As we have warranty. Her death was doubtful."

He means, as we English professors sometimes have to explain to students, that because Ophelia might have been a suicide, she isn't entitled to the Church's full "obsequys"—its usual funerary rituals.

Like me, Laertes is panicky. "Must there no more be done?" he asks plaintively.

Have we done everything we can? Is it all over now?

Laertes stands by his sister's grave, silent and sullen. I sit silent and sullen on the edge of my bed.

"No more be done," replies the indifferent doctor in *Hamlet*.

No ceremony else, my love.

21

There's no sign of blood, not anywhere.
I've searched everywhere.
The executioner's hands are clean, his nails transparent.
The sleeves of each assassin are spotless.
No sign of blood: no trace of red,
not on the edge of the knife, not on the point of the sword.
The ground is without stains, the ceiling white.

This blood which has disappeared without leaving a trace
isn't part of written history: who will guide me to it?
It wasn't spilled in service of emperors—
it earned no honor, had no wish granted.
It wasn't offered in rituals of sacrifice—
no cup of absolution holds it in a temple.
It wasn't shed in any battle—
no one calligraphed it on banners of victory.

But unheard, it still kept crying out to be heard.

—FAIZ AHMED ALI,
"In Search of Vanished Blood"
trans. Agha Shahid Ali

BERKELEY, CALIFORNIA
SUNDAY, JANUARY 31, 1993, 3 P.M.

Dear Doctors deVere White, Reitan, Poonamallee—and, yes, Doctor Tupin—and yes, you, too, Dean Castle, because I want to address not just my husband's physicians but the administrators of the medical center where he died, the ones who are responsible for recovery room procedures:

At just about this time, exactly two years ago, my daughters and I were driving Elliot home from the hospital, after your surgical team's failure to intubate him meant you had to cancel the operation that had been scheduled for Wednesday, January 30, 1991.

He was red-faced, angry, and agitated, not only because the procedure that was supposed to save his life had been put off, but also (at least in my opinion) because the steroids that had been given him to reduce the swelling in his throat hadn't been properly tapered. Nevertheless, he insisted that we stop in Davis on the way back to Berkeley so that he could check his mail and, more important, so that, always a raconteur, he could tell the remarkable story of the "failed intubation" to anybody who would listen.

Laughing too hard and too hoarsely, "How do you like *that?*" he said to the administrative assistant of our department, and to the acting chair, and to several students who gathered around him in the mailroom.

I was worried and tried, as gently as possible, to pry him loose from the little band of interlocutors.

But it wasn't easy. He seemed compelled, like some sort of medicalized Ancient Mariner, to repeat his tale again and again, each time with further details. How, for instance, we had told the anesthesiology resident that his chart *indicated* he was "diffi-

cult to intubate." How the resident assured us we shouldn't
worry, even though he agreed that the chart *did* say what we
said it said. How the very next day the frustrated anesthesiologists "poked and poked" at his throat with a horrifyingly sharp
instrument, or so he seemed to remember. How much, in fact, he
did remember.

By the time we got over to the Humanities Institute—where,
although the girls and I were increasingly desperate to get him
home and to bed, he insisted we should go to pick up some books
I'd forgotten—his narrative was even longer and more detailed.
What the nurses on the floor said; what you, Dr. deVere White
said; what comments critics of the UCDMC might make on this
event and how, despite his annoyance and discomfort, he would
refute such comments, *although*, he warned, he would definitely
sue if his vocal cords had been damaged.

Perhaps somehow, from beyond the grave, he transmitted his
obsession with telling his story to me. Perhaps that's why I too
feel obliged to rehearse the chain of events that began on January 30, 1991, over and over again, adding more details, remembering more and trying to understand more, each time.

———

When we finally cajoled Elliot into the car at around 5 P.M. on
the afternoon of January 31, we all agreed that I should take
him up to Sea Ranch as soon as possible and stay there until we
had to come back to Davis to get ready for the surgery that had
been rescheduled for February 11. But now, and for the last
twenty-four months, I have regularly marked January 30 as the
day on which his death, or the little I know of his death, began.

After all, I speculate, if he *had* been properly intubated on
January 30, and the surgery had proceeded as it should have,
*whatever it was that happened in the OR to cause postoperative hem-
orrhaging* (the "brisk bleeding" you mentioned when you were
deposed, Dr. deVere White? or something else we don't know

about?) *mightn't have happened.* Or maybe, *whoever it was who was on duty in the recovery room and failed to get the 3 P.M. hematocrit back* (a nurse? a resident?) *mightn't have been on duty* so that whoever *was* on duty might actually have noticed the severe drop in his hematocrit and done something about it. Or perhaps *whatever else it was that happened* (whatever you have all discussed among yourselves, as you, Dr. deVere White, told Dan Kelly you had—in "M and M" or in "Quality Assurance") *whatever it is that you haven't ever told me and my children and haven't ever offered to tell us,* perhaps *that* mysterious thing, whatever it is or was, *mightn't have happened.*

Maybe, in other words, if your team had intubated Elliot properly on January 30, 1991, on January 31, at just this hour, two years ago, instead of driving him back to Berkeley while with sometimes real and sometimes mock irascibility he reiterated his tale of the failed intubation yet again, I might have been sitting by his bedside, holding his hand or watching a video or doing whatever loving wives do when their husbands are successfully recovering from radical prostatectomies, and maybe therefore he'd be alive today, watching the Super Bowl probably (he liked football on TV) and probably thinking about what we'd have for dinner tonight, which is what my friend Bob (who is "Yaddo-ing" right now so I can feel safe enough to write you this letter) is thinking about at the moment. Or maybe Elliot and Bob would be watching the Super Bowl together and *I* would be thinking about dinner. Maybe some more people would be coming over because it's such a beautiful day here that we'd have decided to have a late-afternoon, midwinter barbecue so others, too, could admire the quince that has just begun to flower on the back deck and the tubbed rhododendron that has tentatively extended one somewhat premature blossom and the magnolia in my neighbor's yard that has all week been opening big pink blooms the size and shape of wine goblets.

Instead, as you know—though you haven't ever really talked

to me about it—Elliot's death, whatever caused it, however it happened, and however it felt to him (and to you), actually began two years ago yesterday, so that yesterday afternoon, at this same time (exactly the hour when you, Dr. DeVere White, came downstairs, and, looking chagrined, indeed quite sheepish, confessed that "they couldn't intubate, they were there with their fiber optics but they couldn't intubate") Susan and I went to the Sunset View Cemetery to bring some flowers to my husband's grave.

January 30, 1993, was as beautiful a day as January 31, 1993, has been. One of those ravishingly clear blue-and-gold days that always made Elliot grateful to be living in northern California. From the hillside where he lies, we could see Mount Tamalpais, the Golden Gate, and a sparkly swath of San Francisco Bay.

"It won't be like this in Indiana tomorrow," Susan remarked. She was visiting for only a week, so we could get some collaborative work done, and knowing she had to fly out this morning, she wasn't looking forward to going back into the cold.

We brought egg-yellow daffodils and brisk, yellow-white daisies, to remind Elliot of what spring used to be like, and I crossed myself three times, without even hiding the gesture from Susan, although she knows I'm not religious and may have thought I was being cornily theatrical, and then I silently said three Hail Marys in my head. *Holy Mary, Mother of God, pray for us sinners, now and at the hour of our death.* And, Holy Mary, after the hour of our death, let us go in peace on whatever unimaginable journeys we have to go on—under the hillside, among the roots of the flowers that are struggling to thrust themselves toward the light, and into the light, whatever light there is, wherever it is, the kindly light that my grief books talk about when they recount the "near-death experience" as a way of comforting the bereaved.

Perhaps you'll remember, Doctor deVere White, that I crossed myself obsessively when I found out that my husband was dead. "We've had a problem, a big problem," you said.

Yes, it was a big problem. He was dead, less than eight hours after surgery, on February 11, 1991.

Was his death, Doctor Reitan, a bigger problem than what you called, when you came to Elliot's room at twilight on February 10, the "problem of defensive medicine"?

I can assure you that it's been, to put it mildly, a major problem for me and for the kids.

You visited him that evening, in his "special amenities" room at the UCDMC, out of kindness. I know that. As chair of anesthesiology, you were even more embarrassed than deVere White was about your staff's inability to intubate my husband on January 30. You chatted amiably about English literature to show your concern, your collegiality. And when Elliot asked you about the state of medicine you explained that malpractice suits have lately become serious problems for physicians.

Do you remember? I can't know whether you do because after February 11, you and I never met again, despite the fact that as head of the anesthesiology team you were at least technically in charge of what went on in the recovery room, and despite the fact that it was you to whom the telling diagnosis of "acute posthemorrhagic anemia" was attributed on my husband's chart.

Standing by Elliot's bed at dusk on February 10, 1991, you shrugged your shoulders helplessly, comically bemused, probably to keep on demonstrating collegiality as you discussed the vagaries of "defensive medicine." You and my husband were both professors on the same faculty, your gesture implied, so you'd confide in him a little about what was going on in *your* field since he'd told you something about his. "We all have to practice defensive medicine nowadays," you said.

Elliot laughed sympathetically. Now that I've become something of a minor expert on medical malpractice myself, I realize that he very likely didn't have a clue what you meant by the phrase "defensive medicine." But do any of the countless physicians, politicians, and journalists who use these words so freely have a clue? No doubt most people believe they mean "unnecessary procedures," procedures performed to satisfy lawyers or insurance companies or other outsiders—for example, anxious patients and their families, "laypersons" who want desperately to be sure that, as the saying goes, "everything that can possibly be done has been done."

But was the vexing hematocrit, the lost hematocrit that has so troubled all of us for the last two years—was that what anyone might have meant by an "unnecessary procedure"? Surely even the most contemptuous critic of "defensive medicine" wouldn't consider such medicine foolish because it meant doing needless hematocrits?

Or do opponents of defensive medicine worry that physicians might spend excessive time listening to patients? (Studies have shown—I imagine many are aware of this—that doctors who practice defensive medicine *do* spend more time not only ordering such tests as hematocrits but also talking to their patients.) So would a doctor who engaged in defensive medicine have paid a little more attention to Elliot's complaint that he was "feeling awful"?

"He was woozy comin' out of the anaesthesia, woozy just the way he was after the biopsy," you said, Doctor deVere White.

We met outside the hospital some time after six o'clock.

My husband was dying upstairs—"terminating," as you later called it—on the second floor, in the recovery room. "He said somethin' like 'I feel lousy,' " you told us, rather dismissively we thought.

February 11, 1991. Blue and windy. After six, maybe six-thirty already. I can only place the hour by trying to remember what the sky was like. How its color was fading and failing. How the lights were on in the windows of the tall hospital.

But so far as I can tell from the records, within a half-hour or less the code team would be summoned to the recovery room to administer seven transfusions to my husband, to do a "trache," and try to insert a pacemaker (and they had to do the trache because, as on January 30, they couldn't intubate him).

You walked away from the hospital, Doctor deVere White. Walked, I guess, through the blue twilight to the professional building on the other side of the parking lot, where your office is. You had to go to a meeting, you later explained to our attorney.

If you had practiced defensive medicine would you have stayed at my husband's bedside, asked to see the result of the hematocrit, wondered why your patient was pale and "feeling awful"?

———

"In much popular discussion," notes Harvard Law School Professor Paul C. Weiler in a sweeping recent study of our nation's medical malpractice system, the "label [defensive medicine] is applied to any steps taken by doctors because of their concern about being sued." But, he adds dryly, "In other contexts, evidence that this kind of response was occurring would be viewed as a positive compliment to the law. Consider what our reaction would be to finding that motor vehicle litigation was inducing widespread defensive driving."

In fact, Weiler goes on to say, medical malpractice litigation— or the threat of such litigation—appears to have had a considerable effect on "the percentage of adverse events . . . judged negligent." In addition, he observes, the "somewhat more expensive mode of defensive medicine fortunately appears to have produced some of the hoped-for reduction in doctor negligence and patient injuries." Nor is there evidence, observes Weiler, "that tort law"—the law that made it possible for me and my kids to seek reparation by suing the Regents of the University of California—has been producing higher medical costs without any reduction in patient injuries.

In other words, it looks as though, in the present state of things, the very potential for patients to sue negligent doctors may actually have, in some cases, a beneficial effect: the effect of making doctors a little more careful about their procedures.

Nevertheless, as I imagine you also know, the first version of the Clinton health care proposal urges the handling of malpractice cases through out-of-court proceedings—processes of "alternative dispute resolution"—in which injured patients (or, presumably, their survivors) would be required to "submit . . . claims to trained mediators or panels of experts" before actually filing suit. This, as Edward Felsenthal has noted in the *Wall Street Journal,* despite considerable evidence that such strategies have "already been tried in many states . . . with disappointing results." In fact, Felsenthal cites Law Professor Weiler's misgivings: " 'It's strange, . . . the verdict across the country in the bulk of the jurisdictions that have tried [alternate dispute resolution] is that it has been a failure.' "

Even more radically, during the 1992 presidential election campaign, the Republican platform included a crucial plank that may well have articulated your own positions on the problem of defensive medicine as it has been constituted by the supposed "crisis" in medical malpractice litigation. The Republican party, wrote the framers of the platform, intended to address "the medical malpractice problem by a cap on non-economic damage recoveries in malpractice claims [as well as] an alternative dispute resolution before going to court," explaining that "[m]eaningful medical tort reform would assure that doctors would not have to practice medicine under a cloud of potential litigation."

And, as you may also recall, President Bush actually sent Vice-President Quayle out on the road to push his plan.

But Quayle, as you may also remember, had significant problems with the whole unnerving situation. According to the *New York Times:* " 'I can't tell you exactly what we do on that pain and suffering in the—' the Vice-President said, his voice trailing off as he looked offstage toward Kevin E. Moley, the deputy secretary of the Department of Health and Human Services, who [had] been coaching him. 'Kevin, what do we do on the pain and suffering on our malpractice proposal?' "

Indeed. What do we do, Doctor Reitan and Doctor deVere White, "on the pain and suffering"?

———

But after all, you may wish to say, and I won't disagree with you, how could I?, *your lawsuit hasn't brought your husband back to life, has it? And why, after all, should you, Sandra, deserve any compensation for* his *pain and suffering*—for what you (perhaps foolishly, perhaps just ignorantly) imagine as the "white clicking, the white hissing"—*or in fact for your* own *misery?*

Aren't we all, in any case, in every case, doomed sooner or later to "the pain and suffering"? How can money *make any part of that catastrophe better? If you've lost a gorgeous orange, no number of delicious apples can replace its glow and sweetness, right?*

As Weiler rather grimly puts it elsewhere in his study of our malpractice system, "what is the point of paying money now to repair a harm that cannot be affected by the payment? It is lamentable but true that the parent who loses a child has less, not more, need of family income after the fatal accident." As for a widow who has lost her spouse, she can be at least minimally compensated, as I have been, for her *economic* loss—but how can dollars substitute for her loss of a husband's "care, comfort, and consortium"?

Indeed, even if we define payments for a family's pain and suffering as in some sense punitive damages—damages designed to remind physicians and other health care providers of the famous tenet *At least do no harm*—it is questionable whether any kind of punishment *I* can inflict upon you will mean very much to any of you personally, since, as Patricia Danzon, another medical malpractice expert, observes, "insurance tends to insulate the physician from the penalties meted out by the legal process." Not one of you is out of pocket because of Elliot's death; not one of you has even been asked to apologize to me, much less *compensate* me for my loss.

And to go back to apples and oranges, how could you compensate me anyway?

Here is what, when I started my book at Yaddo a year-and-a-half ago, I planned to end it with:

POSTSCRIPT: A MEMO ON COMPENSATION
To the Judge: In behalf of decedent, plaintiff requests compensation for all items and events decedent has missed in consequence of his wrongful death on February 11, 1991.

—He has missed the plum blossoms.

—He has missed the end of the Gulf War.

—He has missed the Kurdish exodus.

—He has missed the California rains of March 1991.

—He has missed the trappers who caught the opossum outside the house where he lived in Berkeley.

—He has missed the publication of his son's first book.

—He has missed his grandson's graduation from nursery school.

—He has missed the fourth of July picnic where no one could light the barbecue without him.

—He has missed the Clarence Thomas/Anita Hill hearings.

—He has missed the firestorm in the Oakland hills.

—He has missed the publication of three of his own essays.

—He has missed Halloween; he is going to miss Thanksgiving, Christmas, and New Year's.
—He will miss the plum blossoms again.

How odd, how obsolete, this list looks now! Think of all the other history he's missed and will miss: the Mike Tyson case, Iraqgate, the L. A. riots, the Clinton campaign, "ethnic cleansing" in Bosnia, starvation in Somalia, the Clinton victory, the explosion at the World Trade Center, the crisis in Haiti—and the plum blossoms.

And again the plum blossoms.

And over and over again the plum blossoms.

For which loss, what compensation?

———

THE SEA RANCH, CALIFORNIA
SATURDAY, FEBRUARY 6, 1993, 3 P.M.

Dear Doctors:

Although it's been threatening rain and heavy surf, although there were floods around the Russian river and some scary-looking mudslides on Route 1, Bob and I came up here yesterday so I can try to bring this letter to an end, this *book* to an end. Bob's nobly Yaddoing again—listening to music and grading papers—while I pull my thoughts together.

Two years ago, at around this time, Elliot and I had already left this house. He had to be back in Berkeley for an appointment with his own pulmonary specialist on Wednesday, February 6, 1991. And the next day he had to see another pulmonary specialist at the UCDMC. They were trying to figure out why he was so hard to intubate.

I *am* struggling to pull my thoughts together, but frankly, as I approach February 11, I find it harder and harder to think clearly. To be sure, I've had certain mental glitches since 2/11/

91. For example, during much of the last two years, every time I had to date a letter or a check, I began with 2/, even if it was, say, the middle of June and I was supposed to begin with 6/. Every day really *was* 2/11/91, the originatory day on which this nightmare began.

It's getting a little worse right now, though. Suddenly, just this week, I found myself writing anything *but* 2/, even though 2/ is what I have to write this month.

And a few days ago, talking on the phone with an old friend, I said the strangest thing, "I *have* to finish the book," I told him. "I really have to finish the book *before Elliot dies.*"

Maybe Elliot hasn't died in my mind because I know so little about his death—not just the why of it but the how of it, the when and where of it, the look and sound and feel of it.

You didn't just take away his life, you took away his death. Whether or not you knew what you were doing, no matter how kind your intentions were, you stole his death when you sent us away from the hospital, Doctor deVere White. And you stole it, all of you, with your silence, your secrecy, your privileged conversations in "M and M" and "quality assurance."

And when you stole his death, or what might have been the moment of his almost-death, what might have been his (later to be cherished, later to be recounted and marveled over) "near-death experience," perhaps you stole his chance of life. Perhaps, if you'd summoned us into the recovery room and confessed his peril, perhaps, Doctor deVere White, if you'd said, "We *have* a problem, a big problem, Dad may be *dying,*" perhaps we could have *called him back.*

Survivors of "near-death experiences" are often in some sense "called back" by loved ones.

And if we hadn't been able to persuade him to live, or if he was already too defeated by the hemorrhaging and the waiting for help, at least we would have been there with him, there when he was forced through the enormous wall between what we know and what we don't know, there to try to comfort him as he was dragged away from us.

"Sooner or later, to all, to each, serenely arriving," says Whitman, "delicate death." We have each of us a death prepared for us, says some other poet, maybe Rilke. "It *will* come," concedes Hamlet. "The readiness is all."

And surely the readiness must include the awesome ceremony, the concession that *it* is happening and that the living must bear witness to the translation of the dying.

The translation. Not the "termination."

Just as we've come to understand the right of parents to see their infant draw its first breath, to welcome their child into life, we should understand the right of those who love to be with the one they love at the hour of death.

In 1991 Susanna had a roommate whose mother was a surgery nurse. When this nurse heard our story, she was shocked. At *her* hospital, she said, they don't send the families of critically ill patients *away*. On the contrary, she said, they insist that the families should be there.

"Isn't that a matter of medical ethics?" she asked.

Hasn't the Catholic Church, whatever you think of the Church, always known this? Isn't it what the Last Rites are about, are *for*?

Who administered what "Last Rites" to my husband? What were his final words, Doctor Poonamallee? Did you hear them, or did some nurse listen to them? Did she turn away, ignoring what he said? Or did she take his hand and console him?

Was there a moment when he realized what was happening, a moment of transition and recognition? Was he frightened? Was he resigned? Did he ask for me? Did he remember me? Did he remember *himself*?

That moment (surely, as they knew in the nineteenth century, a majestic one in every life), that moment is what you stole from us, along with everything else for which you can never compensate us or him.

———

A few nights ago I had dinner with another old friend, a therapist who was helping me grapple with the torment of my absolute ignorance about my husband's last hours. "What survivors could be in worse shape than *we* are?" I wondered. "Maybe the families of MIAs?"

"Yes, the families of MIAs. That's a good analogy," she said.

But no, I told her. After all, the families of MIAs have to admit that their loved ones knew they were going into battle, knew they had to go warily.

But Elliot went trustingly. We *sent* him trustingly. He went to be made well. We *sent* him to be made well.

Sent him because we believed not just in the skill but (naively?) in the ethics—the morality—of the hospital.

Believed that the hospital will cure, will comfort, will assuage. *Will tell you what happened.*

Ah but—you may say—*ah but, what could we do when you filed a case against us? Our lawyers forbade us to speak. The university counsel's office forbade us to speak. The Regents wouldn't let us speak. No one would let us speak, for fear of what we might tell you and how you might use it against us.*

Yet it's been, now, six months since the case was settled, since my kids and I officially "absolved" you of blame in exchange for the trivial compensation your attorneys offered.

And still you have told me nothing.

Maybe, though, you've told me nothing not just for legal reasons but because you've told *yourselves* nothing. Perhaps, Doctor deVere White, you meant every word you said when you were deposed. What *you* saw, you want to believe, was *not* "red blood" but merely "serous sanguinous fluid," because it would have been too disturbing for you to have seen "red blood." For you to have had to confront the horror of what had happened to a man whom, I'm sure, you genuinely liked.

Meditating on "The Anatomy and Economics of Surgical Mishaps" in the *New England Journal of Medicine*, a team of researchers wrote in 1981 that among the origins of medical error "familiar to most experienced clinicians" is *misplaced optimism.* . . . It is often apparent in progress notes of the hospital record, in which the physician primarily responsible for the patient displays the least capacity for facing bad news."

Richard Selzer, that elegant surgeon-stylist, made the same point more felicitously in his *Mortal Lessons*. "Like an asthmatic hungering for air, longing to take just one deep breath, the surgeon struggles not to feel," he admitted. "It is suffocating to press the feeling out. It would be easier to weep or mourn—for you know that the lovely precise world of proportion contains, just beneath, *there* all disaster, all disorder."

Remember what you said, Doctor deVere White, as we faced each other across my husband's body in the little white chamber around the corner from the recovery room, as you glanced uncomfortably down at your gold watch, as he lay between us, faintly chilly, like someone who had just taken a long walk in the snow, and grimacing ruefully? "For you, this is unpleasant, awful, I know. For *me*, it's shattering."

And while your appraisal of *my* plight was curiously—how shall I put it?—*anesthetized*, you were certainly right about yourself. It was shattering. Perhaps too shattering to acknowledge?

"Surgeons must be very careful," declared Emily Dickinson, "When they take the knife!/Underneath their fine incisions/Stirs the Culprit—*Life!*"

FEBRUARY 6, 1993, 6:30 P.M.

Dear Doctors:

Of course it isn't just to you I'm writing, nor is it just in behalf of myself and my dead husband and my living children. I want to wake you and other doctors up, to make you *feel*, in behalf of all those who have been, like me and him and them, through "the pain and suffering" of an absurdly unnecessary death.

Last week, as I worried about finishing this book "before Elliot dies" and as I compared the miseries of the families of MIAs to my own miseries and as I found myself incapable of dating anything 2/, I read an interesting column called "Medical Overkill," by Ellen Goodman, an essayist whose work I admire almost as much as I admire the writing of Richard Selzer.

Like so many other recent thinkers about American health care and its discontents, Goodman was brooding on what (apart from the problem of insurance coverage) I, too, until February 1991, considered perhaps *the* major medical problem we face today. Studies show, she remarked, "that Americans worry that at the end of life they will receive too much medical treatment and too little pain relief. Now there is, as well, a survey that says doctors and nurses who treat dying patients worry that they give too much treatment and too little pain relief." In addition, she notes, "Health-care providers who answered [a recent survey] were four times as likely to be concerned about overtreatment as about undertreatment."

Overtreatment v. undertreatment. Sounds a bit like a lawsuit, doesn't it?

Except that, from Jack Kevorkian, the celebrated "death doctor," to many minions of the Bush administration, to the well-known prioritizings advocated by the Canadian health care program and (for example) those instituted lately in Oregon, "overtreatment" is a problem that has been much addressed.

Not "undertreatment," though. "Undertreatment" has only been defined in the negative. As in the 1992 Republican platform, whose malpractice plank assumes that for the most part medical negligence suits are brought through a conspiracy between predatory plaintiffs and ambulance-chasing lawyers.

Yet as almost all the responsible literature about malpractice indicates, the incidence of iatrogenic "adverse events" due to medical negligence in this country has been deeply underestimated. Most victims of "adverse events," say the countless articles I have read, *just don't know what has happened to them or to their loved ones.*

In my own experience this is true. After Elliot died, I found that almost everyone I talked to had some story involving a medical mystery. "My dad died in a hospital in Mexico," said a carpenter who came to fix my fence. "They told us he had pneumonia but we never really knew what was wrong with him." "They told me my father couldn't have survived the operation," a famous novelist confided. "But I was sure he could have." "My brother-in-law was misdiagnosed," another well-known writer told me. "He could have lived if they'd been more careful and found out what was really wrong." "We'll never really know what happened to my husband," said another woman. "And my mother—she went in healthy and came out dead," someone else insisted. "We were always suspicious, but what could we do?"

Now and then, to be sure, we hear about a few sensational cases—the Andy Warhol case, the Libby Zion case. But even those are problematic. Hospitals stonewall. Doctors concede nothing. Frantic families complain, complain and, usually, are silenced. Silenced with money. Silenced with disapproval.

In our own situation, we had the good fortune to know someone who could read the records, to find an attorney who'd believe our story and who was expert enough to prosecute the matter, and—perhaps most important—to belong to a social/ economic class in which my husband's income (and my consequent monetary loss) was sufficient to make a lawsuit worthwhile for all concerned.

But my suit wasn't about money, really, as I've been trying to assure you. My suit was for the dead one. My suit was motivated by William Blake's great proverb of Hell: *"A dead body revenges not injuries."*

Because my husband, superb storyteller though he was, could not tell his own story, I have had to tell his story for him.

What can one do in the face of death? Confronting the dead body that revenges no injuries, that is forced to lie there in its mild factuality, its hopeless and helpless irrevocability?

Just a week ago today, Susan and I brought Elliot daffodils and daisies to remind him of what spring used to be like.

Glitter of the bay. Peak of Mount Tam in the distance. The Golden Gate opening out into the huge space of the Pacific.

What can I do? Nothing, of course. The notion of *doing* is merely an illusion in this context.

Well, there's one thing, maybe, that I can do.

As I looked back over the first two sections of this book in preparation for writing my letter to you, Doctors deVere White and Reitan *et al.*, I found a scribbled note from my youngest child on page one of part one: "Add: Susanna wore 'hand' earrings day of surgery & never again."

Susanna (who at first only reluctantly read a portion of this manuscript because, she confessed, it was too painful to her) was referring to a pair of earrings that Elliot and I bought her in Israel a few years ago. *Hamsa* earrings: that is, earrings featuring beautiful little silver hands designed to ward off evil.

She wore them to ensure her father's safety, the way I wore the Puerto Rican healing beads, the way my colleague Gary

Snyder arranged for a Buddhist service in the foothills of the Sierra, the way Susan's friend Mary Jo asked the convent in Indianapolis to pray for him, the way my colleague Michael Kramer asked his whole Orthodox congregation in Sacramento to think of Elliot on the day of the surgery. She wore them, I wore them, we prayed, we begged, we meditated—and it did no good, did it?

There are things we may never do again. Never wear *hamsa* earrings. Never wear Puerto Rican healing beads or, maybe, believe—if we ever did—in the protective efficacy of Buddhist services or Carmelite prayers or Orthodox Jewish meditations.

Yet my kids did tell me what I should do and what I was going to do. When I began this book, I thought it would be an article. My fantasy was of an essay in the *New York Times Magazine.*

"I *know* you, Mom," Roger said. "You're going to write a book."

And my daughters agreed. Yes, I was going to write a book, and yes, that was what I should do. Because, sad as it is, there isn't and wasn't and never was anything else to do.

This is how Elizabeth Barrett Browning, one of my heroines, puts it in a somewhat different context:

> Weep and write.
> A curse from the depths of womanhood
> Is very salt, and bitter, and good.

I didn't want to curse. I don't. But I want to *talk* to you. I want you to hear me. I want to tell you, among other things, why Susanna will never wear her *hamsa* earrings again. And I guess this is the only way.

Says Barrett Browning, at the end of her poem, "THIS is the curse. Write."

———

And just the other day, as I sat at my computer writing, I noticed that there was a file cryptically entitled *A* in its directory. When, merely out of idle curiosity, I opened it, I saw that it had been put there quite some time ago by my husband, who had an odd habit of giving casual files unfathomable names like *A*, *B*, *X*, *Y*, and *Z*.

This is what the file said:

Video Tapes for Hospital

FLIGHT OF THE PHOENIX, THE	Robert Aldrich
VERDICT, THE	Sidney Lumet
STING, THE	George Roy Hill
NINOTCHKA	Ernst Lubitsch
PURPLE ROSE OF CAIRO, THE	Woody Allen
WITNESS	Peter Weir
HOW THE WEST WAS WON	Ford/Hathaway/Marshall

So he *was* expecting to live. To survive the surgery and even, if necessary, to endure what he saw as its direst consequences (impotence, incontinence). Elliot was an organized man—he was holding *on* by being an "organized man"—and he was planning ahead. He wanted to be sure that he wouldn't forget to take a select group of his favorite videos along. So that he could watch them while he was recovering in his "special amenities room" (one of the special amenities was a VCR) at the UCDMC.

Interesting, isn't it?, that he decided to bring *The Verdict*, that gripping detective story/courtroom drama (Paul Newman v. James Mason) about medical negligence. A film in which, though the hapless patient never recovers, at least the survivors find out what happened.

His choice of that movie probably meant he considered its

342

subject fascinating but not so close to the bone that it would disturb him as he lay there in his hospital bed, watching and sipping, let's say, the apple juice or cranberry juice that they give you just before they bring you your evening pills on whatever floor they've put you on.

He imagined a near future in which we'd have called the kids together, and then he'd have said goodnight to me, I'd have gone back to the condo, and alone and peaceful in his room he'd raise himself to a cosy sitting position in the white bed (by now he'd be wearing his striped pajamas instead of that dumb hospital gown), glance conspiratorially over at Raggedy Andy and Orlando Furrioso, perky on their windowsill, sip his apple juice, flick the set on with his remote, and admire the performances of Newman and Mason. *Performances*, fictions: that's all those roles would be.

I'm glad, I'm relieved, that Elliot wrote down the video list telling me he imagined this. He wrote it down, printed it out, and then, I guess, forgot to delete the file.

I'm glad he didn't delete it. I'm glad he wrote it down, though I wept when I found it.

———

"Weep and write."

I have written it, dear doctors. I have done "the real mourning thing": I have written it down.

In behalf of myself and my children, but most of all in my husband's behalf, in his honor—and in his memory.

POSTSCRIPT

January 23, 1994

Dear Doctors,

As I finish my final revisions on this book, just a week before Super Bowl Sunday and a week before the third anniversary of the day on which, as I have told you, I believe my husband's death "began," I find myself obsessively poring over a newspaper clipping that was just sent me by the daughter of a dear friend. From the November 7, 1993, edition of the *Sacramento Bee*, it's entitled " 'What Really Happened to My Baby': A Mother Fights for the Truth," and it tells the sad story of four-year-old Camelia Plaza, who was allegedly the victim of several acts of medical negligence—from an ambulance company and from the UCDMC—in December 1991.

Camelia is severely brain damaged, says Sam Stanton, the *Bee* staff writer who produced the article. "She cannot hear. She cannot speak. She will not eat most solid foods and has to be fed a liquid protein diet through a tube in her stomach every four hours."

Andrea Plaza, Camelia's mother, retained Noel Ferris, a personal injury attorney, who brought suit against both the ambulance company and the medical center. Just a few months ago, both organizations settled the case—without, of course, admitting guilt.

Andrea Plaza testifies that what especially tormented her was the refusal of Camelia's doctors and nurses at the UCDMC to tell her what had happened to her little girl. I have used one of her statements as an epigraph for this book because it so concisely expresses my own anguish and bewilderment: *"None of the doctors told me. I asked them what really happened to my baby. . . . I asked them crying and I asked them OK and I asked them mad. And they didn't tell me."*

In fact, elsewhere in her deposition Plaza implies that such bewilderment was crucial to the feelings of betrayal that motivated her lawsuit, a notion with which Dan Kelly would likely agree.

"A lot of these doctors can be really *something,*" Kelly told us at our first meeting on July 23, 1991. "If only they'd level with people, half the time they wouldn't get to this kind of point, things like this wouldn't come to *my* office."

Because the chief pediatrician in charge of her daughter's case "did not explain it to me," testified Andrea Plaza, "I felt really bad and very sad. . . . I felt betrayed and I was, I am very frustrated, still at this time because I couldn't trust them."

To my astonishment, however, the *Bee* story continues as follows:

> The charge that Plaza was not fully informed of what happened to her daughter does not fit with the medical center's existing policy.

That policy requires that families always be kept informed of such things, said Carol Robinson, the medical center official who agreed to discuss general aspects of hospital policy.

"They're always told when there's an error, and they're always told when that error has been associated with an apparent consequence," she said. "There are no reasons for not telling a patient."
[italics mine]

I study these sentences with amazement at 5:45 P.M. as, once again, the way I have almost every evening at this time of year since the month, three years ago, of Elliot's death, I scrutinize the light—how blue is it? how gray? how bright or dull?—to try to be absolutely certain of the exact minute when we returned to the UCDMC on February 11, 1991, to be told that we couldn't see my husband yet because "they" (the nurses? the doctors?) were "still waiting for a bed in the ICU."

Upstairs, although we didn't know it, he lay dying in the recovery room.

Yes, it was after six, about six-fifteen. It was probably just a little grayer than it is right now. It was a gray-blue minute when we left the hospital to go to dinner at the Chinese restaurant, a windy gray-blue minute three hours before the gray-black nighttime minute when the elevator doors slid open and the surgeon and the resident and the Decedent Services woman hurried out into the deserted lobby to inform us of my husband's shattering, inexplicable death.

NOTES

13 *Perhaps it's easier* See, for instance, the remarks on "Unclear Assignment of Responsibility for Hospitalized Patients," in Steward Wolf, "The Medicine of the Lateral Pass," *Perspectives in Biology and Medicine* 35, no. 2 (Winter 1992): 196.

23 *Every year* Some researchers even suggest that one out of ten hospital admissions could conceivably issue in a claim of medical negligence or malpractice. For some pertinent statistics, see, for instance, Howard H. Hiatt et al., "A Study of Medical Injury and Medical Malpractice," *New England Journal of Medicine* 321, no. 7 (August 1989): 480–84; A. Russell Localio et al., "Relation between Malpractice Claims and Adverse Events Due to Negligence: Results of the Harvard Medical Practice Study III," *New England Journal of Medicine* 325, no. 4 (July 1991): 245–51; Troyen A. Brennan et al., "Identification of Adverse Events Occurring during Hospitalization: Across-Sections Study of Litigation, Quality Assurance, and Medical Records at Two Teaching Hospitals," *Annals of Internal Medicine* 112 (February 1990): 221–26; and Troyen A. Brennan et al., "Incidence of Adverse Events and Negligence in Hospitalized Patients: Results of the Harvard Medical Practice Study I," *New England Journal of Medicine* 324, no. 6 (February 1991): 370–76.

23 *one in every 388 hospitalizations* See Troyen A. Brennan et al., "Incidence of Adverse Events and Negligence in Hospitalized Patients: Results of the Harvard Medical Practice Study I," *New England Journal of Medicine* 324, no. 6 (February 1991): 373. ". . . among the 2,671,863 discharges from New York hospitals in 1984, we estimate that there were 98,609 adverse events. . . ."

We estimated that 27,179 injuries, including 6895 deaths and 877 cases of permanent and total disability, resulted from negligent care in New York in 1984."

23 *"Less than two"* Quoted in "Study Says Few Sue Over Malpractice," *San Francisco Chronicle*, July 25, 1991, p. D6. A recent article in the *Journal of the American Medical Association* gives rather different statistics: according to this piece, acts of medical negligence are eight to ten times more common than malpractice suits. See John Glasson and David Orentlicher, "Not Caring for the Poor and Professional Liability: Is There a Need for Tort Reform?" *Journal of the American Medical Association* 270, no. 14 (October 1993): 1740–41.

24 *"the civil-justice"* A. Russell Localio et al., "Relation between Malpractice Claims and Adverse Events Due to Negligence," *New England Journal of Medicine* 325, no. 4 (July 1991): 250.

24 *"it is the question"* Arnold Simanowitz, "Accountability," in Charles Vincent at al., *Medical Accidents* (Oxford: Oxford University Press, 1993), p. 209. Charles Inlander, Lowell Levin, and Ed Weiner formulate the problem more bitterly in their crusading *Medicine on Trial: The Appalling Story of Medical Ineptitude and the Arrogance That Overlooks It* (New York: Pantheon/The People's Medical Society, 1988), 122: "As long as disclosure laws do not exist (or, if they do exist, do not have teeth), as long as mortality and morbidity statistics are not made readily available at all to the public, and as long as the medical profession covers up for its faulty own despite review committees designed to weed out the bad practitioners, surgery will be a crap shoot." For further comment on this last point, see also Joel Brinkley, "You Bet Your Life. Do You Know the Odds?" *New York Times*, May 29, 1994, sec. 4. p. 4.

24 *More recently* For problems associated with this, see Edward Felsenthal, "Clinton's Plan for Malpractice Has Failed Tests," *Wall Street Journal*, September 16, 1993, p. B1: "In fact . . . the procedures [of alternate dispute resolution] often do little more than gum up the works, building in extra delays and legal costs." And for a searing comment on the move to cap com-

pensatory payments to victims, see Frank Cornelius, "Crushed by My Own Reform," *New York Times,* October 7, 1994, Op-Ed, p. A31.

25 *"credible systems"* A. Russell Localio et al., "Relation between Malpractice Claims and Adverse Events Due to Negligence," *New England Journal of Medicine* (August 1991): 250.

25 *"With cash reserves"* In-house newsletter of the San Francisco law firm Walkup, Shelby, Melodia, Bastian, Kelly, Echevarria and Link (Summer 1991).

26 *"malpractice suits"* William Ira Bennett, "Pluses of Malpractice Suits," *New York Times Magazine,* 24 July 1988, p. 31.

28 *Although it has received* The recent deaths of a number of well-known and relatively youthful men from prostate cancer (e.g., Frank Zappa, Bill Bixby) have lately brought the disease (and its relative obscurity) more attention. Newly vehement popular journalism on the subject has appeared both here and abroad in, for instance, the *London Times* (Thomas Stuttaford, "Why Zappa Died So Young," Tuesday, 7 December 1993, p. 17) and *Newsweek* (Jerry Adler, "The Killer We Don't Discuss," and Geoffrey Cowley, "To Test or Not to Test," both 27 December 1993, pp. 40–43). Excellent overviews of current research on the disease, its treatments, and the dilemmas they pose are offered by Mark B. Garnick, "The Dilemmas of Prostate Cancer," *Scientific American* 270, no. 4 (April 1994): 72–81; and Charles C. Mann, "The Prostate Cancer Dilemma," *Atlantic Monthly* 272, no. 5 (November 1993): 102–18.

30 *Perhaps, I speculated* For a useful discussion of the surprisingly low funding of prostate cancer research compared to research into breast cancer (a comparably threatening disease in its assault on sexual self-images) see Marc B. Garnick, "The Dilemmas of Prostate Cancer," *Scientific American* 270, no. 4 (April 1994): 81. "For fiscal year 1994, the NCI is estimated to have spent some $40 million for [prostate cancer research]. . . . By comparison, more than $250 million is expected to be spent for breast cancer."

61 *The UCDMC had almost lost* For one account of the problems that the UCDMC had in the seventies, see Thomas J. Moore, *Heart Failure: A Critical Inquiry into American Medicine and the Revolution in Heart Care* (New York: Random House, 1989), 222–99. For a more recent difficulty, see Sam Stanton, " 'What Really Happened to My Baby?' " *Sacramento Bee*, 7 November, 1993, p. A1.

180 *"Perhaps the most dangerous"* Jonathan Miller, *The Body in Question* (New York: Random House, 1978), 122.

181 *"The body is unable"* Ibid.

270 *in favor of plaintiffs* See Kevin M. Clermont and Theodore Eisenberg, "Trial by Jury or Judge," *Cornell Law Review* 77, no. 5 (July 1992): 1125–77.

304 *"Surgical shock"* Jonathan Miller, *The Body in Question* (New York: Random House, 1978), 118–24.

329–30 *"In much popular discussion"* Paul C. Weiler, *Medical Malpractice on Trial* (Cambridge and London: Harvard University Press, 1991), 88.

329–30 *In fact, Weiler* Ibid., 88–90.

330 *This, as Edward Felsenthal* Edward Felsenthal, "Clinton's Plan for Malpractice Has Failed Tests," *Wall Street Journal*, 16 September 1993, p. B1.

330 *"the medical malpractice problem"* "The Platform: Party Stresses Family Values, Decentralized Authority," *Congressional Quarterly*, 22 August 1992: 2564.

331 *"what is the point"* Weiler, *Medical Malpractice*, 57.

332 *"insurance tends"* Patricia Danzon, *Medical Malpractice: Theory, Evidence, and Public Policy* (Cambridge and London: Harvard University Press, 1985), 5.

337 *"misplaced optimism"* Nathan P. Couch, Nicholas L. Tilney, Anthony A. Rayner, and Francis D. Moore, "the Hight Cost of Low-Frequency Events: The Anatomy and Economics of Surgical Mishaps," *New England Journal of Medicine* 304, no. 11 (March 1981): 636.

337 *"Like an asthmatic hungering"* Richard Selzer, *Mortal Lessons: Notes on the Art of Surgery* (New York: Simon & Schuster, 1976), 101.

338 *"that Americans worry"* Ellen Goodman, "Medical Overkill," *San Francisco Chronicle* (2 February 1993): p. A15.

339 *In our own situation* As many commentators on medical malpractice litigation have observed, contingency fee arrangements—while useful for those who can't afford to pay legal fees up front—nevertheless prevent attorneys from taking cases in which monetary compensation is likely to be insignificant. Thus the "wrongful death" of a retiree living on Social Security might not be worth investigating, no matter how egregious its circumstances. See Helen R. Burstin et al., "Do the Poor Sue More? A Case-Control Study of Malpractice Claims of Socioeconomic Status." *Journal of the American Medical Association* 270, no. 14 (October 1993): 1697–1701.

BIBLIOGRAPHY

The following bibliography is by no means complete. Rather, it is meant to suggest the range of books and articles that bear on issues raised by the story I have told here. I have myself spent considerable time with many of the works listed: some are quoted in the text or cited in my notes; others have also shaped my thinking; a number will, I hope, be useful to people coping with problems similar to those I have confronted or to researchers interested in the dilemmas of contemporary medicine.

I should add that I have generally omitted materials on specific cases (for instance, the Libby Zion and Andy Warhol cases), although articles about particular instances of medical negligence and the course of ensuing litigation have also been illuminating for me.

Ethics and Quality

Annas, George J. "The Hospital: A Human Rights Wasteland." In *Judging Medicine*. Clifton, N.J.: Humana Press, 1988.

Arnold, Robert M., and Forrow, Lachlan. "Rewarding Good Medicine: Good Doctors and Good Behavior." *Annals of Internal Medicine* 113, no. 2 (November 1990).

Astrow, Alan B. "The French Revolution and the Dilemma of Medical Training." *Perspectives in Biology and Medicine* 33, no. 3 (Spring 1990).

Bogadanich, Walt. *The Great White Lie: How America's Hospitals Betray Our Trust and Endanger Our Lives.* New York: Simon & Schuster, 1991.

Brody, Jane. "How Educated Patients Get Proper Health Care." *New York Times*, 30 January 1976, sec. 1, p. 10.

Brook, Robert H. "Quality of Care: Do We Care?" *Annals of Internal Medicine* 115, no. 6 (September 1991).

Feinstein, Alvin R. "The Intellectual Crisis in Clinical Science: Med-
aled Models and Muddled Mettle." *Perspectives in Biology and Medicine* 30, no. 2 (Winter 1987).

Fox, Renee C. "Ethical and Existential Developments in Contempo-
raneous American Medicine: Their Implications for Culture and
Society." *Milbank Memorial Fund Quarterly/Health and Society*
(Fall 1974).

Inlander, Charles B., Levin, Lowell S., and Weiner, Ed. *Medicine on
Trial: The Appalling Story of Medical Ineptitude and the Arrogance
That Overlooks It.* New York: Pantheon Books, 1988.

Light, Donald, Jr. "Uncertainty and Control in Professional Training." *Journal of Health and Social Behavior* 20 (December 1979).

Miller, Jonathan. *The Body in Question.* New York: Random House,
1978.

Peters, J. Douglas, and Peraino, Jeanette C. "Malpractice in Hospitals: Ten Theories for Direct Liability." *Law, Medicine and Health
Care* 12, no. 5 (October 1994).

Selzer, Richard. *Mortal Lessons: Notes on the Art of Surgery.* New
York: Simon & Schuster, 1976.

Siegel, Bernie S. *Love, Medicine and Miracles: Lessons Learned about
Self-Healing from a Surgeon's Experience with Exceptional Patients.*
New York: Harper & Row, 1986.

Sommerville, Margaret A. "Examination on Discovery of 'Death at a
New York Hospital': Searching for the Governing Values, Poli-
cies, and Attitudes." *Law, Medicine, and Health Care* 13, no. 6
(December 1985).

Wolf, Stewart. "The Medicine of the Lateral Pass." *Perspectives in
Biology and Medicine* 35, no. 2 (Winter 1992).

Grief, Grieving, Widowhood, Memoirs

Brothers, Joyce. *Widowed.* New York: Simon & Schuster, 1990.

Broyard, Anatole. *Intoxicated by My Illness: And Other Writings on
Life and Death.* Alexandra Broyard, ed. New York: C. Potter, 1992.

Caine, Lynn. *Being a Widow.* New York: Penguin, 1988.

————. *Widow.* New York: William Morrow, 1974.

L'Engle, Madeleine. *Two-Part Invention: The Story of a Marriage.* San
Francisco: HarperCollins, 1988.

Lerner, Gerda. *A Death of One's Own.* New York: Simon & Schuster, 1978.

Lewis, C. S. *A Grief Observed.* New York: Bantam, 1961.

Lightner, Candy, and Hathaway, Nancy. *Giving Sorrow Words: How to Cope with Grief and Get On with Your Life.* New York: Warner Books, 1990.

Moffat, Mary Jane, ed. *In the Midst of Winter: Selections from the Literature of Mourning.* New York: Vintage Books, 1982.

Mukand, Jon, ed. *Sutured Words: Contemporary Poems About Medicine.* Brookline, Mass: Aviva Press, 1987.

Rando, Therese A. *How To Go On Living When Someone You Love Dies.* New York: Bantam, 1988.

Staudacher, Carol. *Beyond Grief: A Guide for Recovering from the Death of a Loved One.* Oakland: New Harbinger Publications, 1987.

Viorst, Judith. *Necessary Losses: The Loves, Dependencies and Impossible Expectations That All of Us Have to Give Up in Order to Grow.* New York: Fawcett Gold Medal Books, 1986.

Weinman-Lear, Martha. *Heartsounds.* New York: Simon & Schuster, 1980.

Wertenbaker, Lael. *Death of a Man.* New York: Random House, 1957.

Malpractice Theory

Bebchuk, L. "Suing Solely to Extract a Settlement Offer." *Journal of Legal Studies* 17 (1988).

Bovbjerg, R. "Legislation on Medical Malpractice: Further Developments and Preliminary Report Card." *UC Davis Law Review* 22 (1989).

———. "Medical Malpractice on Trial." *Law and Contemporary Problems* 49 (Spring 1986).

Burstin, Helen R., et al. "Do the Poor Sue More? A Case-Control Study of Malpractice Claims and Socioeconomic Status." *Journal of the American Medical Association* 270, no. 14 (October 1993).

Cooter, R., and Rubinfeld, D. "Economic Analysis of Legal Disputes and Their Resolution." *Journal of Economic Literature* 27, no. 3 (September 1989).

Cornelius, Frank. "Malpractice Damage Caps Won't Help." *Wall Street Journal,* 13 October 1993, A21.

Cornell, B. "The Incentive to Sue: An Option Pricing Analysis." *Journal of Legal Studies* 19 (1990).

Danzon, P. M. "The Contingent Fees for Personal Injury Litigation." *Bell Journal of Economics* 14 (Spring 1983).

————. "The Crises in Medical Malpractice: A Comparison of the Trends in the US, Canada, UK and Australia." *Law, Medicine, and Health Care* 18, nos. 1–2 (Spring 1990).

————. *The Disposition of Medical Malpractice Claims.* New York: Random House, 1980.

————. "The Frequency and Severity of Medical Malpractice Claims." *Law and Contemporary Problems* 49, no. 2 (Spring 1986).

————. "Incentive Effects of Medical Malpractice: The Effects of Medical Malpractice on Physicians' Fees and Incomes." *American Economic Review* 80, no. 2 (1990).

————. "Liability and Liability Insurance for Medical Malpractice." *Journal of Health and Economics* 4 (December 1985).

————. "Liability for Medical Malpractice." *Journal of Economic Perspectives* 5, no. 3 (Summer 1991).

————. *Medical Malpractice: Theory, Evidence, and Public Policy.* Cambridge: Harvard University Press, 1985.

Danzon, P. M., and Lillard, L. "Settlement Out of Court: The Disposition of Medical Malpractice Claims." *Journal of Legal Studies* 12 (1982).

Dietz, S. B. Baird, and Berull, L. "The Medical Malpractice Legal System." *Department of Health, Education and Welfare, Report of the Secretary's Commission on Medical Malpractice* (1973), Appendix 87, OS 73-89.

Felsenthal, Edward. "Clinton's Plan for Malpractice Has Failed Tests." *Wall Street Journal,* 16 September 1993, B1.

Flahavan, William F., Kelly, Daniel J., Rea, William J., and Tenner, Jack. *California Practice Guide: Personal Injury: 1991, Update* 14.

Fournier, G., and Zuehlke, T. "Litigation and Settlement: An Empirical Approach." *Review of Economics and Statistics* 71 (1989).

Gershonowitz, Aaron. "Tort Reform from Within." *Law Medicine and Health Care* 14, no. 2 (1986).

Glasson, John, and Orentlicher, David. "Not Caring for the Poor and Professional Liability: Is There a Need for Tort Reform?" *Journal of the American Medical Association* 270, no. 14 (October 1993).

Gould, J. "The Economics of Legal Conflicts." *Journal of Legal Studies* 2 (1973).

Griffith, J. "What It Will Take to Solve the Malpractice Crisis." *Medical Economics* (September 1982).

Hammit, J., et al. "Tort Standards and Jury Decisions." *Journal of Legal Studies* 14 (1985).

Jacobson, J. "Medical Malpractice and the Tort System." *Journal of the American Medical Association* 262, no. 23 (December 1989).

Law and Contemporary Problems 49 (Spring 1986). Special Edition on "Information on Medical Malpractice: A Review of Empirical Research on Major Policy Issues." Duke University School of Law.

Law and Contemporary Problems 54 (Winter/Spring 1991). Special Edition on "Medical Malpractice: Lessons for Reform." Duke University School of Law.

Metzloff, T. "Resolving Malpractice Disputes: Imaging the Jury's Shadow." *Law and Contemporary Problems* 54 (Winter 1991).

Miller, Frances H. "Medical Malpractice Litigation: Do the British Have a Better Remedy?" *American Journal of Law and Medicine* 11, no. 4 (1986).

Peterson, M. "Consumer's Knowledge of and Attitudes toward Medical Malpractice." *Department of Health, Education and Welfare, Report of the Secretary's Commission on Medical Malpractice* (1973), Appendix 658, OS 73–89.

P'ng, I. "Litigation, Liability and Incentives for Care." *Journal of Public Economics* 34 (1987).

Priest, G., and Klein, B. "The Selection of Disputes for Litigation." *Journal of Legal Studies* 13 (1984).

Rottenberg, Simon, ed. *The Economics of Medical Malpractice.* Washington, D.C.: American Enterprise Institute, 1978.

Saks, Michael J. "In Search of the 'Lawsuit Crisis.'" *Law, Medicine and Health Care* 14, no. 2 (1986).

Shavell, S. "Suit, Settlement, and Trial: A Theoretical Analysis under Alternative Methods for the Allocation of Legal Costs." *Journal of Legal Studies* XI, no. 1 (January 1982).

Sloan, F. "State Responses to the Malpractice Insurance Crisis of the 1970s." *Journal of Health Policy* 9, no. 4 (1985).

Sloan, F., et al. "Effects of Tort Reforms on the Value of Closed Medical Malpractice Claims: A Microanalysis." *Journal of Health Politics, Policy and Law* 14, no. 4 (Winter 1989).

Sloan, F., et al. "Insuring Medical Malpractice: An Economist's View." *American Bar Foundation Research Journal* (1976).

Sloan F., and Bovbjerg, R. "Medical Malpractice: Crises, Response and Effects." *Health Insurance Association of America Research Bulletin* (May 1989).

Sloan, F., and Hoerger, T. "Uncertainty, Information and Resolution of Medical Malpractice Disputes." *Journal of Risk and Uncertainty* 4, no. 4 (December 1991).

Sloan, F., and Hsieh, C. "Variability in Medical Malpractice Payments: Is the Compensation System Fair?" *Law and Society Review* 24, no. 4 (1994).

Taragin, Mark I., et al. "The Influence of Standard of Care and Severity of Injury on the Resolution of Medical Malpractice Claims." *Annals of Internal Medicine* 117, no. 9 (November 1992).

Trebilcock, M., et al. "Canadian Medical Malpractice Liability: An Empirical Analysis of Recent Trends." In *Scope and Trends in Health Care Liability in Canada*, ed. J. R. Prichard. Toronto: University of Toronto Press, 1990.

Weiler, Paul C. *Medical Malpractice on Trial.* Cambridge: Harvard University Press, 1991.

Medical Negligence

Brennan, Troyen A., et al. "Hospital Characteristics Associated with Adverse Events and Substandard Care." *Journal of the American Medical Association* 265, no. 24 (June 1991).

Brennan, Troyen A., et al. "Identification of Adverse Events Occurring during Hospitalization: Across-Sections Study of Litigation, Quality Assurance, and Medical Records at Two Teaching Hospitals." *Annals of Internal Medicine* 112, no. 3 (February 1990).

Brennan, Troyen A., et al. "Incidence of Adverse Events and Negligence in Hospitalized Patients." *New England Journal of Medicine* 324, no. 6 (February 1991).

Brennan, Troyen A., et al. "Reliability and Validity of Judgments Concerning Adverse Events Suffered by Hospitalized Patients." *Medical Care* 27, no. 12 (December 1989).

Couch, Nathan, et al. "The High Cost of Low-Frequency Events: The Anatomy and Economics of Surgical Mishaps." *New England Journal of Medicine* 304, no. 11 (March 1981).

Dans, Peter E., Weiner, Jonathan P., and Otter, Sharon E. "Peer Review Organizations: Promises and Potential Pitfalls." *New England Journal of Medicine* 313, no. 18 (October 1985).

Dubois, Robert W., and Brook, Robert H. "Preventable Deaths: Who, How Often, and Why?" *Annals of Internal Medicine* 109, no. 7 (October 1988).

Farber, M. A. and Altman, Lawrence K. "A Great Hospital in Crisis." *New York Times Magazine* 24 January 1988.

Hiatt, Howard H., et al. "A Study of Medical Injury and Medical Malpractice." *New England Journal of Medicine* 321, no. 7 (August 1989).

Klawans, Harold L., *Trials of an Expert Witness.* Boston: Little, Brown, 1991.

Leape, Lucian L., et al. "The Nature of Adverse Events in Hospitalized Patients: Results of the Harvard Medical Practice Study II." *New England Journal of Medicine* 324, no. 6 (February 1991).

Localio, A. Russell, et al. "Relation between Malpractice Claims and Adverse Events Due to Negligence: Results of the Harvard Medical Practice Study III." *New England Journal of Medicine* 325, no. 4 (July 1991).

Meyers, Allan R. " 'Lumping It': The Hidden Denominator of the Medical Malpractice Crisis." *American Journal of Public Health* 77, no. 12 (December 1987).

Moore, Thomas J. *Heart Failure: A Critical Inquiry into American Medicine and the Revolution in Heart Care.* New York: Random House, 1989.

Ogilvie, Richard Ian, and Ruedy, John. "Adverse Drug Reactions during Hospitalization." *Canadian Medical Association Journal* 97 (December 1967).

Pear, Robert. "Medical Malpractice Study Finds Unjust Payments Are Rare." *New York Times* 1 November 1992, vol. 142, sec. 1.

Rensenberger, Boyce. "Few Doctors Ever Report Colleagues' Incompetence." *New York Times,* 29 January 1976, sec. 1, p. 18.

———. "Thousands a Year Killed by Faulty Prescriptions." *New York Times,* 28 January 1976, sec. 1, p. 17.

———. "Unfit Doctors Create Worry in Profession." *New York Times,* 26 January 1976, sec. 1, p. 20.

Rowen, Hobart. "Rx Negative." *Seattle Times,* 19 July 1992, p. K1–2.

Schimmel, Elihu M. "The Hazards of Hospitalization." *Annals of Internal Medicine* 60, no. 1 (January 1964).

Schwartz, William B., and Komesar, Neil K. "Doctors, Damages and Deterrence: An Economic View of Medical Malpractice." *New England Journal of Medicine* 298, no. 23 (June 1978).

Sloan, Frank A., et al. "Medical Malpractice Experience of Physicians: Predictable or Haphazard." *Journal of the American Medical Association* 262, no. 23 (December 1989).

Steel, Knight, et al. "Iatrogenic Illness on a General Medical Service at a University Hospital." *New England Journal of Medicine* 340, no. 11 (March 1981).

Vincent, Charles, et. al. *Medical Accidents.* Oxford: Oxford University Press, 1993.

Zion, Sidney. "Doctors Know Best?" *New York Times,* 13 May 1990.

Medicine and Law

Amundsen, Darrel W. "The Liability of the Physician in Classical Greek Legal Theory and Practice." *Journal of the History of Medicine* 49, no. 71 (April 1977).

Barrett, Paul M. "Litigation Boom? Professor Turns Up a New Culprit." *Wall Street Journal,* 17 October 1988, p. B1.

"Bashing Lawyers. Also Justice." *New York Times,* 15 February 1992, p. 14.

Bennett, William Ira. "Pluses of Malpractice Suits." *New York Times Magazine,* 24 July 1988.

Clermont, Kevin M., and Eisenberg, Theodore. "Trial by Jury or Judge: Transcending Empiricism." *Cornell Law Review* 77, no. 5 (July 1992).

Epp, Charles R. "Let's Not Kill All the Lawyers." *Wall Street Journal,* 9 July 1992, p. A13.

Felsenthal, Edward. "Idea of No-Fault in Medical Cases Gains Support." *Wall Street Journal*, 28 September 1993, p. B1.

Furrow, Barry R., et al. *Health Law: Cases, Material and Problems*. St. Paul, Minn.: West Publishing, 1987.

Gage, Sanford M. "Alteration, Falsification, and Fabrication of Records in Medical Malpractice Actions." *Medical Trial Technique Quarterly* 27, no. 4 (Spring 1981).

Geyelin, Milo. "Arbitration Can Cost Defendants More Than Jury Trial, Study Says." *Wall Street Journal*, 19 August 1993, p. B2.

Hall, Mark A. "The Malpractice Standard under Health Care Cost Containment." *Law, Medicine and Health Care* 17, no. 4 (Winter 1989).

Harrison, Louis B., et al. "The Development of the Principles of Medical Malpractice in the United States." *Perspectives in Biology and Medicine* 29, no. 1 (Fall 1985).

Holding, Reynolds. "Doctors Need Not Tell Patients All They Know, Court Rules." *San Francisco Chronicle*, 1 October 1993, p. 1.

———. "Jurors Aren't Pushovers for Plaintiffs, Studies Say: New Legal Research Rebuts Popular View of Personal Injury Trials." *San Francisco Chronicle*, 25 July 1992, p. A6.

Marcotte, Paul. "Study: Arbitration Cheaper for Litigants, but Not Quicker." *American Bar Association Journal* 27 (December 1990).

McDermott, Walsh. "Evaluating the Physician and His Technology." In *Doing Better and Feeling Worse*, ed. John H. Knowles. New York: W. W. Norton, 1977.

Meyers, Allan R. "'Lumping It': The Hidden Denominator of the Medical Malpractice Crises." *American Journal of Public Health* 77, no. 12 (December 1987).

Morreim, E. Haavi. "Stratified Scarcity: Redefining the Standard of Care." *Law, Medicine and Health Care* 17, no. 4 (Winter 1989).

Zaslow, Jerry. "What Is Malpractice in General Surgery?" *Medical Trial Technique Quarterly* 27, no. 3 (Winter 1981).

Sociology of Medicine

Anspach, Renee R. "Notes on the Sociology of Medical Discourse: The Language of Case Presentation." *Journal of Health and Social Behavior* 29 (December 1988).

Bosk, Charles L. *Forgive and Remember: Managing Medical Failure*. Chicago: University of Chicago Press, 1979.

———. "Occupational Rituals in Patient Management." *New England Journal of Medicine* 303, no. 2 (July 1980).

Bosk, Charles L., and Frader, Joel E. "AIDS and Its Impact on Medical Work: The Culture and Politics of the Shop Floor." *Milbank Memorial Fund Quarterly/Health and Society* 68, no. 2 (1990).

Donnely, William J. "Medical Language as Symptom: Doctor Talk in Teaching Hospitals." *Perspectives in Biology and Medicine* 30, no. 1 (Fall 1986).

Fox, Renee C. "The Evolution of Medical Uncertainty." *Milbank Memorial Fund Quarterly/Health and Society* 58, no. 1 (1980).

———. "The Medicalization and Demedicalization of American Society." In *Doing Better and Feeling Worse: Health in the United States*, ed. John H. Knowles New York: W. W. Norton, 1977.

———. "Reflections and Opportunities in the Sociology of Medicine." *Journal of Health and Social Behavior* 26 (March 1985).

Fox, Renee C., and Willis, David P. "Personhood, Medicine, and American Society." *Milbank Memorial Fund Quarterly/Health and Society* 61, no. 1 (1983).

Hafferty, Frederic W. "Cadaver Stories and the Emotional Socialization of Medical Students." *Journal of Health and Social Behavior* 29, no. 4 (December 1988).

Hunter, Kathryn Montgomery. "There Was This One Guy . . .": The Uses of Anecdotes in Medicine." *Perspectives in Biology and Medicine* 29 (Summer 1986).

Leiderman, Deborah B. and Grisso, Jean-Anne. "The Gomer Phenomenon." *Journal of Health and Social Behavior* 26 (September 1985).

Light, Donald W. "Toward a New Sociology of Medical Education." *Journal of Health and Social Behavior*, 29 (December 1988).

Lorber, Judith. "Good Patients and Problem Patients: Conformity and Deviance in a General Hospital." *Journal of Health and Social Behavior* 16 (1975).

Stelling, Joan, and Bucher, Rue. "Vocabularies of Realism in Professional Socialization." *Social Sciences and Medicine* 7 (1973).